SHRIMAD-BHAGAVAD-GITA

With Text, Word-for-word Translation,
English Rendering, Comments
and Index

BY
SWAMI SWARUPANANDA

ADVAITA ASHRAMA
4, Wellington Lane
Calcutta 13

Published by
SWAMI GAMBHIRANANDA
PRESIDENT, ADVAITA ASHRAMA
MAYAVATI, ALMORA, HIMALAYAS

Ninth Impression, 1956
COPYRIGHT REGISTERED UNDER ACT XX OF 1847.

Printed in India
BY B. K. SEN
AT THE MODERN INDIA PRESS
7, WELLINGTON SQUARE
CALCUTTA 13

PREFACE TO THE FIRST EDITION

Swami Swarupananda, the first president of the Advaita Ashrama, Mayavati, and late editor of the *Prabuddha Bharata,* compiled the present edition of the Bhagavad-Gitâ with the collaboration of his brother Sannyâsins at Mayavati, and some of the Western disciples of Swami Vivekananda. The manuscripts were begun in 1901, and were ready for the press by the end of 1903, but through unavoidable circumstances the publication was delayed. It was only after the passing away of Swami Swarupananda that the work was brought out in monthly instalments in the *Prabuddha Bharata,* and this work is now presented to the public in convenient book form, after being carefully edited and enlarged with additional comments.

The object of the compiler was to make accessible to the Indian public who are educated in English but have a limited knowledge in Sanskrit, and also to the Western world, an edition of the Celestial Gitâ, in which they will feel sufficient interest to follow the original text, and thus create a taste for the study and interpretation of holy Sanskrit literature. How far the compiler has been successful in his object can be gleaned from the following pages. His thoughtful comments following the commentaries of the great Âchâryas, and illuminating sidelights thrown on intricate places, will, we trust, be of much help to the study of the Gitâ, especially to a beginner. An elaborate Index has been subsequently added.

A word of explanation as to the paraphrase is necessary here : Though the literal meaning of each word is given, yet to avoid the awkwardness of language and confusion of sense to a beginner, the equivalents of case terminals of such words as are used to qualify some other words in the sentence, are omitted in most cases.

We hope this edition will meet a much-felt want, not only in India but in all English-speaking countries.

THE EDITORS AND PUBLISHERS

ADVAITA ASHRAMA
MAYAVATI, HIMALAYAS
18th October, 1909

CONTENTS

FOREWORD

The Shrimad-Bhagavad-Gîtâ occurs in the Bhishma Parva of the Mahâbhârata and comprises 18 chapters from the 25th to the 42nd. The discourse between Arjuna and Krishna on the battle-field, on the eve of the war which forms the subject-matter of the work, was strung together in seven hundred verses and put in its place in the body of this great history by Vyâsa.

The Gîtâ opens with Dhritarâshtra's query to Sanjaya about the progress of events. In the second chapter of the Bhishma Parva, we find Vyâsa offering the power of sight to the blind king, that he might see the war. Dhritarâshtra declined to have it, saying he did not care to have eyes with which only to see the death of his own people; but he would like to hear what was happening. On this the great Rishi Vyâsa said, that all the occurrences in connection with the war would be reflected in the mind of Sanjaya, and he would faithfully report them to Dhritarâshtra.

The Gîtâ is called an Upanishad, because it contains the essence of Self-knowledge, and because its teachings, like those of the Vedas, are divided into three sections, Karma (work), Upâsanâ (devotion), and Jnâna (knowledge).

The first chapter is introductory. The second is a summary of the whole work, e.g., in II. 48 and the connected Shlokas, selfless work devoid of desire for fruits, is taught for the purification of the heart ; in II. 61 and the connected Shlokas devotion is taught to the pure-hearted, to qualify them further for the highest Sannyâsa, which last is taught in II. 71 and the connected Shlokas.

It is also usual to divide the work into three sections illustrative of the three terms of the Mahâvâkya of the Sâma-Veda, "Thou art That" (Chhând. Upa., VI. viii. 7). In this view the first six chapters explain the path of work without desire for fruits, and the nature of "Thou". The next six chapters deal with devotion and the nature of "That". The last six describe the state of the highest knowledge and the nature of the middle term of the Mahâvâkya, in other words, the means of re-establishing the identity of "Thou" and "That".

The central teaching of the Gitâ is the attainment of Freedom, by the performance of one's Svadharma or duty in life. "Do thy duty without an eye to the results thereof. Thus shouldst thou gain the purification of heart which is essential for

Moksha,"—seems to be the key-note of Krishna's teachings to Arjuna.

It is well known why the Gîtâ came into existence. It was owing to Arjuna's unwillingness to do his duty as a Kshatriya—to fight for a just cause— because it involved the destruction of his own people. Not that Arjuna did not recognise the justice and right of the cause, but he would rather renounce the world and try for Moksha than kill his relatives and friends. Krishna's characterisation of this weakly sentimental attitude of Arjuna is well known. He called it "Un-Ârya-like delusion, contrary to the attainment alike of heaven and honour" and exhorted Pârtha to "yield not to unmanliness" but to "cast off this mean faint-heartedness" (II. 2-3). "Could a coward who fails to do his duty, be worthy to attain Moksha?"—seems to be Krishna's rejoinder. Could a man not purified by the fire-ordeal of Svadharma, could a renegade, a slave, attain Moksha? No! says the Lord. And this is the lesson we Indians have forgotten all these years, though we have been reading and discussing the Gîtâ all the time.

S.

MEDITATION

ॐ पार्थाय प्रतिबोधितां भगवता नारायणेन स्वयं
व्यासेन ग्रथितां पुराणमुनिना मध्ये महाभारतम् ।
अद्वैतामृतवर्षिणीं भगवतीमष्टादशाध्यायिनी-
मम्ब त्वामनुसन्दधामि भगवद्गीते भवद्वेषिणीम् ॥१॥

ओं Om भगवता by the Lord नारायणेन (the one Refuge of all beings) Nârâyana स्वयं Himself पार्थाय प्रतिबोधितां with which Pârtha was enlightened पुराणमुनिना by (through the lips of) the ancient sage व्यासेन Vyâsa महाभारतम् मध्ये in the Mahâbhârata ग्रथितां incorporated भगवतीं the blessed Mother अद्वैतामृतवर्षिणीं showering the nectar of Advaita (the philosophy of non-duality) अष्टादशाध्यायिनीं in the form of eighteen chapters भवद्वेषिणीम् destroyer of rebirth अम्ब loving Mother भगवद्गीते (the Lord's song) Bhagavad-Gitâ त्वाम् Thee अनुसन्दधामि I meditate upon.

1. Om ! O Bhagavad-Gitâ—with which Pârtha was enlightened by the Lord Nârâyana Himself and which was incorporated in the Mahâbhârata by the ancient sage Vyâsa—the blessed Mother, the Destroyer of rebirth, showering down the nectar of Advaita, and consisting of eighteen chapters,—upon

Thee, O Bhagavad-Gitâ !   O loving Mother !
I meditate.

नमोऽस्तु ते व्यास विशालबुद्धे

फुल्लारविन्दायतपत्रनेत्र ।

येन त्वया भारततैलपूर्णः

प्रज्वालितो ज्ञानमयः प्रदीपः ॥२॥

विशालबुद्धे Of mighty intellect फुल्लारविन्दायतपत्रनेत्र with
eyes as large as the petals of a full-blown lotus व्यास
Vyâsa येन त्वया by thee भारततैलपूर्णः full of the oil of the
Mahâbhârata ज्ञानमयः consisting of wisdom प्रदीपः lamp
प्रज्वालितः lighted ते to thee नमः salutation अस्तु be.

2.   Salutation to thee, O Vyâsa, of
mighty intellect and with eyes large like
the petals of a full-blown lotus, by whom
was lighted the lamp of wisdom, full of the
Mahâbhârata-oil.

प्रपन्नपारिजाताय तोत्रवेत्रैकपाणये ।

ज्ञानमुद्राय कृष्णाय गीतामृतदुहे नमः ॥३॥

प्रपन्नपारिजाताय O Thou wish-yielding tree of those
who take refuge in Thee तोत्रवेत्रैकपाणये who holdest
in one hand a cane for driving cows गीतामृतदुहे Thou
milker of the Gitâ-nectar ज्ञानमुद्राय (Jnânamudrâ :
a position of the hands in which the tips of the
forefinger and the thumb of each hand touch each

other; an attitude associated with the highest Yogis and Gurus) the holder of Jnânamudrâ कृष्णाय to Thee, O Krishna नमः salutation.

3. Salutation to Krishna, the holder of the Jnânamudrâ, granter of desires of those who take refuge in Him, the milker of the Gitâ-nectar, in whose hand is the cane for driving cows.

सर्वोपनिषदो गावो दोग्धा गोपालनन्दनः ।
पार्थो वत्सः सुधीर्भोक्ता दुग्धं गीतामृतं महत् ॥४॥

सर्वोपनिषदः All the Upanishads गावः the cows गोपाल- नन्दनः Son of the cowherd (Krishna) दोग्धा the milker पार्थः Pârtha (Arjuna) वत्सः the calf सुधीः (men) of purified intellect भोक्ता the drinkers महत् the supreme अमृतं nectar गीता Gitâ दुग्धं the milk.

4. All the Upanishads are the cows, the Son of the cowherd is the milker, Pârtha is the calf, men of purified intellect are the drinkers and the supreme nectar Gitâ is the milk.

वसुदेवसुतं देवं कंसचाणूरमर्दनम् ।
देवकीपरमानन्दं कृष्णं वन्दे जगद्गुरुम् ॥६॥

वसुदेवसुतं The son of Vasudeva कंसचाणूरमर्दनं the Destroyer of Kamsa and Chânura देवकीपरमानन्दं the supreme bliss of Devaki (mother of Krishna) जगद्गुरुम्

the Guru (Teacher) of the Universe देवं God कृष्णं
Krishna वन्दे I salute.

5. I salute Krishna, the Guru of the
Universe, God, the son of Vasudeva, the
Destroyer of Kamsa and Chânura, the supreme
bliss of Devaki.

भीष्मद्रोणतटा जयद्रथजला गान्धारनीलोत्पला ।

शल्यग्राहवती कृपेण वहनी कर्णेन वेलाकुला ।

अश्वत्थामविकर्णघोरमकरा दुर्योधनावर्तिनी ।

सोत्तीर्णा खलु पाण्डवै रणनदी कैवर्तकः केशवः ॥६॥

भीष्मद्रोणतटा With Bhishma and Drona as the banks
जयद्रथजला with Jayadratha as the water गान्धारनीलोत्पला
with the king of Gândhâra as the blue water-lily
शल्यग्राहवती with Shalya as the shark कृपेण वहनी with
Kripa as the current कर्णेन वेलाकुला with Karna as the
high waves अश्वत्थामविकर्णघोरमकरा with Ashvatthâmâ and
Vikarna as terrible Makaras (a kind of marine
animal) दुर्योधनावर्तिनी with Duryodhana as the whirlpool सा that रणनदी battle-river खलु indeed पाण्डवै: by
the Pândavas उत्तीर्णा crossed over केशवः Keshava
(Krishna) कैवर्तकः the ferry-man.

6. The battle-river—with Bhishma and
Drona as its banks, and Jayadratha as the
water, with the king of Gândhâra as
the blue water-lily, and Shalya as the shark,
with Kripa as the current and Karna

as the breakers, with Ashvatthâmâ and Vikarna as terrible Makaras and Duryodhana as the whirlpool in it—was indeed crossed over by the Pândavas, with Keshava as the ferry-man.

पाराशर्यवचःसरोजममलं गीतार्थगन्धोत्कटं
नानाख्यानककेसरं हरिकथासम्बोधनाबोधितम् ।
लोके सज्जनषट्पदैरहरहः पेपीयमानं मुदा
भूयाद्धारतपङ्कजं कलिमलप्रध्वंसिनः श्रेयसे ॥७॥

अमलं Spotless पाराशर्यवचःसरोजं growing on the waters of the words of the son of Parâshara (Vyâsa) भारतपंकजं the Mahâbhârata-lotus गीतार्थगन्धोत्कटं having the Gitâ as its strong sweet fragrance नानाख्यानककेसरं with many a narrative as its stamens हरिकथासम्बोधना-बोधितं fully opened by the discourses on Hari (the remover of misery) लोके in the world सज्जनषट्पदैः by the Bhramara (a beetle-like insect which lives solely on honey) of the good and the pure अहरहः day after day मुदा joyously पेपीयमानं drunk कलिमलप्रध्वंसिन of the destroyer of the taint of Kali (the age of imperfection) श्रेयसे for the supreme good भूयात् may be.

7. May the taintless lotus of the Mahâbhârata—growing on the waters of the words of Parâshara's son, having the

Gitâ as its strong sweet fragrance, with many a narrative as its stamens, fully opened by the discourses on Hari and drunk joyously day after day by the Bhramara of the good and the pure in the world—be productive of the supreme good to him who is eager to destroy the taint of Kali !

मूकं करोति वाचालं पङ्गुं लङ्घयते गिरिम् ।

यत्कृपा तमहं वन्दे परमानन्दमाधवम् ॥८॥

यत्कृपा Whose compassion मूकं the mute वाचालं eloquent करोति makes पङ्गुं the cripple गिरिं mountain लङ्घयते causes to cross तं that परमानन्दमाधवं the All-bliss Mâdhava (sweetest of the sweet) अहं I वन्दे salute.

8.   I salute that All-bliss Mâdhava whose compassion makes the mute eloquent and the cripple cross mountains.

यं ब्रह्मावरुणेन्द्ररुद्रमरुतः स्तुन्वन्ति दिव्यैः स्तवै-
र्वेदैः साङ्गपदक्रमोपनिषदैर्गायन्ति यं सामगाः ।
ध्यानावस्थिततद्गतेन मनसा पश्यन्ति यं योगिनो
यस्यान्तं न विदुः सुरासुरगणा देवाय तस्मै नमः ॥६॥

ब्रह्मा Brahmâ (The Creator) वरुणः Varuna इन्द्रः Indra रुद्रः Rudra मरुतः the Maruts यं whom दिव्यैः

divine स्तवैः with hymns स्तुन्वन्ति praise सामगाः the singers
of Sâma यं whom साङ्गपदक्रमोपनिषदैः with full complement of parts, consecutive sections, and Upanishads
(crowning knowledge-portions) वेदैः the Vedas गायन्ति
sing योगिनः Yogis यं whom ध्यानावस्थिततद्गतेन मनसा with
the mind absorbed in Him through perfection in
meditation पश्यन्ति see सुरासुरगणाः the hosts of Devas and
Asuras यस्य whose अन्तं limit न not विदुः know तस्मै to that
देवाय God नमः salutation.

9. Salutation to that God Whom the
Creator Brahmâ, Varuna, Indra, Rudra,
and the Maruts praise with divine hymns ;
Whom the singers of Sâma sing, by the
Vedas, with their full complement of parts,
consecutive sections, and Upanishads ; Whom
the Yogis see with their minds absorbed in
Him through perfection in meditation, and
Whose limit the hosts of Devas and Asuras
know not.

INVOCATION*

O blessed Mother
Who showerest (upon us) the nectar of Advaita
In the form of (these) eighteen chapters !
Thou Destroyer of rebirth !
Thou loving Mother !
Thou Bhagavad-Gitâ !
    Upon Thee I meditate.

Thee, O Vyâsa, of lotus-eyes,
And mighty intellect,
Who hast lighted the lamp of wisdom
Filled with the oil of the Mahâbhârata,
    Thee we salute.

O Thou who art the Refuge
Of the (ocean-born) Lakshmi,
Thou in whose right hand is the shepherd's crook,
Who art the milker of the divine nectar of the Gitâ,
    To Thee, O Krishna, to Thee our salutation !

The Upanishads are even as the herd of cows,
The Son of the cowherd as the milker,

*Another rendering of the "Meditation".

Pârtha as the sucking-calf,
And men of purified intellect the drinkers,
    Of this, the supreme nectar, the milk of the Gitâ.

Thou son of Vasudeva,
Destroyer of Kamsa and Chânura,
Thou supreme bliss of Devaki,
Guru of the Worlds,
    Thee, O Krishna, as God, we salute!

Of that great river of battle which the Pândavas
                      crossed over,
Bhishma and Drona were as the high banks;
And Jayadratha as the water of the river;
The King of Gândhâra the water-lily;
Shalya as the shark, Kripa as the current;
Karna the mighty waves;
Ashvatthâmâ and Vikarna dread water-monsters,
And Duryodhana was the very whirlpool;
    But Thou, O Krishna, wast the Ferry-man!

This spotless product of the words of Vyâsa,
This lotus of the Mahâbhârata,—
With the Bhagavad-Gitâ as its strong sweet fragrance,
And tales of heroes as its full-blown petals,
Held ever open by the talk of Hari, of Him
Who is destroyer of the taint of Kali-Yuga;
This lotus to which come joyously

Day after day the honey-seeking souls—
    May this produce in us the highest good !

Him Whose compassion maketh the dumb man
                                 eloquent,
And the cripple to cross mountains,
Him the All-blissful Mâdhava,
    Do I salute !

To that Supreme One Who is bodied forth in
                                 Brahmâ,
In Varuna, in Indra, in Rudra, and Maruts ;
That One Whom all divine beings praise with hymns;
Him Whom the singers of Sâma-Veda tell ;
Him of Whose glory, sing in full choir,
                        the Upanishads and Vedas ;
Him Whom the Yogis see, with mind absorbed
                       in perfect meditation ;
Him of Whom all the hosts of Devas and Asuras
Know not the limitations,
    To Him, the Supreme Good, be salutation,—
Him we salute. Him we salute. Him we salute.

SHRIMAD-BHAGAVAD-GITA

॥ प्रथमोऽध्यायः ॥

FIRST CHAPTER

धृतराष्ट्र उवाच ।

धर्मक्षेत्रे कुरुक्षेत्रे समवेता युयुत्सवः ॥
मामकाः पाण्डवाश्चैव किमकुर्वत सञ्जय ॥१॥

धृतराष्ट्रः Dhritarâshtra उवाच said :

(भोः) सञ्जय O Sanjaya धर्मक्षेत्रे on the centre of religious activity कुरुक्षेत्रे in Kurukshetra युयुत्सवः desirous to fight समवेताः assembled मामकाः my people च and पाण्डवाः the Pândavas किम् what एव indeed अकुर्वत did do.

Dhritarâshtra said :

1. Tell me, O Sanjaya ! Assembled on Kurukshetra, the centre of religious activity, desirous to fight, what indeed did my people and the Pândavas do ?

[True it is that the two parties were gathered together for battle, but was the influence of Kuru-

2

kshetra, the sacred centre of religious and spiritual activity from of old, barren of any result? Did not the spiritual influence of the spot affect any of the leaders in a way unfavourable to the occurrence of the battle?—is the purport of Dhritarâshtra's question.]

सञ्जय उवाच ।

दृष्ट्वा तु पाण्डवानीकं व्यूढं दुर्योधनस्तदा ॥

आचार्यमुपसङ्गम्य राजा वचनमब्रवीत् ॥२॥

सञ्जयः Sanjaya उवाच said :

तदा तु But then पाण्डवानीकं the Pândava forces व्यूढं in battle-array दृष्ट्वा having seen राजा दुर्योधनः King Duryodhana आचार्यम् (द्रोणं) the teacher (Drona) उपसंगम्य approaching वचनम् word अब्रवीत् said.

Sanjaya said :

2. But then King Duryodhana, having seen the Pândava forces in battle-array, approached his teacher Drona, and spoke these words :

[Sanjaya's reply beginning with "But then" and describing Duryodhana's action is a plain hint to the old king that his son was afraid. For he went to his teacher (regarded as father) instead of to the commander-in-chief, as a child in fright would run to its parents in preference to others.]

पश्यैतां पाण्डुपुत्राणामाचार्य महतीं चमूम् ॥

व्यूढां द्रुपदपुत्रेण तव शिष्येण धीमता ॥३॥

आचार्य O teacher तव शिष्येण by your disciple धीमता talented द्रुपदपुत्रेण son of Drupada व्यूढां arrayed पाण्डु-पुत्राणाम् of the sons of Pându एतां this महतीं mighty चमूम् army पश्य behold.

3. "Behold, O Teacher! this mighty army of the sons of Pându, arrayed by the son of Drupada, thy gifted pupil.

[As a scorpion would sting even that whose pro-tection is sought to be free from fear, so did the wicked Duryodhana insult his teacher. His mean-ing in plain words comes to this : thus think of your stupidity in teaching the science of fight to the son of Drupada and to those of Pându. They are now arrayed to kill you !]

अत्र शूरा महेष्वासा भीमार्जुनसमा युधि ॥

युयुधानो विराटश्च द्रुपदश्च महारथः ॥४॥

धृष्टकेतुश्चेकितानः काशिराजश्च वीर्यवान् ॥

पुरुजित् कुन्तिभोजश्च शैब्यश्च नरपुङ्गवः ॥५॥

युधामन्युश्च विक्रान्त उत्तमौजाश्च वीर्यवान् ॥

सौभद्रो द्रौपदेयाश्च सर्व एव महारथाः ॥६॥

अत्र Here महेष्वासा mighty archers युधि in battle भीमार्जुनसमाः equals of Bhima and Arjuna शूराः heroes (सन्ति) (are) महारथः the great warrior युयुधानः (सात्यकिः)

Yuyudhâna (Sâtyaki) च and विराटः Virâta च and द्रुपदः Drupada वीर्यवान् the strong धृष्टकेतुः Dhrishtaketu चेकितानः Chekitâna च and काशिराजः the king of Kâshi नरपुङ्गवः the best of men पुरुजित् Purujit च and कुन्तिभोजः Kuntibhoja च and शैब्यः Shaibya च and विक्रान्तः the powerful युधामन्युः Yudhâmanyu च and वीर्यवान् the brave उत्तमौजाः Uttamaujas सौभद्रः the son of Subhadrâ च and द्रौपदेयाः the sons of Draupadi सर्वे all (these) एव verily महारथाः great warriors.

4-6. "Here (are) heroes, mighty archers, the equals in battle of Bhima and Arjuna— the great warriors Yuyudhâna, Virâta, Drupada ; the valiant Dhrishtaketu, Chekitâna, and the king of Kâshi ; the best of men, Purujit, Kuntibhoja, and Shaibya ; the powerful Yudhâmanyu, and the brave Uttamaujas, the son of Subhadrâ, and the sons of Draupadi —all of whom are lords of great chariots.

[महारथः great-charioted : one who is well-versed in the science of war and commands eleven thousand bowmen.]

अस्माकं तु विशिष्टा ये तान्निबोध द्विजोत्तम ॥
नायका मम सैन्यस्य संज्ञार्थं तान् ब्रवीमि ते ॥७॥

(हे) द्विजोत्तम (O you) Best of the twice-born अस्माकं of us तु also ये (those) who विशिष्टाः distinguished मम my सैन्यस्य of the army नायकाः leaders तान् them निबोध

know ते संज्ञार्थं for your information तान् them ब्रवीमि
I relate.

7. "Hear also, O Best of the twice-
born ! the names of those who (are) distinguished amongst ourselves, the leaders of my
army. These I relate (to you) for your
information.

[However well-versed in the science of war you
might be, you are after all a Brâhmana (best of the
twice-born), a lover of peace, that is to say, a
coward. It is therefore natural for you to be afraid
of the Pândava force. But take heart, we too have
great warriors in our ranks—is the veiled meaning
of Duryodhana's words.]

भवान् भीष्मश्च कर्णश्च कृपश्च समितिञ्जयः ॥
अश्वत्थामा विकर्णश्च सौमदत्तिर्जयद्रथः ॥८॥

भवान् Yourself च and भीष्मः Bhishma च and कर्णः Karna
समितिञ्जयः the victorious in war कृपः Kripa च and
अश्वत्थामा Ashvatthâmâ च and विकर्णः Vikarna सौमदत्तिः the
son of Somadatta जयद्रथः Jayadratha.

8. "Yourself and Bhishma and Karna
and Kripa, the victorious in war. Ashvatthâmâ
and Vikarna and Jayadratha, the son of
Somadatta.

[Afraid lest he had said too much, Duryodhana
is flattering Drona, by mentioning the latter before

even Bhishma and qualifying Drona's brother-in-law
with the phrase "victorious in war", a move likely
to touch the heart of mortals.]

अन्ये च बहवः शूरा मदर्थे त्यक्तजीविताः ॥

नानाशस्त्रप्रहरणाः सर्वे युद्धविशारदाः ॥६॥

मदर्थे For my sake त्यक्तजीविताः determined to lay
down (their lives) नानाशस्त्रप्रहरणाः having diverse weapons and missiles सर्वे all युद्धविशारदाः well-skilled in fight
अन्ये च and other बहवः many शूराः heroes (सन्ति) (are).

9.   "And many other heroes also, well-
skilled in fight, and armed with many kinds
of weapons, are here, determined to lay down
their lives for my sake.

अपर्याप्तं तदस्माकम् बलं भीष्माभिरक्षितम् ॥

पर्याप्तं त्विदमेतेषां बलं भीमाभिरक्षितम् ॥१०॥

अस्माकं Our तत् this भीष्माभिरक्षितम् defended by
Bhishma बलं army अपर्याप्तं unlimited तु while एतेषाम् their
भीमाभिरक्षितम् defended by Bhima इदम् this बलं army पर्याप्तं
limited.

10.   "This our army defended by Bhishma
(is) impossible to be counted, but that army
of theirs, defended by Bhima (is) easy to
number.

[In ancient Indian warfare, one commanding a
force had for his mainstay a defender about him,
whose position was no less important. Here are
given the names of the chief defenders, and not of
the chief commanders.

The verse is often interpreted to mean that
Duryodhana considers his army inefficient and that
of the enemy efficient. But this view seems in-
apposite to the context.]

अयनेषु च सर्वेषु यथाभागमवस्थिताः ॥
भीष्ममेवाभिरक्षन्तु भवन्तः सर्व एव हि ॥११॥

च (expletive) सर्वेषु In all अयनेषु the divisions (of the
army) यथाभागं in (your) respective positions अवस्थिताः
being stationed भवन्तः ye सर्वे all एव हि (used for empha-
sis) भीष्मम् Bhishma एव alone अभिरक्षन्तु protect.

11.   "(Now) do, being stationed in your
proper places in the divisions of the army,
support Bhishma alone."

[Since I cannot expect from you any initiative,
do what you are told to do—seems to be
Duryodhana's intention.]

तस्य संजनयन्हर्षं कुरुवृद्धः पितामहः ॥
सिंहनादं विनद्योच्चैः शङ्खं दध्मौ प्रतापवान् ॥१२॥

प्रतापवान् The powerful कुरुवृद्धः oldest of the Kurus
पितामहः grandsire तस्य his (Duryodhana's) हर्षं cheer

संजनयन् causing उच्चः aloud सिंहनादं lion's roar विनद्य
having sounded शङ्खं conch दध्मौ blew.

12. That powerful, oldest of the Kurus,
Bhishma the grandsire, in order to cheer
Duryodhana, now sounded aloud a lion-roar
and blew his conch.

[All eyes were turned upon Duryodhana and
the penetrating intelligence of Bhishma detected his
fear ; and since Drona took no notice of Duryodhana's
words, knowing his grandson as he did, he had no
difficulty in understanding that the latter had spoken
to his teacher in a way which called forth Drona's
coldness instead of his enthusiasm. The grandsire's
heart was moved with pity and hence the action on
his part described in the above verse. It should here
be noted that this action, amounting to a challenge,
really began the fight. It was the Kaurava side
again which took the aggressor's part.]

तत: शङ्खाश्च भेर्यश्च पणवानकगोमुखाः ॥
सहसैवाभ्यहन्यन्त स शब्दस्तुमुलोऽभवत् ॥१३॥

तत: Then शङ्खाः conches च and भेर्यः kettle-drums
पणवानकगोमुखाः tabors, trumpets, and cowhorns सहसा एव
quite suddenly अभ्यहन्यन्त blared forth सः that शब्द: noise
तुमुल: tremendous अभवत् was.

13. Then following Bhishma, conches
and kettle-drums, tabors, trumpets, and

cowhorns blared forth suddenly from the
Kaurava side, and the noise was tremendous.

ततः श्वेतैर्हयैर्युक्ते महति स्यन्दने स्थितौ ॥
माधवः पाण्डवश्चैव दिव्यौ शङ्खौ प्रदध्मतुः ॥१४॥

ततः Then श्वेतैः हयैः with white horses युक्तैः yoked
महति in the magnificent स्यन्दने chariot स्थितौ stationed
माधवः (the Lord of Fortune : Krishna) Mâdhava च
and पाण्डवः (the best of the Pându princes :
Arjuna) Pândava दिव्यौ divine शङ्खौ conches प्रदध्मतुः
blew in a splendid manner.

14. Then, also, Mâdhava and Pândava,
stationed in their magnificent chariot yoked
with white horses, blew their divine conches
with a furious noise.

पाञ्चजन्यं हृषीकेशो देवदत्तं धनञ्जयः ॥
पौण्ड्रं दध्मौ महाशङ्खं भीमकर्मा वृकोदरः ॥१५॥

हृषीकेशः (The Lord of the senses : Krishna) Hrishikesha पाञ्चजन्यं (the conch named) Pânchajanya धनञ्जयः
(the victor of wealth : Arjuna) Dhananjaya देवदत्तं
(the conch named) Devadatta भीमकर्मा doer of terrific
deeds वृकोदरः (having the belly of a wolf : Bhima)
Vrikodara महाशङ्खं the large conch पौण्ड्रं (named)
Paundra दध्मौः blew.

15. Hrishikesha blew the Pânchajanya, Dhananjaya, the Devadatta, and Vrikodara, the doer of terrific deeds, his large conch Paundra.

अनन्तविजयं राजा कुन्तीपुत्रो युधिष्ठिरः ॥
नकुलः सहदेवश्च सुघोषमणिपुष्पकौ ॥१६॥

कुन्तीपुत्रः Son of Kunti राजा king युधिष्ठिरः Yudhishthira अनन्तविजयं (the conch named) Anantavijaya नकुलः Nakula सहदेवः च and Sahadeva सुघोषमणिपुष्पकौ (conches named) Sughosha and Manipushpaka.

16. King Yudhishthira, son of Kunti, blew the conch named Anantavijaya, and Nakula and Sahadeva, their Sughosha and Manipushpaka.

काश्यश्च परमेष्वासः शिखण्डी च महारथः ॥
धृष्टद्युम्नो विराटश्च सात्यकिश्चापराजितः ॥१७॥

काश्यः च परमेष्वासः And the expert bowman, the king of Kâshi महारथः शिखण्डी च and the great warrior Shikhandi धृष्टद्युम्नः Dhrishtadyumna विराटः च and Virâta अपराजितः सात्यकिः च and the unconquered Sâtyaki.

17. The expert bowman, king of Kâshi, and the great warrior Shikhandi,

Dhrishtadyumna, and Virâta, and the unconquered Sâtyaki ;

द्रपदो द्रौपदेयाश्च सर्वशः पृथिवीपते ॥

सौभद्रश्च महाबाहुः शङ्खान्दध्मुः पृथक् पृथक् ॥१८॥

पृथिवीपते O Lord of Earth (Dhritarâshtra) द्रुपदः
(king) Drupada द्रौपदेयाः च and the sons of Draupadi
च and महाबाहुः the mighty-armed सौभद्रः son of
Subhadrâ (Abhimanyu) सर्वशः all पृथक् पृथक् respective
शङ्खान् conches दध्मुः blew.

18. O Lord of Earth ! Drupada and
the sons of Draupadi, and the mighty-armed
son of Subhadrâ, all, also blew each his own
conch.

स घोषो धार्तराष्ट्राणां हृदयानि व्यदारयत् ॥

नभश्च पृथिवीञ्चैव तुमुलोऽभ्यनुनादयन् ॥१९॥

च And सः that तुमुलः tremendous घोषः noise नभः
sky पृथिवीं च and earth अभ्यनुनादयन् causing to resound
धार्तराष्ट्राणां of Dhritarâshtra's party हृदयानि hearts
व्यदारयत् rent.

19. And the terrific noise resounding
throughout heaven and earth rent the hearts
of Dhritarâshtra's party.

[Verses 14-19 are full of hints about the
superiority of the Pândava party and the conse-

quent sure defeat of Dhritarâshtra. The figure to
which Sanjaya draws the old king's attention as first
taking up Bhishma's challenge, is described by him
as the Lord of Fortune and the Pândava—the best
of the Pându princes. Note also the details in
which the chariot, horses, and conches of the
Pândava party are described ; and finally, though
the army of the Kauravas was more than a third
as much again as that of the Pândavas, the noise
made by the former was only tremendous, whereas
that of the latter was not only tremendous but filled
the earth and sky with reverberations and rent the
hearts of the former.]

अथ व्यवस्थितान् दृष्ट्वा धार्तराष्ट्रान् कपिध्वज: ॥

प्रवृत्ते शस्त्रसम्पाते धनुरुद्यम्य पाण्डव: ॥

हृषीकेशं तदा वाक्यमिदमाह महीपते ॥२०॥

(हे) महीपते O Lord of Earth (Dhritarâshtra)
अथ then कपिध्वज: monkey-ensigned पाण्डव: Pândava
(Arjuna) धार्तराष्ट्रान् Dhritarâshtra's party व्यवस्थितान्
standing marshalled दृष्ट्वा seeing शस्त्रसम्पाते discharge of
missiles प्रवृत्ते about to begin धनु: bow उद्यम्य raising
तदा then हृषीकेशं to Hrishikesha इदं following वाक्यं
words आह said.

20. Then, O Lord of Earth, seeing
Dhritarâshtra's party standing marshalled and
the shooting about to begin, that Pândava,

whose ensign was the monkey, raising his bow,
said the following words to Krishna :

[In view of the sudden change of feeling that is
to come over Arjuna it should be noted how full of
the war-spirit we find him in this verse.]

अर्जुन उवाच ।

सेनयोरुभयोर्मध्ये रथं स्थापय मेऽच्युत ॥२१॥

यावदेतान्निरीक्षेऽहं योद्धुकामानवस्थितान् ॥

कैर्मया सह योद्धव्यमस्मिन्रणसमुद्यमे ॥२२॥

अर्जुनः Arjuna उवाच said :

अच्युत (The changeless : Krishna) Achyuta उभयोः
of both सेनयोः armies मध्ये in the midst मे my रथं
chariot स्थापय place अहं I एतान् these योद्धुकामान् desirous
to fight अवस्थितान् standing यावत् while निरीक्षे scrutinise
अस्मिन् on this रणसमुद्यमे eve of battle कैः सहः with whom
मया by me योद्धव्यम् the battle should be fought.

Arjuna said :
21-22. Place my chariot, O Achyuta !
between the two armies that I may see those
who stand here prepared for war. On this eve
of battle (let me know) with whom I have to
fight.

योत्स्यमानानवेक्षेऽहं य एतेऽत्र समागताः ॥

धार्तराष्ट्रस्य दुर्बुद्धेर्युद्धे प्रियचिकीर्षवः ॥२३॥

अत्र Here (in this Kurukshetra) युद्धे in battle दुर्बुद्धे: of the evil-minded धार्तराष्ट्रस्य Dhritarâshtra's son (Duryodhana) प्रियचिकीर्षवः wishing to please ये who एते these समागताः assembled योत्स्यमानान् with the object of fighting अहं I अवेक्षे observe.

23. For I desire to observe those who are assembled here for fight, wishing to please the evil-minded Duryodhana by taking his side on this battle-field.

[Arjuna is impatient to see who dared face him in fight !]

सञ्जय उवाच ।

एवमुक्तो हृषीकेशो गुडाकेशेन भारत ॥

सेनयोरुभयोर्मध्ये स्थापयित्वा रथोत्तमम् ॥२४॥

भीष्मद्रोणप्रमुखतः सर्वेषां च महीक्षिताम् ॥

उवाच पार्थ पश्यैतान्समवेतान् कुरूनिति ॥२५॥

सञ्जयः Sanjaya उवाच said :

भारत (Descendant of king Bharata : Dhritarâshtra) Bhârata गुडाकेशेन by (the conqueror of sleep : Arjuna) Gudâkesha एवं thus उक्तः told हृषीकेशः Hrishikesha उभयोः of the two सेनयोः armies मध्ये between भीष्मद्रोणप्रमुखतः in front of Bhishma and Drona च and सर्वेषां (in front) of all महीक्षितां rulers of the earth रथोत्तमं best of chariots स्थापयित्वा having stationed

पार्थं (son of Prithâ or Kunti : the name of Arjuna's mother, the first wife of Pându) Pârtha समवेतान् gathered together एतान् these कुरून् Kurus पश्य behold इति thus उवाच spoke.

Sanjaya said :

24-25. Commanded thus by Gudâkesha, Hrishikesha, O Bhârata, drove that grandest of chariots to a place between the two hosts, facing Bhishma, Drona, and all the rulers of the earth, and then spoke thus, "Behold, O Pârtha, all the Kurus gathered together !"

तत्रापश्यत् स्थितान् पार्थः पितॄनथ पितामहान् ॥
आचार्यान् मातुलान् भ्रातॄन् पुत्रान् पौत्रान् सखींस्तथा ॥
श्वशुरान् सुहृदश्चैव सेनयोरुभयोरपि ॥२६॥

अथ then पार्थः Pârtha तत्र there उभयोः अपि both the सेनयोः of armies (मध्ये in the midst) स्थितान् stationed पितॄन् uncles पितामहान् grandfathers आचार्यान् teachers मातुलान् maternal uncles भ्रातन् brothers (and cousins) पुत्रान् (his own and their) sons पौत्रान् and grandsons तथा and सखीन् comrades श्वशुरान् fathers-in-law सुहृदः च एव and friends as well अपश्यत् saw.

26. Then saw Pârtha stationed there in both the armies, grandfathers, fathers-in-law, and uncles, brothers and cousins, his own and

their sons and grandsons, and comrades,
teachers, and other friends as well.

तान्समीक्ष्य स कौन्तेयः सर्वान्बन्धूनवस्थितान् ॥

कृपयापरयाविष्टो विषीदन्निदमब्रवीत् ॥२७॥

सः He कौन्तेयः the son of Kunti (Arjuna) अवस्थितान्
stationed तान् those सर्वान् all बन्धून् kinsmen समीक्ष्य
having seen परया deep कृपया with compassion आविष्टः
filled विषीदन् sorrowfully इदं thus अब्रवीत् spoke.

27. Then he, the son of Kunti, seeing
all those kinsmen stationed in their ranks,
spoke thus sorrowfully, filled with deep
compassion.

अर्जुन उवाच ।

दृष्ट्वेमं स्वजनं कृष्ण युयुत्सुं समुपस्थितम् ॥

सीदन्ति मम गात्राणि मुखं च परिशुष्यति ॥२८॥

वेपथुश्च शरीरे मे रोमहर्षश्च जायते ॥

गाण्डीवं स्रंसते हस्तात्त्वक् चैव परिदह्यते ॥२९॥

अर्जुनः Arjuna उवाच said :

कृष्ण (the dark One : He who draws away all
misery from His devotees) O Krishna समुपस्थितं
present इमं these स्वजनं kinsmen युयुत्सुं desirous to fight
दृष्ट्वा seeing मम my गात्राणि limbs सीदन्ति are failing मुखं
च and mouth परिशुष्यति is parching च and मे my शरीरे

in body वेपथु: shivering च and रोमहर्ष: horripilation जायते are taking place हस्तात् from (my) hand गाण्डीवं (my bow) Gândiva स्रं'सते is slipping त्वक् च and (my) skin परिदह्यते is burning all over.

Arjuna said :

29.   Seeing, O Krishna, these my kinsmen gathered here eager for fight, my limbs fail me, and my mouth is parched up. I shiver all over, and my hair stands on end. The bow Gândiva slips from my hand, and my skin burns.

[Compassion overpowered him. Not that it was due to discrimination, but rather to the lack of this. He lost self-control—the first step into the abyss of ignorance.]

न च शक्नोम्यवस्थातुं भ्रमतीव च मे मन: ॥
निमित्तानि च पश्यामि विपरीतानि केशव ॥३०॥

केशव (the slayer of Keshi, Krishna) Keshava अवस्थातुं to stand न not च also शक्नोमि I am able मे my मन: mind च and भ्रमति इव seems whirling विपरीतानि adverse निमित्तानि omens च and पश्यामि I see.

30.   Neither, O Keshava, can I stand up-right. My mind is in a whirl. And I see adverse omens.

न च श्रेयोऽनुपश्यामि हत्वा स्वजनमाहवे ॥
न कांक्षे विजयं कृष्ण न च राज्यं सुखानि च ॥३१॥

3

कृष्ण O Krishna आह्वे in battle स्वजनं own people हृत्वा killing श्रेय: good च and न nor अनुपश्यामि (I) do see न neither विजयं victory न राज्यं च nor empire सुखानि च and pleasures कांक्षे (I) desire.

31. Neither, O Krishna, do I see any good in killing these my own people in battle. I desire neither victory nor empire, nor yet pleasure.

किं नो राज्येन गोविन्द किं भोगैर्जीवितेन वा ॥
येषामर्थे कांक्षितं नो राज्यं भोगाः सुखानि च ॥३२॥
त इमेऽवस्थिता युद्धे प्राणांस्त्यक्त्वा धनानि च ॥
आचार्याः पितरः पुत्रास्तथैव च पितामहाः ॥३३॥
मातुला: श्वशुराः पौत्राः श्यालाः संबन्धिनस्तथा ॥३४॥

गोविन्द (The presider over and knower of the senses : Krishna) Govinda येषाम् अर्थे for whose sake नः by us राज्यं empire भोगाः enjoyments सुखानि च and pleasures कांक्षितं desired आचार्याः teachers पितरः uncles पुत्राः sons तथा एव च and also पितामहाः grandfathers मातुला: maternal uncles श्वशुराः fathers-in-law पौत्राः grandsons श्यालाः brothers-in-law तथा as well as संबन्धिनः (other) relatives ते they इमे these प्राणान् life धनानि च and wealth त्यक्त्वा having renounced युद्धे in battle अवस्थिताः stand (अतः hence) नः our राज्येन kingdom किं for what purpose भोगैः pleasures वा and even जीवितेन life किं of what avail.

32-34. Of what avail is dominion to us, of what avail are pleasures and even life, if these, O Govinda ! for whose sake it is desired that empire, enjoyment, and pleasure should be ours, themselves stand here in battle, having renounced life and wealth—teachers, uncles, sons, and also grandfathers, maternal uncles, fathers-in-law, grandsons, brothers-in-law, besides other kinsmen.

एतान्न हन्तुमिच्छामि घ्नतोऽपि मधुसूदन ॥
अपि त्रैलोक्यराज्यस्य हेतो: किं नु महीकृते ॥३५॥

मधुसूदन O slayer of Madhu (a demon) घ्नत: अपि even if killed (by them) त्रैलोक्यराज्यस्य dominion over the three worlds (the earth, the intermediate, and the celestial) हेतो: for the sake of अपि even एतान् them हन्तं to kill न not इच्छामि (I do) wish महीकृते for earth किं नु far less indeed.

35. Even though these were to kill me, O slayer of Madhu, I could not wish to kill them—not even for the sake of dominion over the three worlds, how much less for the sake of the earth !

निहत्य धार्तराष्ट्रान्न: का प्रीति: स्याज्जनार्दन ॥
पापमेवाश्रयेदस्मान्हत्वैतानाततायिन: ॥३६॥

जनार्दन (The destroyer of the Asura, Jana; or according to Shankara, He that is prayed to by all for prosperity and salvation : Krishna) Janârdana धार्तराष्ट्रान् sons of Dhritarâshtra निहत्य killing नः ours का what प्रीतिः pleasure स्यात् would be एतान् these आततायिनः felons हत्वा by killing अस्मान् us पापम् sin एव surely आश्रयेत् would take hold.

36. What pleasure indeed could be ours, O Janârdana, from killing these sons of Dhritarâshtra ? Sin only could take hold of us by the slaying of these felons.

[*Felons :* Âtatâyi, one who sets fire to the house of, administers poison to, falls upon with a sword on, steals the wealth, land, and wife of, another person. Duryodhana did all these to the Pândava brothers. According to the Artha-Shâstras, no sin is incurred by killing an Âtatâyi, even if he be thoroughly versed in Vedânta. But Arjuna seems to argue, "True, there may not be incurred the particular sin of slaying one's own kith and kin by killing the sons of Dhritarâshtra inasmuch as they are Âtatâyis, but then the general sin of killing is sure to take hold of us, for the Dharma-Shâstra which is more authoritative than the Artha-Shâstra enjoins non-killing."]

तस्मान्नार्हा वयं हन्तुं धार्तराष्ट्रान् स्वबान्धवान् ॥
स्वजनं हि कथं हत्वा सुखिनः स्याम माधव ॥३७॥

तस्मात् Therefore स्वबान्धवान् our relatives धार्तराष्ट्रान् sons of Dhritarâshtra वयं we हन्तुं to kill न not अर्हाः justified माधव O Mâdhava हि for स्वजनं kinsmen हत्वा by killing कथं how सुखिनः happy स्याम could (we be).

37. Therefore ought we not to kill our kindred, the sons of Dhritarâshtra. For how could we, O Mâdhava, gain happiness by the slaying of our own kinsmen ?

यद्यप्येते न पश्यन्ति लोभोपहतचेतसः ॥

कुलक्षयकृतं दोषं मित्रद्रोहे च पातकम् ॥३८॥

कथं न ज्ञेयमस्माभिः पापादस्मान्निवर्तितुम् ॥

कुलक्षयकृतं दोषं प्रपश्यद्भिर्जनार्दन ॥३९॥

यद्यपि Though लोभोपहतचेतसः with understanding overpowered by greed एते these कुलक्षयकृतं due to decay of a family दोषं evil च and मित्रद्रोहे in hostility to friends पातकं sin न no पश्यन्ति see जनार्दन Janârdana कुलक्षयकृतं due to decay of a family दोषं evil प्रपश्यद्भिः clearly seeing अस्माभिः by us अस्मात् पापात् from this sin निवर्तितुं to turn away कथं why न ज्ञेयं should not be learnt.

38-39. Though these, with understanding overpowered by greed, see no evil due to decay of families, and no sin in hostility to friends, why should we, O

Janârdana, who see clearly the evil due to the decay of families, not turn away from this sin ?

कुलक्षये प्रणश्यन्ति कुलधर्माः सनातनाः ॥
धर्मे नष्टे कुलं कृत्स्नमधर्मोऽभिभवत्युत ॥४०॥

कुलक्षये On the decay of a family सनातनाः immemorial कुलधर्माः family religious practices प्रणश्यन्ति disappear धर्मे नष्टे spirituality being destroyed कृत्स्नं the whole उत also कुलं family अधर्मः impiety अभिभवति overcomes.

40. On the decay of a family the immemorial religious rites of that family die out. On the destruction of spirituality, impiety further overwhelms the whole of the family.

अधर्माभिभवात् कृष्ण प्रदुष्यन्ति कुलस्त्रियः ॥
स्त्रीषु दुष्टासु वार्ष्णेय जायते वर्णसङ्करः ॥४१॥

कृष्ण O Krishna अधर्माभिभवात् from the prevalence of impiety कुलस्त्रियः the women of the family प्रदुष्यन्ति become corrupt वार्ष्णेय (descendant of the Vrishni clan : Krishna) Vârshneya स्त्रीषु women दुष्टासु being corrupted वर्णसङ्करः caste admixture जायते arises.

41. On the prevalence of impiety, O Krishna, the women of the family become corrupt ; and women being corrupted,

there arises, O Vârshneya, intermingling of castes.

सङ्करो नरकायैव कुलघ्नानां कुलस्य च ॥
पतन्ति पितरो ह्येषां लुप्तपिण्डोदकक्रियाः ॥४२॥

सङ्करः Admixture (of castes) कुलघ्नानां of the family-destroyers कुलस्य of the family नरकाय for the hell च also एव indeed हि sure एषां their पितरः ancestors लुप्त-पिण्डोदकक्रियाः deprived of the offerings of rice-ball and water पतन्ति fall.

42. Admixture of castes, indeed, is for the hell of the family and the destroyers of the family ; their ancestors fall, deprived of the offerings of rice-ball and water.

[Verily, confusion of family is the hell of destroyers of family. (For then do) their own ancestors fall, deprived etc. This refers to the well-known Shrâddha ceremony of the Hindus, the main principle of which consists in sending helpful thoughts to the dead relations, as well as to all the occupants of Pitri-loka (a temporary abode, immediately after death) accompanied with (to make the thoughts more forcible) concrete offerings. The poor are also fed to secure their good wishes.]

दोषैरेतैः कुलघ्नानां वर्णसङ्करकारकैः ॥
उत्साद्यन्ते जातिधर्माः कुलधर्माश्च शाश्वताः ॥४३॥

कुल्घ्नानां of the family-destroyers वर्णसङ्करकारकैः causing admixture of castes एतैः दोषैः by these misdeeds शाश्वताः immemorial जातिधर्माः caste religious practices कुलधर्माः च and family religious practices उत्साद्यन्ते are destroyed.

43. By these misdeeds of the destroyers of the family, bringing about confusion of castes, are the immemorial religious rites of the caste and the family destroyed.

उत्सन्नकुलधर्माणां मनुष्याणां जनार्दन ॥

नरके नियतं वासो भवतीत्यनुशुश्रुम ॥४४॥

जनार्दन Janârdana उत्सन्नकुलधर्माणां मनुष्याणां of the men whose family religious practices are destroyed नियतं inevitably नरके in hell वासः dwelling भवति is इति thus अनुशुश्रुम have we heard.

44. We have heard, O Janârdana, that inevitable is the dwelling in hell of those men in whose families religious practices have been destroyed.

अहो बत महत्पापं कर्तुं व्यवसिता वयम् ॥

यद्राज्यसुखलोभेन हन्तुं स्वजनमुद्यताः ॥४५॥

यत् That राज्यसुखलोभेन by the greed of pleasure of kingdom स्वजनं kinsmen हन्तुं to kill उद्यताः prepared वयं

we एतत् this महत् great पापं sin कर्तुं to do व्यवसिताः
resolved अहो बत alas.

45. Alas, we are involved in a great
sin, in that we are prepared to slay our
kinsmen, from greed of the pleasures of a
kingdom !

यदि मामप्रतीकारमशस्त्रं शस्त्रपाणयः ॥

धार्तराष्ट्रा रणे हन्युस्तन्मे क्षेमतरं भवेत् ॥४६॥

यदि If अप्रतीकारम् unresisting अशस्त्रं unarmed मां me
शस्त्रपाणयः weapons in hand धार्तराष्ट्राः sons of Dhritarâshtra रणे in the battle हन्युः should slay तत् that मे
my क्षेमतरं better भवेत् would be.

46. Verily, if the sons of Dhritarâshtra,
weapons in hand, were to slay me, unresisting
and unarmed, in the battle, that would be
better for me.

सञ्जय उवाच ।

एवमुक्त्वार्जुनः संख्ये रथोपस्थ उपाविशत् ॥

विसृज्य सशरं चापं शोकसंविग्नमानसः ॥४७॥

सञ्जयः Sanjaya उवाच said :

अर्जुनः Arjuna एवं thus उक्त्वा saying संख्ये in the battle
सशरं with arrows चापं bow (named Gândiva) विसृज्य
casting away शोकसंविग्नमानसः with a mind distressed

with sorrow रथोपस्थे on the seat of the chariot उपाविशत् sat down.

Sanjaya said :

47. Speaking thus in the midst of the battle-field, Arjuna, casting away his bow and arrows, sank down on the seat of his chariot, with his mind distressed with sorrow.

इति अर्जुनविषादयोगो नाम प्रथमोऽध्यायः ॥१॥

The end of chapter first, designated, *The Grief of Arjuna.*

।। द्वितीयोऽध्यायः ।।

SECOND CHAPTER

सञ्जय उवाच ।

तं तथा कृपयाविष्टमश्रुपूर्णाकुलेक्षणम् ।।

विषीदन्तमिदं वाक्यमुवाच मधुसूदनः ।।१।।

सञ्जयः Sanjaya उवाच said :

मधुसूदनः Madhusudana तथा thus कृपया with pity आविष्टं overwhelmed अश्रुपूर्णाकुलेक्षणम् eyes dimmed with tears विषीदन्तं sorrowing तं him (Arjuna) इदं this वाक्यं word उवाच spoke.

Sanjaya said :

1. To him who was thus overwhelmed with pity and sorrowing, and whose eyes were dimmed with tears, Madhusudana spoke these words.

[*Overwhelmed with pity :* Not Arjuna, but Arjuna's feeling was master of the situation.]

श्रीभगवानुवाच ।

कुतस्त्वा कश्मलमिदं विषमे समुपस्थितम् ।।

अनार्यजुष्टमस्वर्ग्यमकीर्तिकरमर्जुन ।।२।।

श्रीभगवान् The Blessed Lord उवाच said :

अर्जुन O Arjuna विषमे in (such a) crisis कुतः whence इदं this अनार्यजुष्टम् un-Arya-like (unworthy of a religious man) अस्वर्ग्यम् contrary to the attainment of heaven अकीर्तिकरम् disgraceful कश्मलम् dejection त्वा upon thee समुपस्थितम् comes.

The Blessed Lord said :

2. In such a crisis, whence comes upon thee, O Arjuna, this dejection, un-Arya-like, disgraceful, and contrary to the attainment of heaven ?

[Mark with what contempt Krishna regards Arjuna's attitude of weakness masked by religious expression !]

क्लैब्यं मास्म गमः पार्थ नैतत्त्वय्युपपद्यते ॥
क्षुद्रं हृदयदौर्बल्यं त्यक्त्वोत्तिष्ठ परन्तप ॥३॥

पार्थ Son of Prithâ क्लैब्यं unmanliness मास्म गमः do not get एतत् it त्वयि in thee न उपपद्यते ill becomes परन्तप O scorcher of foes क्षुद्रं mean हृदयदौर्बल्यं faint-heartedness त्यक्त्वा casting off उत्तिष्ठ arise.

3. Yield not to unmanliness, O son of Prithâ ! Ill doth it become thee. Cast off this mean faint-heartedness and arise, O scorcher of thine enemies !

अर्जुन उवाच ।
कथं भीष्ममहं संख्ये द्रोणं च मधुसूदन ॥
इषुभिः प्रतियोत्स्यामि पूजार्हावरिसूदन ॥४॥

अर्जुनः Arjuna उवाच said :
अरिसूदन O destroyer of foes मधुसूदन O slayer of
Madhu अहं I संख्ये in battle पूजार्हौ worthy to be
worshipped भीष्मं Bhisma द्रोणं च and Drona इषुभिः with
arrows कथं how प्रतियोत्स्यामि shall fight against.

Arjuna said :

4. But how can I, in battle, O
slayer of Madhu, fight with arrows against
Bhishma and Drona, who are rather
worthy to be worshipped, O destroyer of
foes !

गुरूनहत्वा हि महानुभावान्
श्रेयो भोक्तुं भैक्ष्यमपीह लोके ॥
हत्वार्थकामांस्तु गुरूनिहैव
भुञ्जीय भोगान् रुधिरप्रदिग्धान् ॥५॥

महानुभावान् Great-souled गुरून् masters अहत्वा instead
of slaying हि surely इह लोके in this life भैक्ष्यं bread of
beggary अपि even भोक्तुं to eat श्रेयः better तु but गुरून्
masters हत्वा killing इह in this world एव even अर्थकामान्

wealth and desires भोग्यान् enjoyments रुधिर-प्रदिग्धान् stained with blood भुञ्जीय enjoy.

5. Surely it would be better even to eat the bread of beggary in this life than to slay these great-souled masters. But if I kill them, even in this world, all my enjoyment of wealth and desires will be stained with blood.

[i.e. even in this world I shall be in hell.]

न चैतद्विद्मः कतरन्नो गरीयो
यद्वा जयेम यदि वा नो जयेयुः ॥
यानेव हत्वा न जिजीविषाम-
स्तेऽवस्थिताः प्रमुखे धार्तराष्ट्राः ॥६॥

नः for us कतरत् which of the two गरीयः better एतत् this न च विद्मः and I know not यद्वा whether जयेम we should conquer यदि वा or that नः us जयेयुः they should conquer यान् whom एव very हत्वा after slaying न जिजीविषामः we should not care to live ते those धार्तराष्ट्राः sons of Dhritarâshtra प्रमुखे in front अवस्थिताः stand.

6. And indeed I can scarcely tell which will be better, that we should conquer them, or that they should conquer us. The very sons of Dhritarâshtra—after slaying whom we should not care to live—stand facing us.

कार्पण्यदोषोपहतस्वभावः

पृच्छामि त्वां धर्मसंमूढचेताः ॥

यच्छ्रेयः स्यान्निश्चितं ब्रूहि तन्मे

शिष्यस्तेऽहंशाधि मां त्वां प्रपन्नम् ॥७॥

कार्पण्यदोषोपहतस्वभावः with (my Kshatriya) nature
overpowered by the taint of weak commiseration
धर्मसंमूढचेताः with a mind in confusion about Dharma
(duty) त्वां Thee पृच्छामि I ask मे for me यत् which श्रेयः
good स्यात् is तत् that निश्चितं decidedly ब्रूहि say अहं I
ते Thy शिष्यः disciple त्वां Thee प्रपन्नं taken refuge मां me
शाधि instruct.

7. With my nature overpowered by
weak commiseration, with a mind in confusion about duty, I supplicate Thee. Say
decidedly what is good for me. I am Thy
disciple. Instruct me who have taken refuge
in Thee.

[Dharma is the *ness,* the law of the inmost
constitution of a thing. The primary meaning of
Dharma is not virtue or religion, but that is only its
secondary significance. Fighting in a just cause is
the religious duty or Dharma of a Kshatriya, while
the same is a sin to a Brâhmana, because it is contrary to the law of his being. Working out one's
Karma according to the law of one's own being is

therefore the Dharma or religion or way to salvation
of an individual. The cloud of Karma hides the
Self-Sun from view. The means which exhausts this
cloud without adding to it and thus helps in one's
Self-restoration is one's Dharma.

Thy disciple : Until this declaration has been
made, the Master may not give the highest knowledge.]

न हि प्रपश्यामि ममापनुद्याद्

यच्छोकमुच्छोषणमिन्द्रियाणाम् ॥

अवाप्य भूमावसपत्नमृद्धं

राज्यं सुराणामपि चाधिपत्यम् ॥८॥

भूमौ In the earth असपत्न' unrivalled ऋद्ध' flourishing
राज्यं dominion सुराणाम् over the gods अपि even आधिपत्यं
mastery च and अवाप्य obtaining यत् that मम my
इन्द्रियाणां of the senses उच्छोषणं blasting शोकं sorrow
अपनुद्यात् should remove न हि प्रपश्यामि I do not see.

8. I do not see anything to remove this
sorrow which blasts my senses, even were
I to obtain unrivalled and flourishing
dominion over the earth, and mastery over the
gods.

सञ्जय उवाच ।

एवमुक्त्वा हृषीकेशं गुडाकेशः परन्तपः ॥

न योत्स्य इति गोविन्दमुक्त्वा तूष्णीं बभूव ह ॥९॥

सञ्जयः Sanjaya उवाच said :

परन्तपः The scorcher of foes गुडाकेशः Gudâkesha, the conqueror of sleep (Arjuna) हृषीकेशं to Hrishikesha एवं thus उक्त्वा having spoken न योत्स्ये I shall not fight इति thus गोविन्दं to Govinda उक्त्वा saying तूष्णीं silent बभूव ह became.

Sanjaya said :

9. Having spoken thus to the Lord of the senses, Gudâkesha, the scorcher of foes, said to Govinda, "I shall not fight", and became silent.

[The object of Sanjaya in using these names is to remind Dhritarâshtra—who may naturally be a little elated at the prospect of Arjuna's not fighting —that this is only a temporary weakness, since by the presence of the Lord of the senses all ignorance must eventually be dispelled. Arjuna's own nature also is devoid of darkness. Is he not the conqueror of sleep, and the terror of foes?]

तमुवाच हृषीकेशः प्रहसन्निव भारत ॥
सेनयोरुभयोर्मध्ये विषीदन्तमिदं वचः ॥१०॥

भारत Descendant of king Bharata (after whom India is called Bhârata-Varsha) Bhârata (Dhritarâshtra) हृषीकेशः Hrishikesha प्रहसन् smiling इव as if उभयोः of the two सेनयोः armies मध्ये in the midst विषीदन्तं sorrowing तम् to him इदं this वचः word उवाच spoke.

4

10. To him who was sorrowing in the midst of the two armies, Hrishikesha, as if smiling, O descendant of Bharata, spoke these words.

[*Smiling*—to drown Arjuna in the ocean of shame. Krishna's smile at Arjuna's sorrow is like the lightning that plays over the black monsoon cloud. The rain bursts forth, and the thirsty earth is saturated. It is the smile of the coming illumination.]

श्रीभगवानुवाच।

अशोच्यानन्वशोचस्त्वं प्रज्ञावादांश्चभाषसे ॥

गतासूनगतासूंश्च नानुशोचन्ति पण्डिताः ॥११॥

श्रीभगवान् The Blessed Lord उवाच said :

त्वं Thou अशोच्यान् those who should not be mourned for अन्वशोचः hast been mourning प्रज्ञावादान् words of wisdom भाषसे thou speakest च but पण्डिताः the wise गतासून् the dead अगतासून् the living च and न अनुशोचन्ति grieve not.

The Blessed Lord said :

11. Thou hast been mourning for them who should not be mourned for. Yet thou speakest words of wisdom. The (truly) wise grieve neither for the living nor the dead.

[*Words of wisdom :* Vide I. 35-44.]

न त्वेवाहं जातु नासं न त्वं नेमे जनाधिपाः ॥
न चैव न भविष्यामः सर्वे वयमतः परम् ॥१२॥

अहं I जातु ever न तु आसं did not exist (इति) न एव not
indeed त्वं thou (न आसीः did not exist) न not इमे these
जनाधिपाः kings (न आसन् did not exist) न not अतःपरम्
hereafter सर्वे all वयम् we न not भविष्यामः shall exist च
also न एव not at all.

12. It is not that I have never existed, nor thou, nor these kings. Nor is it
that we shall cease to exist in the future.

[Of course Krishna here does not mean that
the body is immortal, but refers to the true Self,
behind all bodies.]

देहिनोऽस्मिन् यथा देहे कौमारं यौवनं जरा ॥
तथा देहान्तरप्राप्तिर्धीरस्तत्र न मुह्यति ॥१३॥

यथा As देहिनः of the embodied (soul) अस्मिन् देहे in
this body कौमारं childhood यौवनं youth जरा old age तथा
so also देहान्तरप्राप्तिः the attaining of another body
तत्र thereat धीरः the calm soul न मुह्यति is not
deluded.

13. As are childhood, youth, and old
age, in this body, to the embodied soul, so

also is the attaining of another body. Calm souls are not deluded thereat.

[According to this, the continuity of the ego is no more interrupted by death than by the passing of childhood into youth and youth into old age in this body.

Calm souls : Those who have become calm by Self-realisation.]

मात्रास्पर्शास्तु कौन्तेय शीतोष्णसुखदुःखदाः ॥

आगमापायिनोऽनित्यास्तांस्तितिक्षस्व भारत ॥१४॥

कौन्तेय O son of Kunti मात्रास्पर्शाः contacts of senses with their objects तु indeed शीतोष्णसुखदुःखदाः producers of (the notions of) cold and heat, pleasure and pain आगमापायिनः with beginning and end अनित्याः impermanent भारत O Bhârata तान् them तितिक्षस्व bear with.

14. Notions of heat and cold, of pain and pleasure, are born, O son of Kunti, only of the contact of the senses with their objects. They have a beginning and an end. They are impermanent in their nature. Bear them patiently, O descendant of Bharata.

[*They have a beginning and an end :* as distinguished from the Permanent Self. The more one is able to identify oneself with the Permanent

Self, the less one is affected by the agreeable and disagreeable conditions of life.

Impermanent in their nature : That is, the same object which gives pleasure at one moment, gives pain at another, and so on.]

यं हि न व्यथयन्त्येते पुरुषं पुरुषर्षभ ॥

समदुःखसुखं धीरं सोऽमृतत्वाय कल्पते ॥१५॥

पुरुषर्षभ O Bull (i.e. chief) among men एते these समदुःखसुखं same in pain and pleasure धीरं calm यं that पुरुषं (lit. dweller in the body) man न व्यथयन्ति afflict not सः he हि surely अमृतत्वाय for immortality कल्पते is fit.

15. That calm man who is the same in pain and pleasure, whom these cannot disturb, alone is able, O great amongst men, to attain to immortality.

[This perfect sameness, amidst the ills of life, means full and unbroken consciousness of our one-ness with the Immortal Self. Thus is immortality attained.]

नासतो विद्यते भावो नाभावो विद्यते सतः ॥

उभयोरपि दृष्टोऽन्तस्त्वनयोस्तत्त्वदर्शिभिः ॥१६॥

असतः Of the unreal भावः existence न विद्यते is not सतः of the real अपि also अभावः non-existence न विद्यते is

not तत्त्वदर्शिभिः by the knowers of the Truth तु indeed
अनयोः उभयोः of these two अन्तः the final truth दृष्टः seen.

16. The unreal never is. The Real
never is not. Men possessed of the knowledge of the Truth fully know both these.

[*Unreal : Real :* The determination of the
nature of the Real is the quest of all philosophy.
Shri Krishna here states that a thing which never
remains the same for any given period is unreal,
and that the Real on the other hand is always the
same. The whole of the phenomenal world, therefore, must be unreal, because in it no one state
endures for even an infinitesimal division of time.
And that which takes note of this incessant change,
and is therefore itself changeless—the Âtman,
Consciousness—is the Real.]

अविनाशि तु तद्विद्धि येन सर्वमिदं ततम् ॥
विनाशमव्ययस्यास्य न कश्चित्कर्तुमर्हति ॥१७॥

येन By which इदं this सर्वं all ततं is pervaded तत्
That अविनाशि indestructible तु विद्धि know for certain
कश्चित् one अस्य अव्ययस्य of this Immutable विनाशं destruction कर्तुं to do न अर्हति is not able.

17. That by which all this is pervaded—That know for certain to be
indestructible. None has the power to
destroy this Immutable.

[*That by which all this is pervaded* : i.e. He that pervades all this *as the Witness.*]

अन्तवन्त इमे देहा नित्यस्योक्ता: शरीरिण: ॥

अनाशिनोऽप्रमेयस्य तस्मादुध्यस्व भारत ॥१८॥

नित्यस्य Of the ever-changeless अनाशिन: of the inde-structible अप्रमेयस्य of the illimitable शरीरिण: of the Indweller इमे these देहा: bodies अन्तवन्त: having an end उक्ता: are said भारत O Bhârata तस्मात् therefore युध्यस्व fight.

18. Of this indwelling Self—the ever-changeless, the indestructible, the illimit-able—these bodies are said to have an end. Fight, therefore, O descendant of Bharata.

[Arjuna's grief which deters him from his duty of fighting against the Kauravas is born of ignorance as to the true nature of the soul. Hence Shri Bhagavân's strong and repeated attempts to illumine him on the subject.]

य एनं वेत्ति हन्तारं यश्चैनं मन्यते हतम् ॥

उभौ तौ न विजानीतो नायं हन्ति न हन्यते ॥१९॥

य: Who एनं this (Self) हन्तारं slayer वेत्ति knows य: च and who एनं this हतं slain मन्यते thinks उभौ both तौ these न not विजानीत: know अयं this (Self) न not हन्ति slays न not हन्यते is slain.

19. He who takes the Self to be the slayer, and he who takes It to be the slain, neither of these knows. It does not slay, nor is It slain.

[Cf. Katha Up. I ii. 19-20]

न जायते म्रियते वा कदाचि-
न्नायं भूत्वा भविता वा न भूयः ॥
अजो नित्यः शाश्वतोऽयं पुराणो
न हन्यते हन्यमाने शरीरे ॥२०॥

अयं this (Self) कदाचित् ever न not जायते is born वा or म्रियते dies वा or न भूत्वा not having been भूयः again भविता comes into being (इति) न (it is) not. (Another paraphrase) वा Or भूत्वा having been भूयः again न भविता ceases to be (इति) न (it is) not. अजः unborn नित्यः eternal शाश्वतः changeless पुराणः ever-Itself अयं this (Self) शरीरे the body हन्यमाने being killed न not हन्यते is killed.

20. This is never born, nor does It die. It is not that not having been It again comes into being. (Or according to another view : It is not that having been, It again ceases to be). This is unborn, eternal, changeless, ever-Itself. It is not killed when the body is killed.

[This shloka refers in the sense of denial to the six kinds of modification inherent in matter : birth, subsistence, growth, transformation, decay, and death.]

वेदाविनाशिनं नित्यं य एनमजमव्ययम् ॥
कर्थं स पुरुषः पार्थ कं घातयति हन्ति कम् ॥२१॥

पार्थ O Pârtha यः who एनम् this (Self) अविनाशिनं inde-structible नित्यं changeless अजम् unborn अव्ययम् immutable वेद knows सः that पुरुषः person कथं how कं whom हन्ति kills कं whom घातयति causes to slay.

21. He that knows This to be inde-structible, changeless, without birth, and immutable, how is he, O son of Prithâ, to slay or cause another to slay ?

[*How is he to slay?*—referring to Arjuna. *To cause another to slay*—referring to Krishna's own part.]

वासांसि जीर्णानि यथा विहाय
नवानि गृह्णाति नरोऽपराणि ॥
तथा शरीराणि विहाय जीर्णा-
न्यन्यानि संयाति नवानि देही ॥२२॥

नरः A man यथा as जीर्णानि worn-out वासांसि clothes विहाय casting off अपराणि others नवानि new गृह्णाति takes

तथा so देही the embodied जीर्णानि worn-out शरीराणि
bodies विहाय casting off अन्यानि others नवानि new संयाति
enters.

22. Even as a man casts off worn-out
clothes, and puts on others which are new, so
the embodied casts off worn-out bodies, and
enters into others which are new.

[As one only puts off the old, when one already
possesses the new garment, so the embodied is
already entering a new body in the act of leaving
this. The Upanishad compares this to the movement
of a leech, which has already established a new foot-
hold before leaving the old.]

नैनं छिन्दन्ति शस्त्राणि नैनं दहति पावकः ॥
न चैनं क्लेदयन्त्यापो न शोषयति मारुतः ॥२३॥

शस्त्राणि Weapons एनं this (Self) न छिन्दन्ति cut not
पावकः fire एनं This न दहति burns not आपः waters एनं
This न क्लेदयन्ति wet not च and मारुतः wind न शोषयति
dries not.

23. This (Self), weapons cut not ; This,
fire burns not ; This, water wets not ; and
This, wind dries not.

अच्छेद्योऽयमदाह्योऽयमक्लेद्योऽशोष्य एव च ॥
नित्यः सर्वगतः स्थाणुरचलोऽयं सनातनः ॥२४॥

अयं This (Self) अच्छेद्यः cannot be cut अयं This
अदाह्यः cannot be burnt अक्लेद्यः cannot be wetted अशोष्यः
च एव and cannot also be dried अयं This नित्यः changeless सर्वगतः all-pervading स्थाणुः unmoving अचलः immovable सनातनः eternal.

24. This Self cannot be cut, nor burnt,
nor wetted, nor dried. Changeless, all-pervading, unmoving, immovable, the Self is
eternal.

अव्यक्तोऽयमचिन्त्योऽयमविकार्योऽयमुच्यते ॥
तस्मादेवं विदित्वैनं नानुशोचितुमर्हसि ॥२५॥

अयम् This (Self) अव्यक्तः unmanifested अयम् This अचिन्त्य
unthinkable अयम् This अविकार्यः unchangeable उच्यते is
said तस्मात् therefore एवं thus एनं This विदित्वा knowing
अनुशोचितुम् to mourn न अर्हसि oughtest not.

25. This (Self) is said to be unmanifested, unthinkable, and unchangeable.
Therefore, knowing This to be such, thou
oughtest not to mourn.

[This Self is infinite and partless, so can be
neither subject nor object of any action.]

अथ चैनं नित्यजातं नित्यं वा मन्यसे मृतम् ॥
तथापि त्वं महाबाहो नैनं शोचितुमर्हसि ॥२६॥

अथ च But if एनं This (Self) नित्यजातं constantly born नित्यं constantly वा or मृतं dead मन्यसे thinkest तथापि even then महाबाहो mighty-armed त्वं thou एनं This शोचितुं to mourn न अर्हसि oughtest not.

26. But if thou shouldst take This to have constant birth and death, even in that case, O mighty-armed, thou oughtest not to mourn for This.

[Krishna here, for the sake of argument, takes up the materialistic supposition, and shows that even if the Self were impermanent, sorrow ought to be destroyed, since in that case there would be no here-after, no sin, and no hell.]

जातस्य हि ध्रुवो मृत्युर्ध्रुवं जन्म मृतस्य च ॥
तस्मादपरिहार्येऽर्थे न त्वं शोचितुमर्हसि ॥२७॥

हि For जातस्य of that which is born मृत्युः death ध्रुवः certain मृतस्य च and of that which is dead जन्म birth ध्रुवं certain तस्मात् therefore अपरिहार्ये अर्थे in an unavoidable matter त्वं thou शोचितुं to grieve न अर्हसि oughtest not.

27. Of that which is born, death is certain ; of that which is dead, birth is certain. Over the unavoidable, therefore, thou oughtest not to grieve.

[This shloka concerns only those who are not yet free. So long as there is desire, birth and death are inevitable.

Therefore thou oughtest not to grieve : Since you cannot control the inevitable and preserve the bodies of your relations, work out your own Karma and go beyond both birth and death.]

अव्यक्तादीनि भूतानि व्यक्तमध्यानि भारत ॥
अव्यक्तनिधनान्येव तत्र का परिदेवना ॥२८॥

भारत O Bhârata भूतानि beings अव्यक्तादीनि unmanifested in the beginning व्यक्तमध्यानि manifested in the middle state अव्यक्तनिधनानि एव unmanifested again in the end तत्र there का what परिदेवना grief.

28. All beings are unmanifested in their beginning, O Bhârata, manifested in their middle state, and unmanifested again in their end. What is there then to grieve about ?

[*Beings :* In their relationships as sons and friends, who are mere combinations of material elements, correlated as causes and effects.

The idea here is that that which has no existence in the beginning and in the end, must be merely illusory in the interim, and should not therefore be allowed to have any influence upon the mind.]

आश्चर्यवत्पश्यति कश्चिदेन-

माश्चर्यवद्वदति तथैव चान्यः ॥

आश्चर्यवच्चैनमन्यः शृणोति

श्रुत्वाप्येनं वेद न चैव कश्चित् ॥२९॥

कश्चित् Some one एनम् This (Self) आश्चर्यवत् as a wonder पश्यति looks upon तथा एव च and so also अन्यः another आश्चर्यवत् as a wonder वदति speaks अन्यः च another again एनम् This आश्चर्यवत् as a wonder शृणोति hears कश्चित् च and yet another श्रुत्वा अपि though hearing एनं This न एव वेद knows not at all.

29. Some look upon the Self as marvellous. Others speak of It as wonderful. Others again hear of It as a wonder. And still others, though hearing, do not understand It at all.

[The shloka may also be interpreted in the sense that those who see, hear, and speak of the Self are wonderful men, because their number is so small. It is not therefore remarkable that you should mourn, because the Âtman is so difficult to comprehend.]

देही नित्यमवध्योऽयं देहे सर्वस्य भारत ॥

तस्मात्सर्वाणि भूतानि न त्वं शोचितुमर्हसि ॥३०॥

भारत O Bhârata अयं this देही Indweller सर्वस्य of all देहे in the body नित्यम् ever अवध्यः indestructible तस्मात्

therefore त्वं thou सर्वाणि all भूतानि beings शोचितुं to
mourn न अर्हसि oughtest not.

30. This, the Indweller in the bodies
of all, is ever indestructible, O descendant of
Bharata. Therefore thou oughtest not to
mourn for any creature.

[Krishna here returns to His own point of
view.]

स्वधर्ममपि चावेक्ष्य न विकम्पितुमर्हसि ॥

धर्म्याद्धि युद्धाच्छ्रेयोऽन्यत्क्षत्रियस्य न विद्यते ॥३१॥

स्वधर्मं Own Dharma अपि च and also अवेक्ष्य looking
at न not विकम्पितुम् to waver अर्हसि oughtest हि for धर्म्यात्
युद्धात् than a righteous war क्षत्रियस्य of a Kshatriya
अन्यत् any other श्रेयः higher न विद्यते exists not.

31. Looking at thine own Dharma,
also, thou oughtest not to waver, for there is
nothing higher for a Kshatriya than a righteous
war.

[That is to say, it is the duty of a Kshatriya
to fight in the interest of his country, people, and
religion.]

यदृच्छया चोपपन्नं स्वर्गद्वारमपावृतम् ॥

सुखिनः क्षत्रियाः पार्थ लभन्ते युद्धमीदृशम् ॥३२॥

पार्थ O Pârtha यदृच्छया of itself उपपन्नं come अपावृतं
opened स्वर्गद्वारम् the gate of heaven ईदृशम् such युद्धम्

battle सुखिनः happy क्षत्रियाः Kshatriyas च verily लभन्ते gain.

32.   Fortunate certainly are the Kshatriyas, O son of Prithâ, who are called to fight in such a battle that comes unsought as an open gate to heaven.

[The Shâstras say that if a Kshatriya, fighting for a righteous cause, falls in the battle-field, he at once goes to heaven.]

अथ चेत्त्वमिमं धर्म्यं संग्रामं न करिष्यसि ॥

ततः स्वधर्मं कीर्तिं च हित्वा पापमवाप्स्यसि ॥३३॥

अथचेत् But if त्वं thou इमं this धर्म्यं righteous संग्रामं warfare न करिष्यसि wouldst not do ततः then स्वधर्मं own Dharma कीर्तिं च and honour हित्वा forfeiting पापम् sin अवाप्स्यसि shalt incur.

33.   But if thou refusest to engage in this righteous warfare, then forfeiting thine own Dharma and honour, thou shalt incur sin.

अकीर्तिंश्चापि भूतानि कथयिष्यन्ति तेऽव्ययाम् ॥

संभावितस्य चाकीर्तिर्मरणादतिरिच्यते ॥३४॥

अपिच And also भूतानि beings ते of thee अव्ययाम् everlasting अकीर्तिं dishonour कथयिष्यन्ति will tell संभावितस्य of the honoured अकीर्तिः dishonour मरणात् than death च surely अतिरिच्यते exceeds.

34. The world also will ever hold thee in reprobation. To the honoured, disrepute is surely worse than death.

[The present argument —shlokas 33-36— assumes that the cause in hand is already proved to be right. Hence it could only be from cowardice that Arjuna could abandon it. Even a hero may be weakened by the stirring of his deepest emotions.]

भयाद्रणादुपरतं मंस्यन्ते त्वां महारथाः ॥
येषां च त्वं बहुमतो भूत्वा यास्यसि लाघवम् ॥३५॥

महारथाः च And the great chariot-warriors त्वां thee भयात् from fear रणात् from battle उपरतं withdrawn मंस्यन्ते will regard येषां of those त्वं thou बहुमतः much-thought-of भूत्वा having been लाघवं lightness यास्यसि wilt receive.

35. The great chariot-warriors [1] will believe that thou hast withdrawn from the battle through fear. And thou wilt be lightly esteemed by them who have thought much of thee.

अवाच्यवादांश्च बहून्वदिष्यन्ति तवाहिताः ॥
निन्दन्तस्तव सामर्थ्यं ततो दुःखतरं नु किम् ॥३६॥

तव Thine अहिताः च enemies also तव thy सामर्थ्यं

<hr>

[1] *Vide* commentary 1.6.

5

prowess निन्दन्तः cavilling बहून् many अवाच्यवादान्
unutterable things वदिष्यन्ति will say ततः than this
दुःखतरं more painful नु किं what (could be).

36.   Thine enemies also, cavilling at thy
great prowess, will say of thee things that are
not to be uttered. What could be more
intolerable than this ?

हतो वा प्राप्स्यसि स्वर्गं जित्वा वा भोक्ष्यसे महीम् ॥
तस्मादुत्तिष्ठ कौन्तेय युद्धाय कृतनिश्चयः ॥३७॥

हतः Slain वा or स्वर्गं heaven प्राप्स्यसि shalt gain जित्वा
conquering वा or महीं earth भोक्ष्यसे shalt enjoy तस्मात्
therefore कौन्तेय O son of Kunti युद्धाय for fight कृतनिश्चय
resolved उत्तिष्ठ arise.

37.   Dying thou gainest heaven ; conquering thou enjoyest the earth. Therefore,
O son of Kunti, arise, resolved to
fight.

सुखदुःखे समे कृत्वा लाभालाभौ जयाजयौ ॥
ततो युद्धाय युज्यस्व नैवं पापमवाप्स्यसि ॥३८॥

सुखदुःखे Pain and pleasure समे the same कृत्वा having
made लाभालाभौ gain and loss जयाजयौ conquest and
defeat ततः then युद्धाय for battle युज्यस्व be ready एवं thus
पापं sin न no अवाप्स्यसि shalt incur.

38. Having made pain and pleasure, gain and loss, conquest and defeat, the same, engage thou then in battle. So shalt thou incur no sin.

[It is always the desire for one of the pairs of opposites that binds. When an act is done without attachment either for itself or its fruit, then Karma can be worked out without adding to its store, and this leads to Freedom.]

एषा तेऽभिहिता सांख्ये बुद्धियोंगे त्विमां श्रृणु ॥

बुद्ध्या युक्तो यया पार्थ कर्मबन्धं प्रहास्यसि ॥३६॥

सांख्ये In regard to Self-realisation एषा this बुद्धि: wisdom ते to thee अभिहिता declared योगे तु but in regard to Yoga इमां it श्रृणु hear पार्थ O Pârtha यया with which बुद्ध्या wisdom युक्त: endued कर्मबन्धं bondage of Karma प्रहास्यसि shalt break through.

39. The wisdom of Self-realisation has been declared unto thee. Hearken thou now to the wisdom of Yoga, endued with which, O son of Prithâ, thou shalt break through the bonds of Karma.

[*Yoga* : Karma-Yoga, or that plan of conduct which secures the working out of past Karma, non-accumulation of new, and the striving for Self-realisation with the whole of the will. In this discipline, one's sole object in life is Self-realisation ; hence no importance is attached to anything else. Thus all actions are performed without attachment,

or care for results. So no new Karma is made : only
the already accumulated is exhausted. And at the
same time, the whole will is left free to devote itself
to the achievement of Self-realisation alone.

In the preceding shlokas, 11-25, Krishna has
given the point of view of the highest knowledge,
the ancient Brahmajnâna. In the 26th and 27th we
have a purely materialistic standpoint. Shlokas 28
to 37 give the attitude of a man of the world. In
the 38th we have an anticipation of the Yoga. And
in what is to follow, we have Shri Krishna's own con-
tribution to the philosophy of life.]

नेहाभिक्रमनाशोऽस्ति प्रत्यवायो न विद्यते ॥

स्वल्पमप्यस्य धर्मस्य त्रायते महतो भयात् ॥४०॥

इह In this अभिक्रमनाशः waste of attempt नअस्ति is not
प्रत्यवायः(च and) production of contrary results न विद्यते
exists not अस्य धर्मस्य of this Dharma स्वल्पं very little अपि
even महतः भयात् from great terror त्रायते protects.

40. In this, there is no waste of the
unfinished attempt, nor is there production
of contrary results. Even very little
of this Dharma protects from the great
terror.

[*Waste of the unfinished attempt :* A religious
rite or ceremony performed for a definite object, if
left uncompleted, is wasted, like a house unroofed
which is neither serviceable nor enduring. In Karma-
Yoga, however, that is, action and worship performed

without desire, this law does not apply, for every
effort results in immediate purification of the heart.
Production of contrary results : In worship for an
object, any imperfection in the process produces
positive loss instead of gain. As in cases of
sickness, the non-use of the right medicine results in
death. *The great terror :* Being caught in the
wheel of birth and death.]

व्यवसायात्मिका बुद्धिरेकेह कुरुनन्दन ॥

बहुशाखा ह्यनन्ताश्च बुद्धयोऽव्यवसायिनाम् ॥४१॥

कुरुनन्दन O scion of Kuru इह in this व्यवसायात्मिका one-
pointed बुद्धिः determination एका single (एव only)
अव्यवसायिनां of the undecided बुद्धयः purposes हि indeed
बहुशाखाः many-branching च and अनन्ताः innumerable.

41.   In this, O scion of Kuru, there is but
a single one-pointed determination. The
purposes of the undecided are innumerable
and many-branching.

[In Karma-Yoga, the one goal is Self-realisation.
The undecided (that is, about the highest), naturally
devote themselves to lower ideals, no one of which
can satisfy. Thus they pass from plan to plan.]

यामिमां पुष्पितां वाचं प्रवदन्त्यविपश्चितः ॥

वेदवादरताः पार्थ नान्यदस्तीतिवादिनः ॥४२॥

कामात्मानः स्वर्गपरा जन्मकर्मफलप्रदाम् ॥

क्रियाविशेषबहुलां भोगैश्वर्यगतिं प्रति ॥४३॥

भोगैश्वर्यप्रसक्तानां तयापहृतचेतसाम् ॥

व्यवसायात्मिका बुद्धि: समाधौ न विधीयते ॥४४॥

पार्थ O Pârtha अविपश्चित: the unwise वेदवादरता:taking
pleasure in the panegyric statements of the Vedas
अन्यत् anything else न अस्ति does not exist इति this वादिन:
declaring कामात्मान: full of desires स्वर्गपरा: with heaven
as their highest goal याम् which इमां this (well-known)
पुष्पितां flowery जन्मकर्मफलप्रदाम् leading to (new) birth as
the result of their works भोगैश्वर्यगतिं प्रति for the attainment of pleasure and power क्रियाविशेषबहुलां exuberant
with various specific actions वाचं word प्रवदन्ति expatiate
upon भोगैश्वर्यप्रसक्तानां of (people) deeply attached to
pleasure and power तया by that अपहृतचेतसाम् with their
discrimination stolen away व्यवसायात्मिका set बुद्धि: determination समाधौ in the mind न विधीयते is not formed.

42-44. O Pârtha, no set determination is
formed in the minds of those that are
deeply attached to pleasure and power,
and whose discrimination is stolen away
by the flowery words of the unwise, who
are full of desires and look upon heaven
as their highest goal and who, taking
pleasure in the panegyric words of the
Vedas, declare that there is nothing else.
Their flowery words are exuberant with
various specific rites as the means to pleasure
and power and are the causes of (new) births

as the result of their works (performed with desire).

[Samâdhi has been rendered into "mind" in the above. The generally accepted significance of the term (absorption in God-consciousness produced by deep meditation) would give an equally consistent and happy meaning : Persons attached to pleasure and power cannot have perfect steadiness of mind in divine meditation.

Panegyric words of the Vedas : The Karma Kânda or the sacrificial portion of the Vedas which lays down specific rules for specific actions and their fruits, and extols these latter unduly. *Nothing else :* Beyond the heavenly enjoyments procurable by the sacrificial rites of the Vedas.]

त्रैगुण्यविषया वेदा निस्त्रैगुण्यो भवार्जुन ॥

निर्द्वन्द्वो नित्यसत्त्वस्थो निर्योगक्षेम आत्मवान् ॥४५॥

वेदाः The Vedas त्रैगुण्यविषयाः deal with the three Gunas अर्जुन O Arjuna (त्वं thou) निस्त्रैगुण्यः free from the triad of Gunasभव be निर्द्वन्द्वः free from the pairs of opposites नित्यसत्त्वस्थः ever-balanced निर्योगक्षेमः free from getting and keeping आत्मवान् established in the Self.

45. The Vedas deal with the three Gunas. Be thou free, O Arjuna, from the triad of the Gunas, free from the pairs of opposites, ever-balanced, free from (the thought of) getting and keeping, and established in the Self.

[*The Vedas deal with etc.:* That is to say, the Vedas treat of relativity. *Pairs of opposites :* Dvandva, all correlated ideas and sensations, e.g., good and bad, pleasure and pain, heat and cold, light and darkness, etc.

Guna is a technical term of the Sânkhya philosophy : also used in the same sense by the Vedânta. Prakriti or Nature is constituted of three Gunas ; Sattva (equilibrium), Rajas (attraction), Tamas (inertia). Prakriti *is* the three Gunas, *not* that she *has* them. Guna is wrongly translated as quality ; it is substance as well as quality, matter, *and* force. Wherever there is name and form, there is Guna. Guna also means a rope, that which binds.]

यावानर्थ उदपाने सर्वतः संप्लुतोदके ॥
तावान्सर्वेषु वेदेषु ब्राह्मणस्य विजानतः ॥४६॥

सर्वतः Everywhere संप्लुतोदके being flooded उदपाने in a reservoir यावान् as much अर्थः 'use विजानतः of the knowing ब्राह्मणस्य Brâhmana सर्वेषु in all वेदेषु the Vedas तावान् so much (use).

46. To the Brâhmana who has known the Self, all the Vedas are of so much use as a reservoir is, when there is a flood everywhere.

[A man possessed of Self-knowledge has no need whatever of the Vedas. This does not, however, mean that the Vedas are useless ; only to the knower of Brahman they have no value, as the transient

pleasures derivable from them are comprehended in
the infinite bliss of Self-knowledge.]

कर्मण्येवाधिकारस्ते मा फलेषु कदाचन ॥
मा कर्मफलहेतुर्भूर्मा ते सङ्गोऽस्त्वकर्मणि ॥४७॥

कर्मणि In work एव only ते thy अधिकारः right कदाचन
ever फलेषु in fruits मा not कर्मफलहेतुः the producer of
the results of acts मा भूः shouldst not be अकर्मणि in
inaction ते thy सङ्गः attachment मा not अस्तु let be.

47. Thy right is to work only ; but
never to the fruits thereof. Be thou not
the producer of the fruits of (thy) actions ;
neither let thy attachment be towards
inaction.

[*Be thou not the producer, etc.*: That is, do
not work with any desire for results, for actions produce fruits or bondage only if they are performed
with desire.

Karma primarily means action, but a much pro-
founder meaning has come to be attached to this
word. It means the destiny forged by one in one's
past incarnation or present : the store of tendencies,
impulses, characteristics, and habits laid by, which
determines the future embodiment, environment, and
the whole of one's organisation.

Another meaning of Karma often used in
reference to one's caste or position in life, is duty,
the course of conduct which one ought to follow in
pursuance of the tendencies which one acquired in

one's past, with a view to working them out and
regaining the pristine purity of the Self.]

योगस्थः कुरु कर्माणि सङ्गं त्यक्ता धनञ्जय ॥
सिद्ध्यसिद्ध्योः समो भूत्वा समत्वं योग उच्यते ॥४८॥

धनञ्जय O Dhananjaya योगस्थः steadfast in Yoga सङ्गं
attachment त्यक्ता abandoning सिद्ध्यसिद्ध्योः in regard to
success and failure समः the same भूत्वा being कर्माणि
actions कुरु perform समत्वं evenness of mind (in regard
to success and failure) योगः Yoga उच्यते is called.

48. Being steadfast in Yoga, O
Dhananjaya, perform actions, abandoning
attachment, remaining unconcerned as regards
success and failure. This evenness of mind
(in regard to success and failure) is known
as Yoga.

दूरेण ह्यवरं कर्म बुद्धियोगाद्धनञ्जय ॥
बुद्धौ शरणमन्विच्छ कृपणाः फलहेतवः ॥४९॥

धनञ्जय O Dhananjaya हि as बुद्धियोगात् than work
performed with the mind undisturbed by thoughts
of results दूरेण by far कर्म work अवरं inferior बुद्धौ in
evenness of mind शरणं refuge अन्विच्छ seek फलहेतव
seekers after results कृपणाः wretched.

49. Work (with desire) is verily far
inferior to that performed with the
mind undisturbed by thoughts of results. O

Dhananjaya, seek refuge in this evenness
of mind. Wretched are they who act for
results.

बुद्धियुक्तो जहातीह उभे सुकृतदुष्कृते ॥
तस्माद्योगाय युज्यस्व योगः कर्मसु कौशलम् ॥५०॥

बुद्धियुक्तः Endued with evenness of mind इह in this
(life) उभे both सुकृतदुष्कृते virtue and vice जहाति casts off
तस्मात् therefore योगाय to Yoga युज्यस्व devote thyself योगः
Yoga कर्मसु in work कौशलम् dexterity.

50.　Endued with this evenness of mind,
one frees oneself in this life, alike from
vice and virtue. Devote thyself, therefore,
to this Yoga. Yoga is the very dexterity of
work.

[*Alike from vice and virtue :* A follower of
Karma-Yoga can have no personal motive for any
action. Our action without motive becomes colour-
less, loses its character of vice or virtue.

Dexterity of work : It is the nature of work to
produce bondage. Karma-Yoga is the dexterity of
work, because it not only robs work of its power to
bind, but also transforms it into an efficient means
of freedom.]

कर्मजं बुद्धियुक्ता हि फलं त्यक्त्वा मनीषिणः ॥
जन्मबन्धविनिर्मुक्ताः पदं गच्छन्त्यनामयम् ॥५१॥

बुद्धियुक्ता: Possessed of evenness of mind मनीषिण: the wise कर्मजं फलं the fruit of action त्यक्त्वा abandoning जन्मबन्धविनिर्मुक्ता: freed from the fetters of birth अनामयं beyond evil पदं state हि verily गच्छन्ति go to.

51. The wise, possessed of this evenness of mind, abandoning the fruits of their actions, freed for ever from the fetters of birth, go to that state which is beyond all evil.

यदा ते मोहकलिलं बुद्धिर्व्यतितरिष्यति ॥

तदा गन्तासि निर्वेदं श्रोतव्यस्य श्रुतस्य च ॥५२॥

यदा When ते thy बुद्धि: intellect मोहकलिलं taint of illusion व्यतितरिष्यति crosses beyond तदा then श्रोतव्यस्य of what is to be heard श्रुतस्य च and of what is heard निर्वेदं indifference गन्तासि thou shalt attain.

52. When thy intellect crosses beyond the taint of illusion, then shalt thou attain to indifference, regarding things heard and things yet to be heard.

[*The taint of illusion :* the identifying of the Self with the non-Self, the ego.]

श्रुतिविप्रतिपन्ना ते यदा स्थास्यति निश्चला ॥

समाधावचला बुद्धिस्तदा योगमवाप्स्यसि ॥५३॥

यदा When ते thy श्रुतिविप्रतिपन्ना tossed about by the conflict of opinions बुद्धि: intellect अचला firmly established

सभाधौ in the Self निश्चला immovable स्थास्यति will remain तदा then योगं Self-realisation अवाप्स्यसि shalt attain.

53. When thy intellect, tossed about by the conflict of opinions has become immovable and firmly established in the Self, then thou shalt attain Self-realisation.

अर्जुन उवाच ।

स्थितप्रज्ञस्य का भाषा समाधिस्थस्य केशव ॥

स्थितधीः किं प्रभाषेत किमासीत व्रजेत किम् ॥५४॥

अर्जुनः Arjuna उवाच said :

केशव O Keshava स्थितप्रज्ञस्य of the (man of) steady wisdom समाधिस्थस्य of the (man) merged in Samâdhi का what भाषा description स्थितधीः (the man of) steady wisdom किं what प्रभाषेत speaks किं what (how) आसीत sits किं what (how) व्रजेत walks.

Arjuna said :

54. What, O Keshava, is the description of the man of steady wisdom, merged in Samâdhi ? How (on the other hand) does the man of steady wisdom speak, how sit, how walk ?

[Arjuna is asking, (1) what is the state of the mind of the man of realisation when in Samâdhi ? and (2) how is its influence shown in his conduct when out of it ?

Steady wisdom : Settled conviction of one's identity with Brahman gained by direct realisation.]

श्रीभगवानुवाच ।

प्रजहाति यदा कामान्सर्वान्पार्थ मनोगतान् ॥

आत्मन्येवात्मना तुष्टः स्थितप्रज्ञस्तदोच्यते ॥५५॥

श्रीभगवान् The Blessed Lord उवाच said :

पार्थ O Pârtha यदा when सर्वान् all मनोगतान् of the mind कामान् desires प्रजहाति casts off आत्मनि एव in the Self alone आत्मना by the Self तुष्टः satisfied तदा then स्थितप्रज्ञ of steady wisdom उच्यते is said.

The Blessed Lord said :

. 55. When a man completely casts away, O Pârtha, all the desires of the mind, satisfied in the Self alone by the Self, then is he said to be one of steady wisdom.

[This answers the first part of Arjuna's question.]

दुःखेष्वनुद्विग्नमनाः सुखेषु विगतस्पृहः ॥

वीतरागभयक्रोधः स्थितधीर्मुनिरुच्यते ॥५६॥

दुःखेषु In adversity अनुद्विग्नमनाः of unshaken mind सुखेषु in happiness विगतस्पृहः without hankering वीतरागभयक्रोधः free from affection, fear, and wrath मुनिः Muni स्थितधीः of steady wisdom उच्यते is said.

56. He whose mind is not shaken by adversity, who does not hanker after happiness, who has become free from affection, fear, and warth, is indeed the Muni of steady wisdom.

[This and the following two shlokas answer the second part of Arjuna's question, as to the conduct of one of perfect realisation.

Muni : Man of meditation.]

यः सर्वत्रानभिस्नेहस्तत्तत्प्राप्य शुभाशुभम् ॥

नाभिनन्दति न द्वेष्टि तस्य प्रज्ञा प्रतिष्ठिता ॥५७॥

यः Who सर्वत्र everywhere अनभिस्नेहः without attachment तत् तत् whatever शुभाशुभं good and evil प्राप्य receiving न अभिनन्दति does not rejoice न द्वेष्टि is not vexed तस्य his प्रज्ञा wisdom प्रतिष्ठिता is fixed.

57. He who is everywhere unattached, not pleased at receiving good, nor vexed at evil, his wisdom is fixed.

[*Not pleased, etc.* : consequently he does not praise or blame. This is an answer to the query : "How does he speak ?"]

यदा संहरते चायं कूर्मोऽङ्गानीव सर्वशः ॥

इन्द्रियाणीन्द्रियार्थेभ्यस्तस्य प्रज्ञा प्रतिष्ठिता ॥५८॥

यदा When च also अयं this (Yogi) कूर्मः tortoise अङ्गानि limbs इव like इन्द्रियार्थेभ्यः from sense-objects इन्द्रियाणि

senses सर्वशः completely संहरते withdraws तस्य his प्रज्ञा wisdom प्रतिष्ठिता is steadied.

58. When also, like the tortoise drawing its limbs, he can completely withdraw the senses from their objects, then his wisdom becomes steady.

[*Withdraw the senses :* bring the mind back upon the Self from all sense-objects. This is known as Pratyâhâra in Yoga.

To explain the shloka more fully : a man of the highest realisation can, at any moment, shake himself clear of all impressions of the sense-world and go into Samâdhi, with the ease and naturalness of a tortoise drawing its limbs within itself.]

विषया विनिवर्तन्ते निराहारस्य देहिनः ॥
रसवर्जं रसोऽप्यस्य परं दृष्ट्वा निवर्तते ॥५९॥

निराहारस्य Abstinent देहिनः of the man विषयाः objects विनिवर्तन्ते fall away रसवर्जं leaving the longing (तु but) परं the Supreme दृष्ट्वा having seen अस्य of this (man of settled wisdom) रसः longing अपि even निवर्तते falls away.

59. Objects fall away from the abstinent man, leaving the longing behind. But his longing also ceases, who sees the Supreme.

[Abstinent man : An unillumined person abstaining from sense-pleasure for penance, or because of physical incapacity.]

यततो ह्यपि कौन्तेय पुरुषस्य विपश्चित ॥

इन्द्रियाणि प्रमाथीनि हरन्ति प्रसभं मनः ॥६०॥

कौन्तेय O Kaunteya यततः striving विपश्चितः पुरुषस्य of a wise man अपि even हि indeed प्रमाथीनि turbulent इन्द्रियाणि senses प्रसभं violently मनः mind हरन्ति snatch away.

60. The turbulent senses, O son of Kunti, do violently snatch away the mind of even a wise man, striving after perfection.

तानि सर्वाणि संयम्य युक्त आसीत मत्परः ॥

वशे हि यस्येन्द्रियाणि तस्य प्रज्ञा प्रतिष्ठिता ॥६१॥

युक्तः The steadfast तानि them सर्वाणि all संयम्य having controlled मत्परः focussed on Me as the Supreme आसीत sits हि verily यस्य whose इन्द्रियाणि senses वशे under control तस्य his प्रज्ञा wisdom प्रतिष्ठिता settled.

61. The steadfast, having controlled them all, sits focussed on Me as the Supreme. His wisdom is steady, whose senses are under control.

ध्यायतो विषयान्पुंसः सङ्गस्तेषूपजायते ॥

सङ्गात् संजायते कामः कामात् क्रोधोऽभिजायते ॥६२॥

विषयान् Objects ध्यायतः thinking पुंसः of a man तेषु in them सङ्गः attachment उपजायते is produced सङ्गात् from attachment कामः longing संजायते is born कामात् from longing क्रोधः anger अभिजायते grows.

6

62. Thinking of objects, attachment to them is formed in a man. From attachment longing, and from longing anger grows.

क्रोधाद्भवति सम्मोह: सम्मोहात्स्मृतिविभ्रमः ॥

स्मृतिभ्रंशाद्बुद्धिनाशो बुद्धिनाशात्प्रणश्यति ॥६३॥

क्रोधात् From anger सम्मोह: delusion भवति comes सम्मोहात् from delusion स्मृतिविभ्रमः loss of memory स्मृति-भ्रंशात् from loss of memory बुद्धिनाश: the ruin of discrimination बुद्धिनाशात् from the ruin of discrimination प्रणश्यति (he) perishes.

63. From anger comes delusion, and from delusion loss of memory. From loss of memory comes the ruin of discrimination, and from the ruin of discrimination he perishes.

[A beautiful image appears. The tendency of the mind is to repeat it. Then, if the image is allowed to recur, a liking grows. With the growth of liking the wish to come close, to possess, appears. Any obstacle to this produces wrath. The impulse of anger throws the mind into confusion, which casts a veil over the lessons of wisdom learnt by past experience. Thus deprived of his moral standard, he is prevented from using his discrimination. Failing in discrimination, he acts irrationally, on the impulse of passion, and paves the way to moral death.

Thus Krishna traces moral degradation to those

first breaths of thought that come softly and almost
unconsciously to the mind.]

रागद्वेषवियुक्तैस्तु विषयानिन्द्रियैश्चरन् ॥
आत्मवश्यैर्विधेयात्मा प्रसादमधिगच्छति ॥६४॥

तु But रागद्वेषवियुक्तैः free from attraction and aversion आत्मवश्यैः self-restrained इन्द्रियैः with senses विषयान्
objects चरन् moving (amongst) विधेयात्मा the self-controlled प्रसादम् tranquillity अधिगच्छति attains.

64.　But the self-controlled man, moving
among objects with senses under restraint,
and free from attraction and aversion, attains
to tranquillity.

[The above is in answer to Arjuna's fourth question, "How does he move?"]

प्रसादे सर्वदुःखानां हानिरस्योपजायते ॥
प्रसन्नचेतसो ह्याशु बुद्धिः पर्यवतिष्ठते ॥६५॥

प्रसादे In tranquillity अस्य of him सर्वदुःखानां of all
sorrows हानिः destruction उपजायते happens प्रसन्नचेतसः of
the tranquil minded हि because आशु soon बुद्धिः intellect
पर्यवतिष्ठते is established in firmness.

65.　In tranquillity, all sorrow is
destroyed. For the intellect of him, who
is tranquil-minded, is soon established in
firmness.

[That is, firmly concentrates itself on the Self.]

नास्ति बुद्धिरयुक्तस्य न चायुक्तस्य भावना ॥

न चाभावयतः शान्तिरशान्तस्य कुतः सुखम् ॥६६॥

अयुक्तस्य Of the unsteady बुद्धिः knowledge (of the Self) नास्ति is not अयुक्तस्य of the unsteady भावना meditation च also न not अभावयतः च and of the unmeditative शान्तिः peace न not अशान्तस्य of the peaceless सुखं happiness कुतः whence.

66. No knowledge (of the Self) has the unsteady. Nor has he meditation. To the unmeditative there is no peace. And how can one without peace have happiness ?

इन्द्रियाणां हि चरतां यन्मनोऽनुविधीयते ॥

तदस्य हरति प्रज्ञां वायुर्नावमिवाम्भसि ॥६७॥

हि For चरतां wandering इन्द्रियाणां senses यत् which मनः mind अनुविधीयते follows तत् that अस्य his वायुः wind अम्भसि in water नावम् boat इव like प्रज्ञां discrimination हरति scatters.

67. For, the mind, which follows in the wake of the wandering senses, carries away his discrimination, as a wind (carries away from its course) a boat on the waters.

तस्माद्यस्य महाबाहो निगृहीतानि सर्वशः ॥

इन्द्रियाणीन्द्रियार्थेभ्यस्तस्य प्रज्ञा प्रतिष्ठिता ॥६८॥

महाबाहो Mighty-armed तस्मात् therefore यस्य whose इन्द्रियाणि senses इन्द्रियार्थेभ्यः from sense-objects सर्वशः completely निगृहीतानि restrained तस्य his प्रज्ञा knowledge प्रतिष्ठिता (is) steady.

68. Therefore, O mighty-armed, his knowledge is steady, whose senses are completely restrained from their objects.

[This does not mean that the senses remain completely estranged, but that they are all estrangeable at will.]

या निशा सर्वभूतानां तस्यां जागर्ति संयमी ॥

यस्यां जाग्रति भूतानि सा निशा पश्यतो मुनेः ॥६९॥

सर्वभूतानां Of all beings या what निशा night संयमी the self-controlled तस्यां in that जागर्ति keeps awake यस्यां in what भूतानि all beings जाग्रति are awake पश्यतः seeing (the Self) मुनेः of the Muni सा that निशा night.

69. That which is night to all beings, in that the self-controlled man wakes. That in which all beings wake, is night to the Self-seeing Muni.

[Where all beings are in darkness, there the Muni sees, and vice versa. The consciousness of the man of realisation is so full of God that he cannot see anything apart from Him. The ignorant man, on the other hand, lives in the world of plurality alone and God is a non-entity to him.

It follows, that non-susceptibility to the influences of Nature, that is, perfect self-control (spoken of in the preceding shloka) is quite as natural a trait of the illumined soul as its opposite is of the ignorant.]

आपूर्यमाणमचलप्रतिष्ठं

समुद्रमापः प्रविशन्ति यद्वत् ॥

तद्वत्कामा यं प्रविशन्ति सर्वे

स शान्तिमाप्रोति न कामकामी ॥७०॥

यद्वत् As आपूर्यमाणम् filled from all sides अचलप्रतिष्ठं based in stillness समुद्रम् ocean आपः waters प्रविशन्ति enter तद्वत् so सर्वे all कामाः desires यं to which (मुनि Muni) प्रविशन्ति enter सः he शान्तिम् peace आप्रोति attains कामकामी desirer of desires न not.

70. As into the ocean—brimful, and still—flow the waters, even so the Muni into whom enter all desires, he, and not the desirer of desires, attains to peace.

[The ocean is not at all affected by the waters flowing into it from all sides. Similarly, that man alone finds true peace in whom no reaction of desire is produced by the objects of enjoyment, which he happens to come across during his sojourn on earth.]

विहाय कामान्यः सर्वान्पुमांश्चरति निस्पृहः ॥

निर्ममो निरहङ्कारः स शान्तिमधिगच्छति ॥७१॥

यः that पुमान् man सर्वान् all कामान् desires विहाय abandoning निस्पृहः devoid of longing निरहंकारः without the sense of "I" निर्ममः without the sense of "mine" चरति moves (lives) सः he शान्तिं peace अधिगच्छति attains.

71. That man who lives devoid of longing, abandoning all desires, without the sense of "I" and "mine", he attains to peace.

[*The man who lives*—merely to work out his past Karma.]

एषा ब्राह्मी स्थितिः पार्थ नैनां प्राप्य विमुह्यति ।

स्थित्वाऽस्यामन्तकालेऽपि ब्रह्मनिर्वाणमृच्छति ॥७२॥

पार्थ O Pârtha एषा this ब्राह्मी स्थितिः (having one's) being in Brahman एनां this प्राप्य attaining न not विमुह्यति is deluded अन्तकाले at the end of life अपि even अस्यां therein स्थित्वा having stayed ब्रह्मनिर्वाणम् oneness with Brahman ऋच्छति attains.

72. This is to have one's being in Brahman, O son of Prithâ. None, attaining to this, becomes deluded. Being established therein, even at the end of life, a man attains to oneness with Brahman.

इति सांख्ययोगो नाम द्वितीयोऽध्यायः ॥२॥

The end of second chapter, designated, *The Way of Knowledge.*

॥ तृतीयोऽध्याय ॥

THIRD CHAPTER

अर्जुन उवाच ।

ज्यायसी चेत्कर्मणस्ते मता बुद्धिर्जनार्दन ॥

तत्किं कर्मणि घोरे मां नियोजयसि केशव ॥१॥

अर्जुनः Arjuna उवाच said :

जनार्दन O Janârdana केशव O Keshava चेत् if कर्मणः to action बुद्धिः knowledge ज्यायसी superior ते by Thee मता considered तत् then किं why घोरे terrible कर्मणि in action मां me नियोजयसि engagest.

Arjuna said :

1. If, O Janârdana, according to Thee, knowledge is superior to action, why then, O Keshava, dost Thou engage me in this terrible action ?

व्यामिश्रेणेव वाक्येन बुद्धिं मोहयसीव मे ॥

तदेकं वद निश्चित्य येन श्रेयोऽहमाप्नुयाम् ॥२॥

व्यामिश्रेण Conflicting वाक्येन with words इव seemingly मे my बुद्धिं understanding मोहयसि art bewildering इव as it were तत् that एकं one निश्चित्य for certain वद tell येन by which अहं । श्रेयः highest आप्नुयाम् shall attain.

2. With these seemingly conflicting words, Thou art, as it were, bewildering my understanding ;—tell me that one thing for certain, by which I can attain to the highest.

श्रीभगवानुवाच ।

लोकेऽस्मिन्द्विविधा निष्ठा पुरा प्रोक्ता मयाऽनघ ॥

ज्ञानयोगेन सांख्यानां कर्मयोगेन योगिनाम् ॥३॥

श्रीभगवान् The Blessed Lord उवाच said :

अनघ Sinless अस्मिन् in this लोके world द्विविधा twofold निष्ठा (path of) devotion मया by Me पुरा in the beginning प्रोक्ता said ज्ञानयोगेन by the path of knowledge सांख्यानां of the meditative कर्मयोगेन by the path of action योगिनाम् of the active.

The Blessed Lord said :

3. In the beginning (of creation) O sinless one, the twofold path of devotion was given by Me to this world ;—the path of knowledge for the meditative, the path of work for the active.

[*Meditative*—those who prefer meditation to external action.

Active—those who believe in external work with or without meditation.]

न कर्मणामनारम्भान्नैष्कर्म्यं पुरुषोऽश्नुते ॥

न च संन्यसनादेव सिद्धिं समधिगच्छति ॥४॥

पुरुष: A person कर्मणां of works अनारम्भात् from non-performance नैष्कर्म्यं worklessness न not अश्नुते reaches च and संन्यसनात् from giving up एव merely सिद्धिं perfection न not समधिगच्छति attains.

4. By non-performance of work none reaches worklessness ; by merely giving up action no one attains to perfection.

[*Worklessness and perfection :* These are synonymous terms, meaning, becoming one with the Infinite and free from all ideas of want. A man who has reached this state can have no necessity or desire for work as a means to an end. Perfect satisfaction in the Self is his natural condition. (*Vide* III. 17).]

न हि कश्चित्क्षणमपि जातु तिष्ठत्यकर्मकृत् ॥

कार्यते ह्यवशः कर्म सर्वः प्रकृतिजैर्गुणैः ॥६॥

जातु Ever क्षणं for an instant अपि even कश्चित् any one अकर्मकृत् without performing action न not हि verily तिष्ठति rests हि for प्रकृतिजैः born of Prakriti गुणैः by the Gunas सर्वः all अवशः helpless कर्म action कार्यते are made to do.

5. Verily none can ever rest for even an instant, without performing action ; for all are made to act, helplessly indeed, by the Gunas, born of Prakriti.

[*All are made to act :* All men living under bondage.]

कर्मेन्द्रियाणि संयम्य य आस्ते मनसा स्मरन् ॥

इन्द्रियार्थान्विमूढात्मा मिथ्याचार: स उच्यते ॥६॥

य: Who कर्मेन्द्रियाणि organs of action संयम्य restraining मनसा by the mind इन्द्रियार्थान् sense-objects स्मरन् remembering आस्ते sits स: he विमूढात्मा of deluded understanding मिथ्याचार: hypocrite उच्यते is called.

6. He, who restraining the organs of action, sits revolving in the mind, thoughts regarding objects of senses, he, of deluded understanding, is called a hypocrite.

यस्त्विन्द्रियाणि मनसा नियम्यारभतेऽर्जुन ॥

कर्मेन्द्रियै: कर्मयोगमसक्त: स विशिष्यते ॥७॥

अर्जुन O Arjuna य: who तु but इन्द्रियाणि senses मनसा by the mind नियम्य controlling असक्त: unattached कर्मेन्द्रियै: by the organs of action कर्मयोगं path of work आरभते follows स: he विशिष्यते excels.

7. But, who, controlling the senses by the mind, unattached, directs his organs of action to the path of work, he, O Arjuna, excels.

नियतं कुरु कर्म त्वं कर्म ज्यायो ह्यकर्मण: ॥

शरीरयात्रापि च ते न प्रसिध्येदकर्मण: ॥८॥

त्वं Thou नियतं obligatory कर्म action कुरु perform हि
for अकर्मणः to inaction कर्म action ज्यायः superior अकर्मणः
(of the) inactive ते thy शरीरयात्रा maintenance of the
body अपि even च and न not प्रसिध्येत् would be possible.

8. Do thou perform obligatory[1]
action ; for action is superior to inaction ;
and even the bare maintenance of thy
body would not be possible if thou art
inactive.

यज्ञार्थात्कर्मणोऽन्यत्र लोकोऽयं कर्मबन्धनः ॥
तदर्थं कर्म कौन्तेय मुक्तसङ्गः समाचर ॥६॥

यज्ञार्थात् For the sake of Yajna कर्मणः of action
अन्यत्र otherwise अयं this लोकः world कर्मबन्धनः bound by
action कौन्तेय O Kaunteya (अतः therefore) तदर्थं for
that मुक्तसङ्गः devoid of attachment कर्म action समाचर
perform.

9. The world is bound by actions
other than those performed for the sake of
Yajna ; do thou, therefore, O son of Kunti,
perform action for Yajna alone, devoid of
attachment.

[*Yajna :* means a religious rite, sacrifice, worship : or an action done with a good or spiritual
motive. It also means the Deity. The Taittiriya-
Samhitâ (I. 7. 4.) says, "Yajna is Vishnu Himself."]

---

[1] See comment on V. 13.

सहयज्ञाः प्रजाः सृष्ट्वा पुरोवाच प्रजापतिः ॥
अनेन प्रसविष्यध्वमेष वोऽस्त्विष्टकामधुक् ॥१०॥

पुरा In the beginning प्रजापतिः the Prajâpati सहयज्ञाः
together with Yajna प्रजाः mankind सृष्ट्वा having created
उवाच said अनेन by this प्रसविष्यध्वम् shall (ye) multiply एषः
this वः your इष्टकामधुक् milch cow of desires अस्तु let be.

10. The Prajâpati, having in the
beginning created mankind together with
Yajna, said, "By this shall ye multiply :
this shall be the milch cow of your desires.

[*Prajâpati*—the creator or Brahmâ.]

देवान् भावयतानेन ते देवा भावयन्तु वः ॥
परस्परं भावयन्तः श्रेयः परमवाप्स्यथ ॥११॥

अनेन With this देवान् the Devas भावयत cherish ते
those देवाः Devas वः you भावयन्तु may cherish परस्परं one
another भावयन्तः cherishing परं highest श्रेयः good अवाप्स्यथ
(ye) shall gain.

11. "Cherish the Devas with this, and
may those Devas cherish you : thus
cherishing one another, ye shall gain the
highest good.

[*Devas :* (lit. the shining ones) beings much
higher than man in the scale of evolution, who are
in charge of cosmic functions.]

इष्टान्भोगान्हि वो देवा दास्यन्ते यज्ञभाविताः ॥
तैर्दत्तानप्रदायैभ्यो यो भुङ्क्ते स्तेन एव सः ॥१२॥

देवाः The Devas यज्ञभाविताः cherished by Yajna इष्टान्
desired-for भोगान् objects वः to you दास्यन्ते will give हि
so तैः by them दत्तान् given एभ्यः to them अप्रदाय without
offering यः who भुङ्क्ते enjoys सः he स्तेनः thief एव verily.

12. "The Devas, cherished by Yajna,
will give you desired-for objects." So, he
who enjoys objects given by the Devas
without offering (in return) to them, is
verily a thief.

यज्ञशिष्टाशिनः सन्तो मुच्यन्ते सर्वकिल्बिषैः ॥
भुञ्जते ते त्वघं पापा ये पचन्त्यात्मकारणात् ॥१३॥

यज्ञशिष्टाशिनः Eating the remnants of Yajna सन्तः the
good सर्वकिल्बिषैः from all sins मुच्यन्ते are freed ये who तु
but आत्मकारणात् for themselves पचन्ति cook ते they पापाः
sinful ones अघं sin भुञ्जते eat.

13. The good, eating the remnants of
Yajna, are freed from all sins : but who
cook food (only) for themselves, those
sinful ones eat sin.

[*Deva-Yajna :* offering sacrifices to the gods,
Brahma-Yajna : teaching and reciting the scriptures,
Pitri-Yajna : offering libations of water to one's

ancestors, *Nri-Yajna :* the feeding of the hungry, and
Bhuta-Yajna : the feeding of the lower animals;—are
the five daily duties enjoined on householders. The
performance of these duties frees them from the five-
fold sin, inevitable to a householder's life, due to the
killing of life, from the use of, (1) the pestle and
mortar, (2) the grinding-stone, (3) the oven, (4) the
water-jar, and (5) the broom.]

अन्नाद्भवन्ति भूतानि पर्जन्यादन्नसम्भवः ॥
यज्ञाद्भवति पर्जन्यो यज्ञः कर्मसमुद्भवः ॥१४॥

भूतानि Beings अन्नात् from food भवन्ति come forth
पर्जन्यात् from rain अन्नसम्भवः production of food पर्जन्यः rain
यज्ञात् from Yajna भवति arises यज्ञः Yajna कर्मसमुद्भवः born
of Karma.

14. From food come forth beings :
from rain food is produced : from Yajna
arises rain ; and Yajna is born of Karma.

[*Yajna :* Here it denotes not the sacrificial
deeds themselves but the subtle principle into which
they are converted, after they have been performed,
to appear, later on, as their fruits. This is techni-
cally known as Apurva.

Karma or sacrificial deeds prescribed in the
Vedas.]

कर्म ब्रह्मोद्भवं विद्धि ब्रह्माक्षरसमुद्भवम् ॥
तस्मात्सर्वगतं ब्रह्म नित्यं यज्ञे प्रतिष्ठितम् ॥१५॥

कर्म Karma ब्रह्मोद्भवं risen from the Veda ब्रह्म Veda अक्षरसमुद्भवं risen from the Imperishable विद्धि know तस्मात् therefore सर्वगतं all-pervading ब्रह्म Veda नित्यं ever यज्ञे in Yajna प्रतिष्ठितं centred.

15. Know Karma to have risen from the Veda, and the Veda from the Imperishable. Therefore the all-pervading Veda is ever centred in Yajna.

[*All-pervading Veda :* because it illumines all subjects and is the store of all knowledge, being the out-breathing of the Omniscient. It is said to be ever centred in Yajna, because it deals chiefly with Yajna, as the means of achieving the end, either of prosperity or final liberation, according as it is performed with or without desire.]

एवं प्रवर्तितं चक्रं नानुवर्तयतीह य ॥
अघायुरिन्द्रियारामो मोघं पार्थ स जीवति ॥१६॥

य: Who इह here एवं thus प्रवर्तितं set revolving चक्रं wheel न not अनुवर्तयति follows पार्थ O Pârtha अघायु: living in sin इन्द्रियाराम: satisfied in the senses स: he मोघं in vain जीवति lives.

16. He, who here follows not the wheel thus set revolving, living in sin, and satisfied in the senses, O son of Prithâ—he lives in vain.

[The *wheel* of action started by Prajâpati on the basis of Veda and sacrifice.]

यस्त्वात्मरतिरेव स्यादात्मतृप्तश्च मानवः ॥
आत्मन्येव च सन्तुष्टस्तस्य कार्यं न विद्यते ॥१७॥

तु But यः मानवः that man आत्मरतिः devoted to the
Self एव alone च and आत्मतृप्तः satisfied with the Self च
and आत्मनि in the Self एव alone सन्तुष्टः content स्यात् may
be तस्य his कार्यं work to be done (i.e., duty) न not विद्यते
exists.

17. But the man who is devoted to
the Self, and is satisfied with the Self, and
content in the Self alone, has no obligatory
duty.

नैव तस्य कृतेनार्थो नाकृतेनेह कश्चन ॥
न चास्य सर्वभूतेषु कश्चिदर्थव्यपाश्रयः ॥१८॥

तस्य Of that man इह in this world कृतेन by action
done अर्थः object न not एव surely (अस्ति is) अकृतेन by action
not done कश्चन any (loss) न not (अस्ति is) च and अस्य of
this man सर्वभूतेषु among all beings कश्चित् any अर्थव्यपाश्रयः
depending for any object न not.

18. He has no object in this world (to
gain) by doing (an action), nor (does he
incur any loss) by non-performance of action
—nor has he (need of) depending on any being
for any object.

7

तस्मादसक्तः सततं कार्यं कर्म समाचर ॥
असक्तो ह्याचरन् कर्म परमाप्नोति पूरुषः ॥१९॥

तस्मात् Therefore असक्तः without attachment सततं
always कार्यं which should be done, i.e., obligatory कर्म
action समाचर perform हि because असक्तःwithout attachment कर्म action आचरन् performing पूरुषः man परम् the
highest आप्नोति attains.

19. Therefore, do thou always perform
actions which are obligatory, without attachment ;—by performing action without attachment, one attains to the highest.

कर्मणैव हि संसिद्धिमास्थिता जनकादयः ॥
लोकसंग्रहमेवापि संपश्यन् कर्तुमर्हसि ॥२०॥

हि Verily जनकादयः Janaka and others कर्मणा by
action एव alone संसिद्धिम् perfection आस्थिताः attained अपि
also लोकसंग्रहम् guidance of men एव only संपश्यन् having
in view कर्तुम् to perform (action) अर्हसि thou shouldst.

20. Verily by action alone, Janaka and
others attained perfection ;—also, simply with
the view for the guidance of men, thou shouldst
perform action.

[*Guidance of men :* the Sanskrit word means,
gathering of men—that is, into the right path.]

यद्यदाचरति श्रेष्ठस्तत्तदेवेतरो जनः ॥

स यत्प्रमाणं कुरुते लोकस्तदनुवर्तते ॥२१॥

श्रेष्ठः The superior यत् यत् whatsoever आचरति does
इतरः inferior जनः man तत् तत् that एव only (does) सः
that (superior) man यत् what प्रमाणं demonstration कुरुते
does तत् that लोकः the world (people) अनुवर्तते follows.

21. Whatsoever the superior person
does, that is followed by others. What he
demonstrates by action, that, people
follow.

न मे पार्थास्ति कर्तव्यं त्रिषु लोकेषु किंचन ॥

नानवाप्तमवाप्तव्यं वर्त एव च कर्मणि ॥२२॥

पार्थ O Pârtha ! मे My कर्तव्यं duty न no अस्ति is त्रिषु
in the three लोकेषु worlds अनवाप्त' unattained अवाप्तव्यं to
be gained किंचन anything न not च yet कर्मणि in action
एव verily वर्ते am.

22. I have, O son of Prithâ, no duty,
nothing that I have not gained, and nothing
that I have to gain, in the three worlds ; yet,
I continue in action.

यदि ह्यहं न वर्तेयं जातु कर्मण्यतन्द्रितः ॥

मम वर्त्मानुवर्तन्ते मनुष्याः पार्थ सर्वशः ॥२३॥

पार्थ O Pârtha ! यदि if अहं I जातु ever अतन्द्रितः without
relaxation कर्मणि in action न not वर्तेयं should be (तदा

then) हि surely मनुष्याः men मम My वर्त्म path सर्वशः in
every way अनुवर्तन्ते (would) follow.

23. If ever I did not continue in work,
without relaxation, men, O son of Prithâ,
would in every way, follow in My wake.

उत्सीदेयुरिमे लोका न कुर्यां कर्म चेदहम् ॥

सङ्करस्य च कर्त्ता स्यामुपहन्यामिमाः प्रजाः ॥२४॥

चेत् If अहं I कर्म action न not कुर्यां would do इमे
these लोकाः worlds उत्सीदेयुः would perish च and संकरस्य
of the admixture (of races) कर्ता author स्याम् would be
इमाः these प्रजाः beings उपहन्याम् would ruin.

24. If I did not do work, these worlds
would perish. I should be the cause of the
admixture of races, and I should ruin these
beings.

सक्ताः कर्मण्यविद्वांसो यथा कुर्वन्ति भारत ॥

कुर्याद्विद्वांस्तथाऽसक्तश्चिकीर्षुर्लोकसंग्रहम् ॥२५॥

भारत O Bhârata ! कर्मणि to action सक्ताः attached
अविद्वांसः the unwise यथा as कुर्वन्ति act असक्तः unattached
लोकसंग्रहं guidance of the world चिकीर्षुः desirous of विद्वान्
the wise तथा so कुर्यात् should act.

25. As do the unwise, attached to
work, act, so should the wise act, O
descendant of Bharata, (but) without

attachment, desirous of the guidance of
the world.

न बुद्धिभेदं जनयेदज्ञानां कर्मसङ्गिनाम् ॥

योजयेत्सर्वकर्माणि विद्वान्युक्तः समाचरन् ॥२६॥

कर्मसङ्गिनां Of the persons attached to action अज्ञानां
the ignorant बुद्धिभेदं unsettlement of the understanding न not जनयेत् should create विद्वान् the wise युक्तः steady
सर्वकर्माणि all actions समाचरन् acting योजयेत् should
engage.

26. One should not unsettle the understanding of the ignorant, attached to action ;
the wise, (himself) steadily acting, should
engage (the ignorant) in all work.

प्रकृतेः क्रियमाणानि गुणैः कर्माणि सर्वशः ॥

अहङ्कारविमूढात्मा कर्ताहमिति मन्यते ॥२७॥

प्रकृतेः Of the Prakriti गुणैः by the Gunas सर्वशः
everywhere कर्माणि works क्रियमाणानि are performed
अहंकारविमूढात्मा one whose understanding is deluded
by egoism अहं I कर्ता doer इति this मन्यते thinks.

27. The Gunas of Prakriti perform all
action. With the understanding deluded by
egoism, man thinks, "I am the doer."

तत्त्ववित्तु महाबाहो गुणकर्मविभागयोः ॥

गुणा गुणेषु वर्तन्त इति मत्वा न सज्जते ॥२८॥

तु But महाबाहो mighty-armed ! गुणकर्मविभागयोः of the divisions of Guna and Karma तत्त्ववित् knower of truth गुणाः Gunas (in the shape of the senses) गुणेषु amidst the Gunas (in the shape of the objects) वर्तन्ते remain इति this मत्वा knowing न not सज्जते becomes attached.

28.   But, one, with true insight into the domains of Guna and Karma, knowing that Gunas as senses merely rest on Gunas as objects, does not become attached.

[*With true insight etc.*: Knowing the truth that the Self is distinct from all Gunas and actions.]

प्रकृतेर्गुणसंमूढाः सज्जन्ते गुणकर्मसु ॥
तानकृत्स्नविदो मन्दान् कृत्स्नविन्न विचालयेत् ॥२६॥

प्रकृतेः Of the Prakriti गुणसंमूढाः persons deluded by Gunas गुणकर्मसु in the functions of the Gunas सज्जन्ते become attached तान् those अकृत्स्नविदः of imperfect knowledge मन्दान् the dull-witted कृत्स्नवित् man of perfect knowledge न not विचालयेत् should unsettle (the understanding).

29.   Men of perfect knowledge should not unsettle (the understanding of) people of dull wit and imperfect knowledge, who deluded by the Gunas of Prakriti attach (themselves) to the functions of the Gunas.

[*Those of imperfect knowledge*—those who can
only see as far as the immediate effect of actions.]

मयि सर्वाणि कर्माणिसंन्य स्याध्यात्मचेतसा ॥

निराशीर्निर्ममो भूत्वा युध्यस्व विगतज्वरः ॥३०॥

सर्वाणि All कर्माणि actions मयि to Me संन्यस्य renouncing अध्यात्मचेतसा with mind centred on the Self निराशीः
devoid of hope निर्ममः devoid of egoism भूत्वा being
विगतज्वरः free from (mental) fever युध्यस्व fight.

30. Renouncing all actions to Me, with
mind centred on the Self, getting rid of hope
and selfishness, fight—free from (mental)
fever.

ये मे मतमिदं नित्यमनुतिष्ठन्ति मानवाः ॥

श्रद्धावन्तोऽनसूयन्तो मुच्यन्ते तेऽपि कर्मभिः ॥३१॥

श्रद्धावन्तः Full of Shraddhâ अनसूयन्तः not cavilling ये
those who मानवाः men मे My इदं this मतं teaching नित्यं
constantly अनुतिष्ठन्ति practise ते they अपि even कर्मभिः
from action मुच्यन्ते are freed.

31. Those men who constantly practise
this teaching of Mine, full of Shraddhâ and
without cavilling, they too, are freed from
work.

[*Shraddhâ :* is a mental attitude constituted
primarily of sincerity of purpose, humility, reverence,
and faith. You have Shraddhâ for your Guru—it

is sincere reverence.   You have Shraddhâ for the Gitâ
—it is admiration for those of its teachings you understand and faith in those that you do not.   You
give alms to a beggar with Shraddhâ—it is a sense of
humility combined with the hope that what you give
will be acceptable and serviceable.]

ये त्वेतदभ्यसूयन्तो नानुतिष्ठन्ति मे मतम् ॥
सर्वज्ञानविमूढांस्तान्विद्धि नष्टानचेतसः ॥३२॥

तु But ये those who एतत् this मे My मतं teaching
अभ्यसूयन्तः decrying न not अनुतिष्ठन्ति practise सर्वज्ञानविमूढान्
deluded in all knowledge अचेतसः devoid of discrimination तान् them नष्टान् ruined विद्धि know.

32.   But those who decrying this teaching
of Mine do not practise (it), deluded in all
knowledge, and devoid of discrimination,
know them to be ruined.

सदृशं चेष्टते स्वस्याः प्रकृतेर्ज्ञानवानपि ॥
प्रकृतिं यान्ति भूतानि निग्रहः किं करिष्यति ॥३३॥

ज्ञानवान् A wise man अपि even स्वस्याः of his own प्रकृतेः
nature सदृशम् in accordance with चेष्टते acts भूतानि
beings प्रकृतिं nature यान्ति follow निग्रहः restraint किं
what करिष्यति will do.

33.   Even a wise man acts in accordance
with his own nature ; beings follow nature :
what can restraint do ?

[The reason why some people do not follow the teaching of the Lord is explained here : Their (lower) nature proves too strong for them.]

इन्द्रियस्येन्द्रियस्यार्थे रागद्वेषौ व्यवस्थितौ ॥
तयोर्न वशमागच्छेत्तौ ह्यस्य परिपन्थिनौ ॥३४॥

इन्द्रियस्य Of the senses इन्द्रियस्य अर्थे in the object of the senses रागद्वेषौ attachment and aversion व्यवस्थितौ ordained by nature तयोः of those two वशं sway न not आगच्छेत् should come under तौ those two हि verily अस्य his परिपन्थिनौ foes.

34. Attachment and aversion of the senses for their respective objects are natural : let none come under their sway : they are his foes.

[*His :* or the seeker after truth.

Though, as has been said in the foregoing Shloka, some are so completely under the sway of their natural propensities, that restraint is of no avail to them, yet the seeker after truth should never think of following their example, but should always exert himself to overrule all attachment and aversion of the senses for their objects.]

श्रेयान् स्वधर्मो विगुणः परधर्मात् स्वनुष्ठितात् ॥
स्वधर्मे निधनं श्रेयः परधर्मो भयावहः ॥३५॥

स्वनुष्ठितात् From the well-performed परधर्मात् Dharma of another विगुणः imperfect स्वधर्मः one's own Dharma

श्रेयान् better स्वधर्मे in one's own Dharma निधनं death
श्रेयः better परधर्मः Dharma of another भयावहः fraught
with fear.

35. Better is one's own Dharma,
(though) imperfect, than the Dharma of
another well-performed. Better is death in
one's own Dharma : the Dharma of another is
fraught with fear.

[The implication is that Arjuna's thought of
desisting from fight and going in for the calm and
peaceful life of the Brâhmana is prompted by man's
natural desire to shun what is disagreeable and
embrace what is agreeable to the senses. He should
on no account yield to this weakness.]

अर्जुन उवाच ।

अथ केन प्रयुक्तोऽयं पापं चरति पूरुषः ॥

अनिच्छन्नपि वार्ष्णेय बलादिव नियोजितः ॥३६॥

अर्जुनः Arjuna उवाच said:
वार्ष्णेय O Vârshneya ! अथ now अनिच्छन् not wishing
अपि even अयं this पूरुषः Purusha केन by what प्रयुक्त
impelled बलात् by force इव as it were नियोजितः constrained पापं sin चरति commits.

Arjuna said :
36. But by what impelled does man
commit sin, though against his wishes,
O Vârshneya, constrained as it were, by
force ?

[*Vârshneya :* a descendant of the race of Vrishni.]

श्रीभगवानुवाच ।

काम एष क्रोध एष रजोगुणसमुद्भवः ॥

महाशनो महापाप्मा विद्ध्येनमिह वैरिणम् ॥३७॥

श्रीभगवान् The Blessed Lord उवाच said :
रजोगुणसमुद्भवः Born of the Rajo-guna महाशनः of great craving महापाप्मा of great sin एष: this कामः desire एष: this क्रोधः anger इह in this world एनं this वैरिणं foe विद्धि know.

The Blessed Lord said :
37. It is desire—it is anger, born of the Rajo-guna : of great craving, and of great sin ; know this as the foe here (in this world).

[*It is desire, etc. :* anger is only another form of desire—desire obstructed.   (See Note, II. 62-63).]

धूमेनात्रियते वह्निर्यथाऽऽदर्शो मलेन च ।

यथोल्बेनावृतो गर्भस्तथा तेनेदमावृतम् ॥३८॥

यथा As वह्निः fire धूमेन by smoke आत्रियते is enveloped (यथा as) आदर्शः mirror मलेन by dust च and यथा as गर्भः embryo उल्बेन by the secundine आवृतः covered तथा so तेन by that इदं this आवृतं covered.

38. As fire is enveloped by smoke, as a mirror by dust, as an embryo by the secundine, so is it covered by that.

["*It*" is knowledge, and "*that*" is desire, as explained in the following Shloka.

Three stages of the overclouding of knowledge or Self by desire are described by the three illustrations here given. The first stage is Sâttvika—"fire enveloped by smoke":—the rise of a slight wind of discrimination dispels the smoke of desire in a Sâttvika heart. The second, the Râjasika—the removal of "the dust on a mirror" requires some time and preparation. While the third—the Tâmasika, takes a much longer time like the release of "the embryo" from the afterbirth.]

आवृतं ज्ञानमेतेन ज्ञानिनो नित्यवैरिणा ॥

कामरूपेण कौन्तेय दुष्पूरेणानलेन च ॥३६॥

कौन्तेय O Kaunteya ज्ञानिनः of the wise नित्यवैरिणा by the constant foe कामरूपेण whose form is desire च and दुष्पूरेण unappeasable एतेन अनलेन by this fire ज्ञानं knowledge आवृतं covered.

39. Knowledge is covered by this, the constant foe of the wise, O son of Kunti, the unappeasable fire of desire.

[Desire is undoubtedly the foe of all mankind. Why it is said to be the constant foe of the wise, is

that they *feel* it to be so even when under its sway.
Fools are awakened for a moment only, when they
suffer from its painful reactions.]

इन्द्रियाणि मनो बुद्धिरस्याधिष्ठानमुच्यते ॥
एतैर्विमोह्यत्येष ज्ञानमावृत्य देहिनम् ॥४०॥

इन्द्रियाणि Senses मनः mind बुद्धिः intellect अस्य its
अधिष्ठानं abode उच्यते is said एषः this एतैः by these ज्ञानं
knowledge आवृत्य covering देहिनं the embodied विमोह्यति
deludes.

40. The senses, the mind and the intellect are said to be its abode : through
these, it deludes the embodied by veiling his
wisdom.

[Like a wise general, Krishna points out the
fortress of the enemy, by conquering which the
enemy is easily defeated.

Through these : by vitiating the senses, mind
and the intellect.]

तस्मात्त्वमिन्द्रियाण्यादौ नियम्य भरतर्षभ ॥
पाप्मानं प्रजहि ह्येनं ज्ञानविज्ञाननाशनम् ॥४१॥

भरतर्षभ O Bull of the Bharata race ! तस्मात् therefore
त्वं you आदौ at the outset इन्द्रियाणि senses नियम्य controlling ज्ञानविज्ञाननाशनं the destroyer of knowledge and
realisation पाप्मानं the sinful हि surely एनं this प्रजहि kill.

41. Therefore, O Bull of the Bharata race, controlling the senses at the outset, kill it—the sinful, the destroyer of knowledge and realisation.

इन्द्रियाणि पराण्याहुरिन्द्रियेभ्यः परं मनः ॥
मनसस्तु परा बुद्धिर्यो बुद्धेः परतस्तु सः ॥४२॥

इन्द्रियाणि Senses पराणि superior आहुः (they) say इन्द्रियेभ्यः to the senses मनः mind परं superior मनसः to mind तु but बुद्धिः intellect परा superior यः who तु but बुद्धेः to the intellect परतः superior सः He (the Âtman).

42. The senses are said to be superior (to the body); the mind is superior to the senses ; the intellect is superior to the mind ; and that which is superior to the intellect is He (the Âtman).

एवं बुद्धेः परं बुद्ध्वा संस्तभ्यात्मानमात्मना ॥
जहि शत्रुं महाबाहो कामरूपं दुरासदम् ॥४३॥

महाबाहो O mighty-armed ! एवं thus बुद्धेः to the intellect परं superior बुद्ध्वा knowing आत्मना by the Self आत्मानं self संस्तभ्य restraining कामरूपं whose form is desire दुरासदं unseizable शत्रुं enemy जहि destroy.

43. Thus, knowing Him who is superior to the intellect, and restraining the self

by the Self, destroy, O mighty-armed, that enemy, the unseizable foe, desire.

इति कर्मयोगो नाम तृतीयोऽध्यायः ॥

The end of the third chapter, designated *The Way of Action.*

॥ चतुर्थोऽध्यायः ॥

FOURTH CHAPTER

श्रीभगवानुवाच ।

इमं विवस्वते योगं प्रोक्तवानहमव्ययम् ॥
विवस्वान्मनवे प्राह मनुरिक्ष्वाकवेऽब्रवीत् ॥१॥

श्रीभगवान् The Blessed Lord उवाच said :

अहं I विवस्वते to Vivasvat इमं this अव्ययं imperishable योगं Yoga प्रोक्तवान् told विवस्वान् Vivasvân मनवे to Manu प्राह told मनुः Manu इक्ष्वाकवे to Ikshvâku अब्रवीत् told.

The Blessed Lord said :

1. I told this imperishable Yoga to Vivasvat ; Vivasvat told it to Manu ; (and) Manu told it to Ikshvâku :

[*Vivasvat :* the Sun. *Manu :* the law-giver. Ikshvâku was the famous ancestor of the Solar dynasty of Kshatriyas.

This Yoga is said to be imperishable, because the end attainable through it is imperishable.]

एवं परम्पराप्राप्तमिमं राजर्षयो विदुः ॥
स कालेनेह महता योगो नष्टः परन्तप ॥२॥

एवं Thus परम्पराप्राप्तं handed down in regular succession इमं it राजर्षयः the royal sages विदुः knew परन्तप O
burner of foes ! इह in this world सः that योगः Yoga
महता by long कालेन lapse of time नष्टः declined.

2. Thus handed down in regular succession, the royal sages knew it. This Yoga, by
long lapse of time, declined in this world,
O burner of foes.

स एवायं मया तेऽद्य योगः प्रोक्तः पुरातनः ॥

भक्तोऽसि मे सखा चेति रहस्यं ह्येतदुत्तमम् ॥३॥

मे My भक्तः devotee सखा friend च and असि (thou) art
इति for this reason सः एव even that पुरातनः ancient योगः
Yoga अयं this अद्य this day मया by Me ते to thee प्रोक्तः
has been told हि for एतत् this उत्तमं profound रहस्यं
secret.

3. I have this day told thee that same
ancient Yoga, (for) thou art My devotee,
and My friend, and this secret is profound
indeed.

[*Secret :* Not as the privilege of an individual
or a sect, but because of its profundity. It is a secret
to the unworthy only.]

अर्जुन उवाच ।

अपरं भवतो जन्म परं जन्म विवस्वतः ॥

कथमेतद्विजानीयां त्वमादौ प्रोक्तवानिति ॥४॥

8

अर्जुनः Arjuna उवाच said :

भवतः Thy जन्म birth अपरं later विवस्वतः of Vivasvat जन्म birth परं prior एतत् this कथं how विजानीयाम् should (I) know त्वम् Thou आदौ in the beginning प्रोक्तवान् told इति this.

Arjuna said :

4. Later was Thy birth, and that of Vivasvat prior ; how then should I understand that Thou toldest this in the beginning ?

श्रीभगवानुवाच ।

बहूनि मे व्यतीतानि जन्मानि तव चार्जुन ॥

तान्यहं वेद सर्वाणि न त्वं वेत्थ परन्तप ॥५॥

श्रीभगवान् The Blessed Lord उवाच said :

परन्तप O scorcher of foes अर्जुन Arjuna मे My तव thy च and बहूनि many जन्मानि births व्यतीतानि have passed away अहं I तानि them सर्वाणि all वेद know त्वं thou न not वेत्थ knowest.

The Blessed Lord said :

5. Many are the births that have been passed by Me and thee, O Arjuna. I know them all, whilst thou knowest not, O scorcher of foes.

अजोऽपि सन्नव्ययात्मा भूतानामीश्वरोऽपि सन् ॥

प्रकृतिं स्वामधिष्ठाय सम्भवाम्यात्ममायया ॥६॥

अजः Unborn सन् being अपि even अव्ययात्मा of changeless nature भूतानाम् of beings ईश्वरः Lord अपि even सन्
being स्वां of one's own प्रकृतिं Prakriti अधिष्ठाय subjugating आत्ममायया by My own Mâyâ सम्भवामि come into
being.

6. Though I am unborn, of changeless
nature and Lord of beings, yet subjugating
My Prakriti, I come into being by My own
Mâyâ.

[*Subjugating My Prakriti :* He does not come
into being as others do, bound by Karma, under
the thraldom of Prakriti (Nature). He is not tied
by the fetters of the Gunas—because He is the Lord
of Mâyâ.

By My own Mâyâ : My embodiment is only
apparent and does not touch My true nature.]

यदा यदा हि धर्मस्य ग्लानिर्भवति भारत ॥
अभ्युत्थानमधर्मस्य तदात्मानं सृजाम्यहम् ॥७॥

भारत O Bhârata यदा यदा whenever हि surely धर्मस्य
of Dharma ग्लानिः decline अधर्मस्य of Adharma अभ्युत्थानं rise
भवति is तदा then अहम् I आत्मानं Myself सृजामि body forth.

7. Whenever, O descendant of Bharata,
there is decline of Dharma, and rise of
Adharma, then I body Myself forth.

[The Dharma and its opposite Adharma imply all the duties (and their opposites) as ordained for men in different stations by the definite scheme of their life and salvation.]

परित्राणाय साधूनां विनाशाय च दुष्कृताम् ॥
धर्मसंस्थापनार्थाय संभवामि युगे युगे ॥८॥

साधूनां Of the good परित्राणाय for the protection च and दुष्कृतां of the wicked विनाशाय for the destruction धर्मसंस्थापनार्थाय for the establishment of Dharma युगे युगे in every age संभवामि I come into being.

8. For the protection of the good, for the destruction of the wicked, and for the establishment of Dharma, I come into being in every age.

[*Destruction of the wicked :* in order to destroy their wickedness, and give them life eternal.]

जन्म कर्म च मे दिव्यमेवं यो वेत्ति तत्त्वतः ॥
त्यक्त्वा देहं पुनर्जन्म नैति मामेति सोऽर्जुन ॥९॥

अर्जुन O Arjuna यः who मे My एवं thus दिव्यं divine जन्म birth च: and कर्म action तत्त्वतः in true light वेत्ति knows सः he देहं body त्यक्त्वा leaving पुनः again जन्म birth न not एति gets माम् Me एति attains.

9. He who thus knows, in true light, My divine birth and action, leaving the body, is not born again : he attains to Me, O Arjuna.

[*He who knows etc.*: He who knows the great truth—that the Lord though apparently born is ever beyond birth and death, though apparently active in the cause of righteousness, is ever beyond all action —becomes illumined with Self-knowledge. Such a man is never born again.]

वीतरागभयक्रोधा मन्मया मामुपाश्रिताः ॥

बह्वो ज्ञानतपसा पूता मद्भावमागताः ॥१०॥

वीतरागभयक्रोधाः Freed from attachment, fear, and anger मन्मयाः absorbed in Me माम् Me उपाश्रिताः taking refuge in ज्ञानतपसा by the fire of knowledge पूताः purified बहवः many मद्भावम् My Being आगताः have attained.

10. Freed from attachment, fear, and anger, absorbed in Me, taking refuge in Me, purified by the fire of knowledge, many have attained My Being.

[*Many have attained* : The import is that the path of liberation here taught by Shri Krishna is not of recent origin, nor is it dependent upon His present manifestation, but has been handed down from time immemorial.]

ये यथा मां प्रपद्यन्ते तांस्तथैव भजाम्यहम् ॥

मम वर्त्मानुवर्तन्ते मनुष्याः पार्थ सर्वशः ॥११॥

ये Who यथा whatever way मां Me प्रपद्यन्ते worship तान् them अहं I तथा in the same way एव verily भजामि

bestow (their desires) पार्थ O Pârtha मनुष्याः men सर्वशः
in all ways मम My वर्त्म path अनुवर्तन्ते follow.

11. In whatever way men worship Me,
in the same way do I fulfil their desires :
(it is) My path, O son of Prithâ, (that) men
tread, in all ways.

[In this shloka Shri Krishna anticipates the ob-
jection that God is partial to some and unkind to
others, since He blesses some with Self-knowledge and
leaves the rest in darkness and misery. This difference is not due to any difference in His attitude
towards them, but is of their own choice.

My path : In the whole region of thought and
action, wherever there is fulfilment of object, no
matter what, the same is due to the Lord. As the
Self within, He brings to fruition all wishes, when
the necessary conditions are fulfilled.]

काङ्क्षन्तः कर्मणां सिद्धिं यजन्त इह देवताः ॥
क्षिप्रं हि मानुषे लोके सिद्धिर्भवति कर्मजा ॥१२॥

कर्मणां Of actions सिद्धिं success काङ्क्षन्तः longing for इह
in this world देवताः gods यजन्ते worship हि because मानुषे
in the human लोके world क्षिप्रं quickly कर्मजा born of
action सिद्धिः success भवति is attained.

12. Longing for success in action, in this
world, (men) worship the gods. Because success, resulting from action, is quickly attained
in the human world.

[*Because success ... human world :* Worldly
success is much easier of attainment than Self-
knowledge. Hence it is that the ignorant do not
go in for the latter.]

चातुर्वर्ण्यं मया सृष्टं गुणकर्मविभागशः ॥
तस्य कर्तारमपि मां विद्ध्यकर्तारमव्ययम् ॥१३॥

मया By Me गुणकर्मविभागशः by the differentiation of
Guna and Karma चातुर्वर्ण्यं fourfold caste सृष्टं was
created तस्य thereof कर्तारम् author अपि even मां Me अव्ययं
changeless अकर्तारं non-doer विद्धि know.

13. The fourfold caste was created
by Me, by the differentiation of Guna
and Karma. Though I am the author
thereof, know Me to be the non-doer, and
changeless.

[This shloka is intended to explain the diversity
of human temperaments and tendencies. All men
are not of the same nature, because of the prepon-
derance of the different Gunas in them.

The caste system was originally meant to make
perfect the growth of humanity, by the special culture
of certain features through the process of discriminate
selection.

Though I am the author, etc.: The Lord, though
the author of the caste system, is yet not the author.
The same dread of being taken as a doer or an agent
crops up again and again. The paradox is explained
in Chap. IX. 5-10. Mâyâ is the real author, but

He is taken as such, because it is His light which gives existence, not only to all actions, but to Mâyâ herself.]

न मां कर्माणि लिम्पन्ति न मे कर्मफले स्पृहा ॥

इति मां योऽभिजानाति कर्मभिर्न स बध्यते ॥१४॥

कर्माणि Actions मां Me न not लिम्पन्ति taint मे My कर्मफले in the result of action स्पृहा desire न not इति thus यः who मां Me अभिजानाति knows सः he कर्मभिः by actions न not बध्यते is fettered.

14.   Actions do not taint Me, nor have I any thirst for the result of action. He who knows Me thus is not fettered by action.

[*Actions do not taint Me :* Karma cannot introduce into Me anything foreign. I never depart from My true self, which is All-fullness.]

एवं ज्ञात्वा कृतं कर्म पूर्वैरपि मुमुक्षुभिः ॥

कुरु कर्मैव तस्मात्त्वं पूर्वैः पूर्वतरं कृतम् ॥१५॥

एवं Thus ज्ञात्वा knowing पूर्वैः by the ancient मुमुक्षुभिः seekers after freedom अपि even कर्म action कृतं was done तस्मात् therefore त्वं thou पूर्वैः by the ancients पूर्वतरं in olden times कृतं done कर्म action एव verily कुरु perform.

15.   Knowing thus, the ancient seekers after freedom also performed action. Do thou, therefore, perform action, as did the ancients in olden times.

[*Knowing thus :* Taking this point of view, that is, that the Self can have no desire for the fruits of action and cannot be soiled by action.]

किं कर्म किमकर्मेति कवयोऽप्यत्र मोहिताः ॥

तत्ते कर्म प्रवक्ष्यामि यज्ज्ञात्वा मोक्ष्यसेऽशुभात् ॥१६॥

किं What कर्म action किम् what अकर्म inaction इति thus अत्र in this कवयः sages अपि even मोहिताः bewildered (अतः therefore) यत् which ज्ञात्वा knowing अशुभात् from evil मोक्ष्यसे will be freed तत् that ते to you कर्म action प्रवक्ष्यामि (I) shall tell.

16. Even sages are bewildered, as to what is action and what is inaction. I shall therefore tell you what action is, by knowing which you will be freed from evil.

[*Evil :* the evil of existence, the wheel of birth and death.]

कर्मणो ह्यपि बोद्धव्यं बोद्धव्यञ्च विकर्मणः ॥

अकर्मणश्च बोद्धव्यं गहना कर्मणो गतिः ॥१७॥

हि Because कर्मणः of actions अपि even (तत्त्वं the true nature) बोद्धव्यं has to be understood विकर्मणः of the forbidden action च and (अपि even) बोद्धव्यं has to be understood अकर्मणः of inaction च and (अपि even) बोद्धव्यं has to be understood कर्मणः of Karma गतिः nature गहना impenetrable.

17. For verily, (the true nature) even of action (enjoined by the Shâstras) should

be known, as also, (that) of forbidden action, and of inaction : the nature of Karma is impenetrable.

कर्मण्यकर्म यः पश्येदकर्मणि च कर्म यः ॥
स बुद्धिमान्मनुष्येषु स युक्तः कृत्स्नकर्मकृत् ॥१८॥

यः Who कर्मणि in action अकर्म inaction पश्येत् would see यः who अकर्मणि inaction च and कर्म action पश्येत् would see सः he मनुष्येषु among men बुद्धिमान् intelligent सः he युक्तः Yogi कृत्स्नकर्मकृत् doer of all action.

18. He who sees inaction in action, and action in inaction, he is intelligent among men, he is a Yogi and a doer of all action.

[An action is an action so long as the idea of actor-ness of the Self holds good. Directly the idea of actor-ness disappears, no matter what or how much is done, action has lost its nature. It has become harmless : it can no longer bind. On the other hand, how much soever inactive an ignorant person may remain, so long as there is the idea of actor-ness in him he is constantly doing action. Action equals to belief in the actor-ness of oneself and inaction its reverse.

He is the doer of all action : He has achieved the end of all action, which is freedom.]

यस्य सर्वे समारम्भाः कामसङ्कल्पवर्जिताः ॥
ज्ञानाग्निदग्धकर्माणं तमाहुः पण्डितं बुधाः ॥१९॥

यस्य Whose सर्वे all समारम्भाः undertakings कामसङ्कल्प-
वर्जिताः devoid of plan and desire for results बुधाः the
sages ज्ञानाग्निदग्धकर्माणं whose actions are burnt by the
fire of knowledge तं him पण्डितं wise आहुः call.

19. Whose undertakings are all devoid
of plan and desire for results, and whose actions
are burnt by the fire of knowledge, him, the
sages call wise.

[*Whose undertakings, etc.:* Who is devoid of
egoism.]

त्यक्त्वा कर्मफलासङ्गं नित्यतृप्तो निराश्रयः ॥
कर्मण्यभिप्रवृत्तोऽपि नैव किञ्चित्करोति सः ॥२०॥

सः He कर्मफलासङ्गं clinging to the fruits of action
यक्त्वा forsaking नित्यतृप्तः ever satisfied निराश्रयः depending
on nothing कर्मणि in action अभिप्रवृत्तः engaged अपि even
किञ्चित् anything एव verily न not करोति does.

20. Forsaking the clinging to fruits of
action, ever satisfied, depending on nothing,
though engaged in action, he does not do
anything.

निराशीर्यतचित्तात्मा त्यक्तसर्वपरिग्रहः ॥
शारीरं केवलं कर्म कुर्वन्नाप्नोति किल्बिषम् ॥२१॥

निराशीः Without hope यतचित्तात्मा one whose mind
and body have been controlled त्यक्तसर्वपरिग्रहः one who

has relinquished all possessions केवलं merely शारीरं
bodily कर्म action कुर्वन् doing किल्बिषं evil न not आप्नोति
incurs.

21. Without hope, the body and mind
controlled, and all possessions relinquished, he
does not suffer any evil consequences, by doing
mere bodily action.

[*Evil consequences :* resulting from good and
bad actions, for both lead to bondage.]

यदृच्छालाभसन्तुष्टो द्वन्द्वातीतो विमत्सरः ॥
समः सिद्धावसिद्धौ च कृत्वापि न निबध्यते ॥२२॥

यदृच्छालाभसन्तुष्टः Content with what comes to him
without effort   द्वन्द्वातीतः unaffected by the pairs of
opposites विमत्सरः free from envy सिद्धौ in success असिद्धौ
in failure च and समः even-minded कृत्वा acting अपि
even न not निबध्यते is bound.

22. Content with what comes to him
without effort, unaffected by he pairs of
opposites, free from envy, even-minded in
success and failure, though acting, he is not
bound.

गतसङ्गस्य मुक्तस्य ज्ञानावस्थितचेतसः ॥
यज्ञायाचरतः कर्म समग्रं प्रविलीयते ॥२३॥

गतसङ्गस्य Of one who is devoid of attachment मुक्तस्य
the liberated ज्ञानावस्थितचेतसः whose mind is centred in
knowledge यज्ञाय for Yajna आचरतः performing समग्रं
whole कर्म Karma प्रविलीयते dissolves away.

23. Devoid of attachment, liberated, with mind centred in knowledge, performing work for Yajna alone, his whole Karma dissolves away.

ब्रह्मार्पणं ब्रह्म हविर्ब्रह्माग्नौ ब्रह्मणा हुतम् ॥

ब्रह्मैव तेन गन्तव्यं ब्रह्मकर्मसमाधिना ॥२४॥

अर्पणं Process of offering ब्रह्म Brahman हविः oblation, as clarified butter ब्रह्म Brahman ब्रह्माग्नौ in the fire of Brahman ब्रह्मणा by Brahman हुतं is offered ब्रह्मकर्म समाधिना by the man who is absorbed in action which is Brahman तेन by him ब्रह्म Brahman एव verily गन्तव्यं should be reached.

24. The process is Brahman, the clarified butter is Brahman, offered by Brahman in the fire of Brahman; by seeing Brahman in action, he reaches Brahman alone.

[How can the whole Karma of a person, engaged in work, melt away as stated here? Because after knowledge, his whole life becomes one act of Yajna, in which the process of oblation, the offering, the fire, the doer of the sacrifice, the work, and the goal, are all Brahman. Since his Karma produces no other result than the attainment of Brahman, his Karma is said to melt away.]

देवमेवापरे यज्ञं योगिनः पर्युपासते ॥

ब्रह्माग्नावपरे यज्ञं यज्ञेनैवोपजुह्वति ॥२५॥

अपरे Other योगिनः Yogis दैवं pertaining to Devas एव
verily यज्ञं sacrifice पर्युपासते perform अपरे others ब्रह्माग्नौ
in the fire of Brahman यज्ञेन by self एव verily यज्ञं the
self उपजुह्वति offer as sacrifice.

25. Some Yogis perform sacrifices to
Devas alone, while others offer the self as
sacrifice by the self in the fire of Brahman
alone.

[*Others offer, etc.:* The sacrifice referred to here,
is, divesting the Self of Its Upâdhis (limiting adjuncts), so that It is found to be the Self.]

श्रोत्रादीनीन्द्रियाण्यन्ये संयमाग्निषु जुह्वति ॥
शब्दादीन्विषयानन्य इन्द्रियाग्निषु जुह्वति ॥२६॥

अन्ये Others संयमाग्निषु in the fire of control श्रोत्रादीनि
organ of hearing, etc. इन्द्रियाणि senses जुह्वति offer as
sacrifice अन्ये others शब्दादीन् sound, etc. विषयान् sense-
objects इन्द्रियाग्निषु in the fire of the senses जुह्वति offer as
sacrifice.

26. Some again offer hearing and
other senses as sacrifice in the fire of control,
while others offer sound and other
sense-objects as sacrifice in the fire of the
senses.

[*Others offer sound, etc.:* Others direct their
senses towards pure and unforbidden objects, and in
so doing regard themselves as performing acts
of sacrifice.]

सर्वाणीन्द्रियकर्माणि प्राणकर्माणि चापरे ॥
आत्मसंयमयोगाग्नौ जुह्वति ज्ञानदीपिते ॥२७॥

अपरे Others ज्ञानदीपिते kindled by knowledge आत्म-
संयमयोगाग्नौ in the fire of control in Self सर्वाणि all इन्द्रिय-
कर्माणि actions of the senses प्राणकर्माणि functions of the
vital energy च and जुह्वति offer as sacrifice.

27. Some again offer all the actions of the
senses and the functions of the vital energy,
as sacrifice in the fire of control in Self, kindled
by knowledge.

द्रव्ययज्ञास्तपोयज्ञा योगयज्ञास्तथापरे ॥
स्वाध्यायज्ञानयज्ञाश्च यतयः संशितव्रताः ॥२८॥

तथा Again अपरे others द्रव्ययज्ञाः those who offer
wealth as sacrifice तपोयज्ञाः those who offer austerity
as sacrifice योगयज्ञाः those who offer Yoga as sacrifice
संशितव्रताः persons of rigid vows यतयः persons of self-
restraint स्वाध्यायज्ञानयज्ञाः those who offer study and
knowledge as sacrifice च and.

28. Others again offer wealth, austerity,
and Yoga, as sacrifice, while still others,
of self-restraint and rigid vows, offer
study of the scriptures and knowledge, as
sacrifice.

[*Offer Yoga as sacrifice :* Practice the eightfold
Yoga as an act of sacrifice.]

अपाने जुह्वति प्राणं प्राणेऽपानं तथाऽपरे ॥

प्राणापानगती रुद्ध्वा प्राणायामपरायणाः ॥

अपरे नियताहारा: प्राणान्प्राणेषु जुह्वति ॥२६॥

तथा Yet अपरे others अपाने into the Apâna प्राणं the
Prâna प्राणे into the Prâna अपानं the Apâna जुह्वति sacrifice प्राणापानगती courses of the out-going and in-coming
breaths रुद्ध्वा stopping प्राणायामपरायणाः constantly practising the regulation of the vital energy   अपरे   others
नियताहारा: persons of regulated food प्राणान् functions of
the Prânas प्राणेषु in the Prânas जुह्वति sacrifice.

29. Yet some offer as sacrifice, the
out-going into the in-coming breath, and
the in-coming into the out-going, stopping
the courses of the in-coming and out-going
breaths, constantly practising the regulation
of the vital energy; while others yet of
regulated food, offer in the Prânas the functions
thereof.

[Offer in the Prânas the functions thereof:
Whatever Prâna has been controlled, into it they
sacrifice all other Prânas; these latter become, as it
were, merged in the former. Or, in another way:
They control the different Prânas and unify them
by the foregoing method; the senses are thus attenua-
ted and are merged in the unified Prâna, as an act
of sacrifice.

All the various acts described in verses 25 to 29, as offerings of sacrifice, are only conceived as such, the study of the scriptures is regarded as an act of sacrifice, and so on.]

सर्वेऽप्येते यज्ञविदो यज्ञक्षयितकल्मषाः ॥३०॥

यज्ञशिष्टामृतभुजो यान्ति ब्रह्म सनातनम् ॥

नायं लोकोऽस्त्ययज्ञस्य कुतोऽन्यः कुरुसत्तम ॥३१॥

सर्वे All अपि even एते these यज्ञविदः knowers of Yajna यज्ञक्षयितकल्मषाः persons having their sins consumed by Yajna कुरुसत्तम O best of the Kurus यज्ञशिष्टामृतभुजः persons eating of the nectar—the remnant of Yajna सनातनं eternal ब्रह्म Brahman यान्ति go अयं this लोकः world अयज्ञस्य of the non-performer of Yajna न not अस्ति is अन्यः another कुतः how.

30-31. All of these are knowers of Yajna, having their sins consumed by Yajna, and eating of the nectar—the remnant of Yajna—they go to the Eternal Brahman. (Even) this world is not for the non-performer of Yajna, how then another, O best of the Kurus ?

[*They go to the Eternal Brahman :* in course of time, after attaining knowledge through purification of heart.

Even this world is not for the non-performer of Yajna : this means—He that does not perform any

9

of the Yajnas above mentioned is not fit even for this
wretched human world—how then could he hope to
gain a better world than this ?]

एवं बहुविधा यज्ञा वितता ब्रह्मणो मुखे ॥
कर्मजान्विद्धि तान्सर्वानेवं ज्ञात्वा विमोक्ष्यसे ॥३२॥

ब्रह्मणः Of the Veda मुखे (lit. mouth), in the store-
house एवं thus बहुविधाः various यज्ञाः Yajnas वितताः are
strewn तान् them सर्वान् all कर्मजान् born of action विद्धि
know एवं thus ज्ञात्वा knowing विमोक्ष्यसे (thou) shalt be free.

32. Various Yajnas, like the above, are
strewn in the store-house of the Veda. Know
them all to be born of action ; and thus knowing, thou shalt be free.

[*Strewn in the store-house of the Veda :* incul-
cated by or known through the Veda.]

श्रेयान्द्रव्यमयाद्यज्ञाज्ज्ञानयज्ञः परन्तप ॥
सर्वं कर्माखिलं पार्थ ज्ञाने परिसमाप्यते ॥३३॥

परन्तप O scorcher of foes द्रव्यमयात् with (material)
objects यज्ञात् to sacrifice ज्ञानयज्ञः knowledge-sacrifice
श्रेयान् superior पार्थ O Pârtha सर्वं all अखिलं in its entirety
कर्म action ज्ञाने in knowledge परिसमाप्यते is culminated.

33. Knowledge-sacrifice, O scorcher of
foes, is superior to sacrifice (performed)
with (material) objects. All action in its

entirety, O Pârtha, attains its consummation
in knowledge.

तद्विद्धि प्रणिपातेन परिप्रश्नेन सेवया ॥
उपदेक्ष्यन्ति ते ज्ञानं ज्ञानिनस्तत्त्वदर्शिनः ॥३४॥

प्रणिपातेन By prostrating thyself परिप्रश्नेन by question
सेवया by service तत् that (ज्ञानं knowledge) विद्धि know
ज्ञानिनः the wise तत्त्वदर्शिनः those who have realised the
Truth ते thee ज्ञानं knowledge उपदेक्ष्यन्ति will instruct.

34.   Know that, by prostrating thyself, by
questions, and by service ; the wise, those
who have realised the Truth, will instruct
thee in that knowledge.

[Prostration before the Guru, questions and personal services to him, constitute discipleship.

Those who have realised the Truth : mere theo-
retical knowledge, however perfect, does not qualify
a person to be a Guru: the Truth, or Brahman, must
be realised, before one can claim that most elevated
position.]

यज्ज्ञात्वा न पुनर्मोहमेवं यास्यसि पाण्डव ॥
येन भूतान्यशेषेण द्रक्ष्यस्यात्मन्यथो मयि ॥३५॥

पाण्डव O Pândava यत् which ज्ञात्वा knowing पुनः again
एवं like this मोहं delusion न not यास्यसि will get येन by
which अशेषेण all भूतानि beings आत्मनि in (thy) Self अथो
and मयि in Me (i.e., highest Self) द्रक्ष्यसि (thou) shalt
see.

35. Knowing which, thou shalt not, O Pândava, again get deluded like this, and by which thou shalt see the whole of creation in (thy) Self and in Me.

[*Which* : the knowledge referred to in the preceding shloka to be learnt from the Guru.]

अपि चेदसि पापेभ्यः सर्वेभ्यः पापकृत्तमः ॥
सर्वं ज्ञानप्लवेनैव वृजिनं सन्तरिष्यसि ॥३६॥

सर्वेभ्यः Among all अपि even पापेभ्यः most sinful चेत् (even) if पापकृत्तमः most sinful असि (thou) be सर्वं all वृजिनं sin ज्ञानप्लवेन by the raft of knowledge एव alone सन्तरिष्यसि shalt go across.

36. Even if thou be the most sinful among all the sinful, yet by the raft of knowledge alone thou shalt go across all sin.

यथैधांसि समिद्धोऽग्निर्भस्मसात्कुरुतेऽर्जुन ॥
ज्ञानाग्निः सर्वकर्माणि भस्मसात्कुरुते तथा ॥३७॥

अर्जुन O Arjuna यथा as समिद्धः blazing अग्निः fire एधांसि wood भस्मसात् reduced to ashes कुरुते makes तथा so ज्ञानाग्निः fire of knowledge सर्वकर्माणि all Karma भस्मसात् reduced to ashes कुरुते makes.

37. As blazing fire reduces wood into ashes, so, O Arjuna, does the fire of knowledge reduce all Karma to ashes.

[Excepting of course the Prârabdha, or Karma which, causing the present body, has begun to bear fruits.]

न हि ज्ञानेन सदृशं पवित्रमिह विद्यते ॥
तत्स्वयं योगसंसिद्धः कालेनात्मनि विन्दति ॥३८॥

हि Verily इह in this world ज्ञानेन knowledge सदृशं like पवित्रं purifying न not विद्यते exists कालेन in time योगसंसिद्धः reaching perfection by Yoga आत्मनि in one's own heart स्वयं oneself तत् that (knowledge) विन्दति realises.

38. Verily there exists nothing in this world purifying like knowledge. In good time, having reached perfection in Yoga, one realises that oneself in one's own heart.

श्रद्धावांल्लभते ज्ञानं तत्परः संयतेन्द्रियः ॥
ज्ञानं लब्ध्वा परां शान्तिमचिरेणाधिगच्छति ॥३९॥

श्रद्धावान् The man of Shraddhâ तत्परः devoted संयतेन्द्रियः the master of one's senses ज्ञानं knowledge लभते attains ज्ञानं knowledge लब्ध्वा having attained अचिरेण at once परां supreme शान्तिं to peace अधिगच्छति goes.

39. The man with Shraddhâ, the devoted, the master of one's senses, attains (this) knowledge. Having attained knowledge one goes at once to the Supreme Peace.

अज्ञश्चाश्रद्दधानश्च संशयात्मा विनश्यति ॥
नायं लोकोऽस्ति न परो न सुखं संशयात्मनः ॥४०॥

अज्ञः The ignorant अश्रद्दधानः the man without Shraddhâ संशयात्मा the doubting self विनश्यति goes to destruction संशयात्मनः of the doubting self अयं this लोकः world
न not अस्ति is न not च and परः the next न not च and
सुखं happiness.

40. The ignorant, the man without
Shraddhâ, the doubting self, goes to destruction. The doubting self has neither this
world, nor the next, nor happiness.

[*The ignorant* : one who knows not the Self.

The man without Shraddhâ : one who has no
faith in the words and teachings of his Guru.

The doubting self has, etc.: One of a doubting
disposition fails to enjoy this world, owing to his
constantly rising suspicion about the people, and
things around him, and is also full of doubt as regards the next world; so do the ignorant and the man
without Shraddhâ.]

योगसंन्यस्तकर्माणं ज्ञानसंछिन्नसंशयम् ॥
आत्मवन्तं न कर्माणि निबध्नन्ति धनञ्जय ॥४१॥

धनञ्जय O Dhananjaya योगसंन्यस्तकर्माणं one who has
renounced work by Yoga ज्ञानसंछिन्नसंशयं one whose
doubts are rent asunder by knowledge आत्मवन्तं poised
in the Self कर्माणि actions न not निबध्नन्ति bind.

41. With work renounced by Yoga and doubts rent asunder by knowledge, O Dhananjaya, actions do not bind him who is poised in the Self.

तस्माद्ज्ञानसंभूतं हृत्स्थं ज्ञानासिनात्मनः ॥

छित्त्वैनं संशयं योगमातिष्ठोत्तिष्ठ भारत ॥४२॥

तस्मात् Therefore आत्मनः of the Self अज्ञानसंभूतं born of ignorance हृत्स्थं residing in the heart एनं this संशयं doubt ज्ञानासिना by the sword of knowledge छित्त्वा cutting योगं Yoga आतिष्ठ take refuge in भारत O Bhârata उत्तिष्ठ arise.

42. Therefore, cutting with the sword of knowledge, this doubt about the Self, born of ignorance, residing in thy heart, take refuge in Yoga. Arise, O Bhârata !

इति ज्ञानकर्मसंन्यासयोगो नाम चतुर्थोऽध्यायः ॥

The end of chapter four, designated, *The Way of Renunciation of Action in Knowledge.*

पञ्चमोऽध्यायः ॥

FIFTH CHAPTER

अर्जुन उवाच ।

संन्यासं कर्मणां कृष्ण पुनर्योगं च शंससि ॥
यच्छ्रेय एतयोरेकं तन्मे ब्रूहि सुनिश्चितम् ॥१॥

अर्जुनः Arjuna उवाच said :
कृष्ण O Krishna कर्मणां of actions संन्यासं renunciation पुनः again योगं performance च and शंससि commendest एतयोः of these two यत् which श्रेयः the better एकं one तत् that (एकं one) सुनिश्चितं decisively मे to me ब्रूहि tell.

Arjuna said :
1. Renunciation of action, O Krishna, thou commendest, and again, its performance. Which is the better one of these ? Do thou tell me decisively.

[In IV. 18, 19, 21, 22, 24, 32, 33, 37, and 41, the Lord has spoken of the renunciation of all actions; and in IV. 42 He has exhorted Arjuna to engage in Yoga, in performance of action. Owing to the mutual opposition between the two, which makes it impossible for one man to resort to both of them at

the same time, doubt arises in the mind of Arjuna,
and hence the question as above.

Its performance—"Yoga" in the text : Yoga
here and in the following verses means Karma-
Yoga.]

श्रीभगवानुवाच

संन्यासः कर्मयोगश्च निःश्रेयसकरावुभौ ॥
तयोस्तु कर्मसंन्यासात्कर्मयोगो विशिष्यते ॥२॥

श्रीभगवान् The Blessed Lord उवाच said :

संन्यासः Renunciation कर्मयोगः performance of action च
and उभौ both निःश्रेयसकरौ leading to freedom तयोः of those
two तु but कर्मसंन्यासात् than renunciation of action
कर्मयोगः performance of action विशिष्यते is superior.

The Blessed Lord said :

2. Both renunciation and performance
of action lead to freedom : of these, performance of action is superior to the renunciation
of action.

[*Performance of action*—is superior to mere renunciation (that is unaccompanied with knowledge)
in the case of the novice in the path of spirituality.
See the 6th shloka of this chapter.]

ज्ञेयः स नित्यसंन्यासी यो न द्वेष्टि न कांक्षति ॥
निर्द्वन्द्वो हि महाबाहो सुखं बन्धात्प्रमुच्यते ॥३॥

यः Who न not द्वेष्टि dislikes न not कांक्षति likes सः he
नित्यसंन्यासी constant Sannyâsi ज्ञेयः should be known

महाबाहो O mighty-armed हि verily निर्द्वन्द्वः one free from the pairs of opposites बन्धात् from bondage सुखं easily प्रमुच्यते is set free.

3. He should be known a constant Sannyâsi, who neither likes nor dislikes : for, free from the pairs of opposites, O mighty-armed, he is easily set free from bondage.

[*Constant Sannyâsi :* he need not have taken Sannyâsa formally, but if he has the above frame of mind, he is a Sannyâsi for ever and aye.

Neither likes nor dislikes : Neither hates pain and the objects causing pain, nor desires pleasure and the objects causing pleasure, though engaged in action.]

सांख्ययोगौ पृथग्बालाः प्रवदन्ति न पण्डिताः ॥
एकमप्यास्थितः सम्यगुभयोर्विन्दते फलम् ॥४॥

बालाः Children सांख्ययोगौ Sânkhya (knowledge) and performance of actions पृथक् distinct (इति this) प्रवदन्ति speak न not पण्डिताः the wise एकं one अपि even सम्यक् truly आस्थितः established in उभयोः of both फलं fruit विन्दते gains.

4. Children, not the wise, speak of knowledge and performance of action, as distinct. He who truly lives in one, gains the fruits of both.

[*Children :* the ignorant people devoid of insight into the purpose of the Shâstra.]

यत्सांख्यैः प्राप्यते स्थानं तद्योगैरपि गम्यते ॥
एकं सांख्यं च योगं च यः पश्यति स पश्यति ॥५॥

सांख्यैः By the Jnânis यत् which स्थानं plane प्राप्यते is
reached योगैः by the Karma-yogis अपि even तत् that गम्यते
is reached यः who सांख्यं knowledge च and योगं performance of action च and एकं one पश्यति sees सः he पश्यति sees.

5. The plane which is reached by the
Jnânis is also reached by the Karma-yogis.
Who sees knowledge and performance of
action as one, he sees.

संन्यासस्तु महाबाहो दुःखमाप्तुमयोगतः ॥
योगयुक्तो मुनिर्ब्रह्म न चिरेणाधिगच्छति ॥६॥

महाबाहो O mighty-armed अयोगतः without performance of action संन्यासः renunciation of action आप्तुं to
attain दुःखं hard तु but योगयुक्तः devoted to the path of
action मुनिः a man of meditation न चिरेण quickly ब्रह्म to
Brahman अधिगच्छति goes.

6. Renunciation of action, O mighty-
armed, is hard to attain to without performance of action; the man of meditation, purified by devotion to action, quickly goes to
Brahman.

[It is not that renunciation of action based on
knowledge is not superior to performance of action,

but that the latter method is easier for a beginner,
and qualifies him for the higher path, by purifying
his mind. Hence it is the proper, and therefore the
superior course, in *his* case.]

योगयुक्तो विशुद्धात्मा विजितात्मा जितेन्द्रियः ॥
सर्वभूतात्मभूतात्मा कुर्वन्नपि न लिप्यते ॥७॥

योगयुक्तः Devoted to the path of action विशुद्धात्मा a man
of purified mind विजितात्मा one with the body conquered
जितेन्द्रियः one whose senses are subdued सर्वभूतात्मभूतात्मा
one who realises his Self as the Self in all beings कुर्वन्
acting अपि though न not लिप्यते is tainted.

7. With the mind purified by devotion
to performance of action, and the body conquered, and senses subdued, one who realises
one's Self, as the Self in all beings, though acting, is not tainted.

नैव किञ्चित्करोमीति युक्तो मन्येत तत्त्ववित् ॥
पश्यञ्शृण्वन्स्पृशञ्जिघ्रन्नश्नन्गच्छन्स्वपञ्श्वसन् ॥८॥
प्रलपन्विसृजन्गृह्णन्नुन्मिषन्निमिषन्नपि ॥
इन्द्रियाणीन्द्रियार्थेषु वर्तन्त इति धारयन् ॥६॥

युक्तः Centred (in the Self) तत्त्ववित् the knower of
truth पश्यन् seeing शृण्वन् hearing स्पृशन् touching जिघ्रन्
smelling अश्नन् eating गच्छन् going स्वपन् sleeping श्वसन्
breathing प्रलपन् speaking विसृजन् letting go गृह्णन् holding
उन्मिषन् opening (the eyes) निमिषन् closing (the eyes) अपि

though इन्द्रियाणि senses इन्द्रियार्थेषु amongst sense-objects
वर्तन्ते move इति this धारयन् being convinced किञ्चित् anything
एव at all न not करोमि (I) do इति this मन्येत should think.

8-9. The knower of Truth, (being)
centred (in the Self) should think, "I do
nothing at all"—though seeing, hearing,
touching, smelling, eating, going, sleeping,
breathing, speaking, letting go, holding,
opening, and closing the eyes—convinced
that it is the senses that move among
sense-objects.

ब्रह्मण्याधाय कर्माणि सङ्गं त्यक्त्वा करोति यः ॥
लिप्यते न स पापेन पद्मपत्रमिवाम्भसा । १०॥

यः Who ब्रह्मणि in Brahman आधाय resigning सङ्गं
attachment त्यक्त्वा forsaking कर्माणि actions करोति does सः
he अम्भसा by water पद्मपत्रं lotus-leaf इव like पापेन by evil
न not लिप्यते soiled.

10. He who does actions forsaking
attachment, resigning them to Brahman,
is not soiled by evil, like unto a lotus-leaf by
water.

[*Evil*: the results, good and bad, producing
bondage.]

कायेन मनसा बुद्ध्या केवलैरिन्द्रियैरपि ॥
योगिनः कर्म कुर्वन्ति सङ्गं त्यक्त्वात्मशुद्धये ॥११॥

योगिनः Devotees in the path of work सङ्गं attachment त्यक्त्वा forsaking आत्मशुद्धये for the purification of the heart केवलैः only कायेन by body मनसा by mind बुद्ध्या by intellect इन्द्रियैः by senses अपि even कर्म action कुर्वन्ति perform.

11. Devotees in the path of work perform action, only with body, mind, senses, and intellect, forsaking attachment, for the purification of the heart.

[*Only with, etc.*—without egotism or selfishness: it applies to body, mind, senses, and intellect.]

युक्तः कर्मफलं त्यक्त्वा शान्तिमाप्नोति नैष्ठिकीम् ।
अयुक्तः कामकारेण फले सक्तो निबध्यते ॥१२॥

युक्तः The well-poised कर्मफलं fruit of action त्यक्त्वा forsaking नैष्ठिकीं born of steadfastness शान्ति peace आप्नोति attains अयुक्तः the unbalanced कामकारेण led by desire फले in the fruit (of action) सक्तः (being) attached निबध्यते is bound.

12. The well-poised, forsaking the fruit of action, attains peace, born of steadfastness; the unbalanced one, led by desire, is bound by being attached to the fruit (of action).

[*Born of steadfastness :* Shankara explains Naisthikim as gradual perfection in the path of knowledge, having the following stages of development : (1) purity of heart, (2) gaining of knowledge, (3) renunciation of action, (4) steadiness in knowledge.]

सर्वकर्माणि मनसा संन्यस्यास्ते सुखं वशी ॥
नवद्वारे पुरे देही नैव कुर्वन्न कारयन् ॥१३॥

वशी Subduer (of the senses) देही embodied soul मनसा by discrimination सर्वकर्माणि all actions संन्यस्य having renounced सुखं happily नवद्वारे in the nine-gated पुरे city न not एव verily कुर्वन् acting न not (एव verily) कारयन् causing (others) to act आस्ते rests.

13. The subduer (of the senses), having renounced all actions by discrimination, rests happily in the city of the nine gates, neither acting, nor causing (others) to act.

[*All actions*: 1st, Nitya, or obligatory—the performance of which does not produce any merit while the non-performance produces demerit. 2nd, Naimittika, those arising on the occurrence of some special events, as the birth of a son: these also are customary. 3rd, Kâmya—those intended for securing some special ends: these are only optional. 4th, Nishiddha—or forbidden. He rests happily in the body (of nine organic openings), seeing inaction in action : just exhausting his Prârabdha—not relating or identifying himself with anything of the dual universe.]

न कर्तृत्वं न कर्माणि लोकस्य सृजति प्रभुः ॥
न कर्मफलसंयोगं स्वभावस्तु प्रवर्तते ॥१४॥

प्रभुः The Lord लोकस्य for the world न neither कर्तृत्वं agency न nor कर्माणि actions न nor कर्मफलसंयोगं union with the fruits of action सृजति creates तु but स्वभावः (Nature) universal ignorance प्रवर्तते leads to action.

14. Neither agency, nor actions does the Lord create for the world, nor (does He bring about) the union with the fruit of action. It is universal ignorance that does (it all).

नादत्ते कस्यचित् पापं न चैव सुकृतं विभुः ॥
अज्ञानेनावृतं ज्ञानं तेन मुह्यन्ति जन्तवः ॥१५॥

विभुः Omnipresent कस्यचित् of any one पापं demerit न not आदत्ते takes सुकृतं merit च एव and न not अज्ञानेन by ignorance ज्ञानं knowledge आवृतं enveloped तेन hence जन्तवः beings मुह्यन्ति get deluded.

15. The Omnipresent takes note of the merit or demerit of none. Knowledge is enveloped in ignorance, hence do beings get deluded.

[In unmistakable words, Krishna describes the position of Ishvara, or the Lord, in relation to the Universe, in these two verses.

He is all-blissful, all-perfect; even the shadow of a motive or relation in Him, would be contradictory to His nature. His mere proximity to Prakriti or Nature endues the latter with power and potency of causing all that is. Jiva is bound so long as it relates itself to, and identifies itself with this Nature. When it ceases to do so, it attains freedom. The whole teaching of the Gitâ, and therefore of the whole Hindu scripture, on this subject, is condensed in the above.]

ज्ञानेन तु तदज्ञानं येषां नाशितमात्मनः ॥

तेषामादित्यवज्ज्ञानं प्रकाशयति तत्परम् ॥१६॥

तु But आत्मनः of Self ज्ञानेन by knowledge येषां whose तत् that अज्ञानं ignorance नाशितं is destroyed तेषां their तत् that ज्ञानं knowledge परं the Supreme (Brahman) आदित्यवत् like the sun प्रकाशयति reveals.

16. But whose ignorance is destroyed by the knowledge of Self—that knowledge of theirs, like the sun, reveals the Supreme (Brahman).

तद्बुद्धयस्तदात्मानस्तन्निष्ठास्तत्परायणाः ॥

गच्छन्त्यपुनरावृत्तिं ज्ञाननिर्धूतकल्मषाः ॥१७॥

तद्बुद्धयः Those who have their intellect absorbed in That तदात्मानः those whose self is That तन्निष्ठाः those who are steadfast in That तत्परायणाः those whose consummation is That ज्ञाननिर्धूतकल्मषाः those whose impurities have been shaken off by knowledge अपुनरावृत्तिं non-return गच्छन्ति attain.

10

17. Those who have their intellect absorbed in That, whose self is That, whose steadfastness is in That, whose consummation is That, their impurities cleansed by knowledge, they attain to Non-return (Moksha).

विद्याविनयसंपन्ने ब्राह्मणे गवि हस्तिनि ॥
शुनि चैव श्वपाके च पण्डिताः समदर्शिनः ॥१८॥

पण्डिताः The knowers of the Self एव verily विद्याविनय-संपन्ने in one endowed with learning and humility ब्राह्मणे in a Brâhmana गवि in a cow हस्तिनि in an elephant शुनि in a dog च and श्वपाके in a pariah (lit. one who cooks or eats a dog) च and समदर्शिनः lookers with an equal eye (भवन्ति become).

18. The knowers of the Self look with an equal eye on a Brâhmana endowed with learning and humility, a cow, an elephant, a dog, and a pariah.

[Because they can see nothing but the Self. It makes no difference to the sun whether it be reflected in the Ganges, in wine, in a small pool, or in any unclean liquid : the same is the case with the Self. No Upâdhi (or limiting adjunct) can attach to it.]

इहैव तैर्जितः सर्गो येषां साम्ये स्थितं मनः ॥
निर्दोषं हि समं ब्रह्म तस्माद्ब्रह्मणि ते स्थिताः ॥१९॥

येषां Whose मनः mind साम्ये in evenness स्थितं fixed इह in this world एव verily तैः by them सर्गः (relative) existence जितः is conquered हि indeed ब्रह्म Brahman समं even निर्दोषं without imperfection तस्मात् therefore ते they ब्रह्मणि in Brahman स्थिताः are established.

19. (Relative) existence has been conquered by them, even in this world, whose mind rests in evenness, since Brahman is even and without imperfection : therefore they indeed rest in Brahman.

[*Relative existence :* All bondage as of birth, death, etc. All possibility of bondage is destroyed when the mind attains perfect evenness, which in other words means—becoming Brahman.]

न प्रहृष्येत् प्रियं प्राप्य नोद्विजेत्प्राप्य चाप्रियम् ॥

स्थिरबुद्धिरसंमूढो ब्रह्मविद्ब्रह्मणि स्थितः ॥२०॥

ब्रह्मवित् Knower of Brahman ब्रह्मणि in Brahman स्थितः established स्थिरबुद्धिः one with intellect steady असंमूढः undeluded प्रियं the pleasant प्राप्य receiving न not प्रहृष्येत् should rejoice अप्रियं the unpleasant च and प्राप्य receiving न not उद्विजेत् should be troubled.

20. Resting in Brahman, with intellect steady, and without delusion, the knower of Brahman neither rejoiceth on receiving what is pleasant, nor grieveth on receiving what is unpleasant.

बाह्यस्पर्शेष्वसक्तात्मा विन्दत्यात्मनि यत्सुखम् ॥

स ब्रह्मयोगयुक्तात्मा सुखमक्षयमश्नुते ॥२१॥

बाह्यस्पर्शेषु In the contacts (of the senses) with the external objects असक्तात्मा one whose heart is unattached आत्मनि in the Self यत् what सुखं joy विन्दति realises सः he ब्रह्मयोगयुक्तात्मा heart devoted to the meditation of Brahman अक्षयं undecaying सुखं happiness अश्नुते attains.

21. With the heart unattached to external objects, he realises the joy that is in the Self. With the heart devoted to the meditation of Brahman, he attains undecaying happiness.

[*Heart*—Antah-karana.]

ये हि संस्पर्शजा भोगा दुःखयोनय एव ते ॥

आद्यन्तवन्तः कौन्तेय न तेषु रमते बुधः ॥२२॥

कौन्तेय O Kaunteya ये which हि verily संस्पर्शजा contact-born भोगाः enjoyments ते they दुःखयोनयः generators of misery एव only आद्यन्तवन्तः with beginning and end बुधः the wise तेषु in them न not रमते seeks pleasure.

22. Since enjoyments that are contact-born are parents of misery alone, and with beginning and end, O son of Kunti, a wise man does not seek pleasure in them.

शक्नोतीहैव यः सोढुं प्राक्शरीरविमोक्षणात् ॥

कामक्रोधोद्भवं वेगं स युक्तः स सुखी नरः ॥२३॥

यः Who शरीरविमोक्षणात् (abl.) liberation from the body प्राक् before कामक्रोधोद्भवं born of lust and anger वेगं impulse इह in this world एव verily सोढुं to withstand शक्नोति is able सः he युक्तः steadfast in Yoga सः he सुखी happy नरः man.

23. He who can withstand in this world, before the liberation from the body, the impulse arising from lust and anger, he is steadfast (in Yoga), he is a happy man.

योऽन्तःसुखोऽन्तरारामस्तथाऽन्तर्ज्योतिरेव यः ॥
स योगी ब्रह्मनिर्वाणं ब्रह्मभूतोऽधिगच्छति ॥२४॥

यः Who अन्तःसुखः one whose happiness is within अन्तरारामः one whose relaxation is within तथा again यः who अन्तर्ज्योतिः one whose light is within सः that योगी Yogi एव alone ब्रह्मभूतः becoming Brahman ब्रह्मनिर्वाणं bliss in Brahman, i.e., absolute freedom अधिगच्छति gains.

24. Whose happiness is within, whose relaxation is within, whose light is within, that Yogi alone, becoming Brahman, gains absolute freedom.

[Within : In the Self.

Absolute Freedom : Brahma-Nirvâna. He attains Moksha while still living in the body.]

लभन्ते ब्रह्मनिर्वाणमृषयः क्षीणकल्मषाः ॥
छिन्नद्वैधा यतात्मानः सर्वभूतहिते रताः ॥२५॥

क्षीणकल्मषाः Those whose imperfections are exhausted छिन्नद्वैधाः those whose doubts are dispelled यतात्मानं those whose senses are controlled सर्वभूतहिते in the good of all beings रताः engaged ऋषयः Rishis ब्रह्मनिर्वाणं absolute freedom लभन्ते obtain.

25. With imperfections exhausted, doubts dispelled, senses controlled, engaged in the good of all beings, the Rishis obtain absolute freedom.

[*Rishis :* Men of right vision and renunciation.]

कामक्रोधवियुक्तानां यतीनां यतचेतसाम् ॥
अभितो ब्रह्मनिर्वाणं वर्तते विदितात्मनाम् ॥२६॥

कामक्रोधवियुक्तानां Of those who have been released from lust and anger यतचेतसां of those whose heart is controlled विदितात्मनां of those who have realised the Self यतीनां of the Sannyâsis अभितः both here and hereafter ब्रह्मनिर्वाणं absolute freedom वर्तते exists.

26. Released from lust and anger, the heart controlled, the Self realised, absolute freedom is for such Sannyâsis, both here and hereafter.

स्पर्शान् कृत्वा बहिर्बाह्यांश्चक्षुश्चैवान्तरे भ्रुवोः ॥
प्राणापानौ समौ कृत्वा नासाभ्यन्तरचारिणौ ॥२७॥
यतेन्द्रियमनोबुद्धिर्मुनिर्मोक्षपरायणः ॥
विगतेच्छाभयक्रोधो यः सदा मुक्त एव सः ॥२८॥

बाह्यान् External स्पर्शान् (contacts) objects हि out-
side कृत्वा shutting out चक्षुः eye च and भ्रुवोः of the
(two) eyebrows अन्तरे in the middle एव thus नासाभ्यन्तर-
चारिणौ moving inside the nostrils प्राणापानौ currents of
Prâna and Apâna समौ even कृत्वा having made यतेन्द्रिय-
मनोबुद्धिः one who has controlled one's senses, mind,
and intellect मोक्षपरायणः one to whom Moksha is the
supreme goal विगतेच्छाभयक्रोधः freed from desire, fear,
and anger यः who मुनिः man of meditation सः he सदा
for ever मुक्तः free एव verily.

27-28. Shutting out external objects ;
steadying the eyes between the eyebrows ;
restricting the even currents of Prâna and
Apâna inside the nostrils ; the senses, mind,
and intellect controlled ; with Moksha as the
supreme goal ; freed from desire, fear, and
anger : such a man of meditation is verily free
for ever.

[*External objects :* Sound and other sense-
objects. External objects are shut out from the
mind by not thinking of them. When the eyes are
half-closed in meditation, the eye-balls remain fixed,
and their gaze converges, as it were, between the
eyebrows. Prâna is the out-going breath, Apâna
the in-coming ; the restriction described is effected by
Prânâyama.

These two verses are the aphorisms of which the
following chapter is the commentary.]

भोक्तारं यज्ञतपसां सर्वलोकमहेश्वरम् ॥

सुहृदं सर्वभूतानां ज्ञात्वा मां शान्तिमृच्छति ॥२६॥

यज्ञतपसां Of Yajnas and asceticisms भोक्तारं dispenser सर्वलोकमहेश्वरं Great Lord of all the worlds सर्वभूतानां of all beings सुहृदं friend मां Me ज्ञात्वा knowing शान्तिं peace ऋच्छति attains.

29. Knowing Me as the dispenser of Yajnas and asceticisms, as the Great Lord of all worlds, as the friend of all beings, he attains Peace.

[*Dispenser :* Both as author and goal, the Lord is the dispenser of the fruit of all actions.

Friend : Doer of good without expecting any return.]

इति संन्यासयोगो नाम पञ्चमोऽध्यायः ॥

The end of the fifth chapter, designated, *The Way of Renunciation.*

॥ षष्ठोऽध्यायः ॥

SIXTH CHAPTER

श्रीभगवानुवाच ।

अनाश्रितः कर्मफलं कार्यं कर्म करोति यः ॥
स संन्यासी च योगी च न निरग्निर्न चाक्रियः ॥१॥

श्रीभगवान् The Blessed Lord उवाच said :

यः Who कर्मफलं fruit of action अनाश्रितः not leaning
to कार्यं bounden कर्म duty करोति performs सः he संन्यासी
renouncer of action च and योगी of steadfast mind च
and न not निरग्निः one without fire न not च and अक्रियः
one without action.

The Blessed Lord said :

1. He who performs his bounden duty
without leaning to the fruit of action—he is a
renouncer of action as well as of steadfast
mind : not he who is without fire, nor he who
is without action.

[*Bounden duty :* Nityakarma.

Renouncer of action as well as of steadfast mind :
Sannyâsi and Yogi.

Without fire : He that has renounced actions
enjoined by the Vedas, requiring fire as adjunct, e.g.,
Agnihotra.

Without action : He who has renounced actions which do not require fire as adjunct, such as austerities and meritorious acts like digging wells etc.]

यं संन्यासमिति प्राहुर्योगं तं विद्धि पाण्डव ॥
न ह्यसंन्यस्तसङ्कल्पो योगी भवति कश्चन ॥२॥

पाण्डव O Pândava यं which संन्यासं renunciation इति this प्राहुः said तं that योगं devotion to action विद्धि know हि for असंन्यस्तसङ्कल्पः one who has not forsaken Sankalpa कश्चन any one योगी a devotee to action न not भवति becomes.

2. Know that to be devotion to action, which is called renunciation, O Pândava, for none becomes a devotee to action without forsaking Sankalpa.

[*Sankalpa*—is the working of the imaging faculty, forming fancies, making plans, and again brushing them aside conceiving future results, starting afresh on a new line, leading to different issues, and so on and so forth. No one can be a Karma-Yogi or a devotee to action, who makes plans and wishes for the fruit of action.]

आरुरुक्षोर्मुनेर्योगं कर्म कारणमुच्यते ॥
योगारूढस्य तस्यैव शमः कारणमुच्यते ॥३॥

योगं Concentration आरुरुक्षोः wishing to climb (i.e., to attain) मुनेः of the man of meditation कर्म work कारणम् means उच्यते is said योगारूढस्य of one who has attained

concentration तस्य his शमः inaction एव verily कारणं way
उच्यते is said.

3.   For the man of meditation wishing to
attain purification of heart leading to concentration, work is said to be the way : For him,
when he has attained such (concentration), inaction is said to be the way.

[*Purification of the heart leading to concentration*
—Yoga. "For a Brâhmana there is no wealth like unto
(the eye of) one-ness, (and) even-ness, true-ness, refine-
ment, steadiness, harmlessness, straightforwardness,
and gradual withdrawal from all action."—Mahâbhârata, Shânti-Parva. 175, 38.]

यदा हि नेन्द्रियार्थेषु न कर्मस्वनुषज्जते ॥
सर्वसंकल्पसंन्यासी योगारूढस्तदोच्यते ॥४॥

यदा When हि verily न neither इन्द्रियार्थेषु in sense-
objects न not कर्मसु in actions अनुषज्जते is attached तदा
then सर्वसङ्कल्पसंन्यासी renouncer of all Sankalpas योगारूढः
to have attained concentration उच्यते is said.

4.   Verily, when there is no attachment,
either to sense-objects, or to actions, having
renounced all Sankalpas, then is one said to
have attained concentration.

[*Attained concentration* : Yogârudha.
Renouncer of all Sankalpas : "O desire, I know
where thy root lies : thou art born of Sankalpa. I

shall not think of thee, and thou shalt cease to exist, together with thy root." Mahâbhârata, Shânti-Parva. 177, 25.]

उद्धरेदात्मनात्मानं नात्मानमवसादयेत् ॥
आत्मैव ह्यात्मनो बन्धुरात्मैव रिपुरात्मनः ॥५॥

आत्मना By self आत्मानं oneself उद्धरेत् should uplift न not (तु but) आत्मानं oneself अवसादयेत् should drag down हि verily आत्मा self एव alone आत्मनः of oneself बन्धुः friend आत्मा self एव verily आत्मनः of oneself रिपुः enemy.

5. A man should uplift himself by his own self, so let him not weaken this self. For this self is the friend of oneself, and this self is the enemy of oneself.

[The self-conscious nature of man is here considered in two aspects as being both the object of spiritual uplift and the subject of spiritual uplift, the ego acted upon and the ego acting upon the former. This latter active principle or ego should be kept strong in its uplifting function, for it is apt to turn an enemy if it is not a friend; and the next verse explains the reason.]

बन्धुरात्मात्मनस्तस्य येनात्मैवात्मना जितः ॥
अनात्मनस्तु शत्रुत्वे वर्तेतात्मैव शत्रुवत् ॥६॥

येन By whom आत्मना by oneself एव verily आत्मा self जितः is conquered तस्य his आत्मा self आत्मनः of oneself बन्धुः friend तु but अनात्मनः of unconquered self आत्मा self

एव verily शत्रुवत् like foe शत्रुत्वे in the position of a foe
वर्तेत would remain.

6. The self (the active part of our
nature) is the friend of the self, for him
who has conquered himself by this self.
But to the unconquered self, this self is
inimical, (and behaves) like (an external) foe.

[The self is the friend of one, in whom the
aggregate of the body and the senses has been
brought under control, and an enemy when such is
not the case.]

जितात्मनः प्रशान्तस्य परमात्मा समाहितः ॥
शीतोष्णसुखदुःखेषु तथा मानापमानयोः ॥७॥ ।

जितात्मनः Of the self-controlled प्रशान्तस्य the serene
one परमात्मा the Supreme Self शीतोष्णसुखदुःखेषु in cold and
heat, pleasure and pain तथा as also मानापमानयोः in
honour and dishonour समाहितः is steadfast.

7. To the self-controlled and serene, the
Supreme Self is the object of constant realisation, in cold and heat, pleasure and pain, as
well as in honour and dishonour.

[Hence he remains unruffled in pleasant and
adverse environments.]

ज्ञानविज्ञानतृप्तात्मा कूटस्थो विजितेन्द्रियः ॥
युक्त इत्युच्यते योगी समलोष्टाश्मकाञ्चनः ॥८॥

ज्ञानविज्ञानतृप्तात्मा One whose heart is satisfied by wisdom and realisation कूटस्थः unshaken विजितेन्द्रियः who has conquered his senses समलोष्टाश्मकाञ्चनः one to whom a lump of earth, stone, and gold are the same योगी Yogi युक्तः steadfast इति this उच्यते is said.

8. Whose heart is filled with satisfaction by wisdom and realisation, and is changeless, whose senses are conquered, and to whom a lump of earth, stone, and gold are the same : that Yogi is called steadfast.

[*Wisdom*—Jnâna : knowledge of Shâstras.

Realisation—Vijnâna : one's own experience of the teachings of Shâstras.

Changeless—like the anvil. Things are hammered and shaped on the anvil, but the anvil remains unchanged : in the same manner he is called Kutastha—whose heart remains unchanged though objects are present.]

सुहृन्मित्रार्युदासीनमध्यस्थद्वेष्यबन्धुषु ॥
साधुष्वपि च पापेषु समबुद्धिर्विशिष्यते ॥९॥

सुहृत् Well-wisher मित्रं friend अरिः foe उदासीनः the neutral मध्यस्थः the arbiter द्वेष्यः the hateful बन्धुः relative (सुहृन्मित्रार्युदासीनमध्यस्थद्वेष्यबन्धुषु in well-wishers, etc.) साधुषु in the righteous अपि even च and पापेषु in the unrighteous समबुद्धिः one whose mind is even विशिष्यते attains excellence.

9. He attains excellence who looks with equal regard upon well-wishers, friends, foes, neutrals, arbiters, the hateful, the relatives, and upon the righteous and the unrighteous alike.

योगी युञ्जीत सततमात्मानं रहसि स्थित: ॥

एकाकी यतचित्तात्मा निराशीरपरिग्रह: ॥१०॥

योगी Yogi सततं constantly रहसि in solitude स्थितः remaining एकाकी alone यतचित्तात्मा one with body and mind controlled निराशीः free from hope अपरिग्रहः free from possession आत्मानं युञ्जीत should practise concentration of the heart.

10. The Yogi should constantly practise concentration of the heart, retiring into solitude, alone, with the mind and body subdued, and free from hope and possession.

शुचौ देशे प्रतिष्ठाप्य स्थिरमासनमात्मनः ॥

नात्युच्छ्रितं नातिनीचं चैलाजिनकुशोत्तरम् ॥११॥

शुचौ In a cleanly देशे spot आत्मनः one's own स्थिरं firm न not अत्युच्छ्रितं too high न not अतिनीचं too low चैलाजिनकुशीत्तरं a cloth, a skin, and Kusha-grass, arranged in consecution आसनं seat प्रतिष्ठाप्य having established.

11. Having in a cleanly spot established his seat, firm, neither too high nor

too low, made of a cloth, a skin, and Kusha-
grass, arranged in consecution :

[*Arranged in consecution* : that is—the Kusha-
grass arranged on the ground ; above that, a tiger or
deer skin, covered by a cloth.]

तत्रैकाग्रं मनः कृत्वा यतचित्तेन्द्रियक्रियः ॥

उपविश्यासने युञ्ज्याद्योगमात्मविशुद्धये ॥१२॥

तत् There आसने on the seat उपविश्य sitting मनः mind
एकाग्रं one-pointed कृत्वा making यतचित्तेन्द्रियक्रियः one who
has subdued the action of mind and senses आत्मविशुद्धये
for the purification of the heart योगं Yoga युञ्ज्यात्
should practise.

12.   There, seated on that seat, making
the mind one-pointed and subduing the action
of the imaging faculty and the senses,
let him practise Yoga for the purification of
the heart.

समं कायशिरोग्रीवं धारयन्नचलं स्थिरः ॥

संप्रेक्ष्य नासिकाग्रं स्वं दिशश्चानवलोकयन् ॥१३॥

कायशिरोग्रीवं Body, head, and neck समं erect अचलं
still धारयन् holding स्थिरः (being) firm स्वं one's own
नासिकाग्रं tip of the nose संप्रेक्ष्य gazing at दिशः directions
च and अनवलोकयन् not looking.

13.   Let him firmly hold his body, head,
and neck erect and still, (with the eye-balls
fixed, as if) gazing at the tip of his nose, and
not looking around.

[*Gazing at the tip of his nose*—could not be literally meant here, because then the mind would be fixed only there, and not on the Self : when the eyes are half-closed in meditation, and the eye-balls are still, the gaze is directed, *as it were,* on the tip of the nose.]

प्रशान्तात्मा विगतभीर्ब्रह्मचारिव्रते स्थितः ॥

मनः संयम्य मच्चित्तो युक्त आसीत मत्परः ॥१४॥

प्रशान्तात्मा Serene-hearted विगतभीः fearless ब्रह्मचारिव्रते in the vow of a Brahmachâri स्थितः established मनः mind संयम्य controlling मच्चित्तः thinking of Me मत्परः having Me as the supreme goal युक्तः steadfast आसीत should sit.

14. With the heart serene and fearless, firm in the vow of a Brahmachâri, with the mind controlled, and ever thinking of Me, let him sit (in Yoga) having Me as his supreme goal.

युञ्जन्नेवं सदात्मानं योगी नियतमानसः ॥

शान्तिं निर्वाणपरमां मत्संस्थामधिगच्छति ॥१५॥

एवं Thus सदा always आत्मानं mind युञ्जन् keeping steadfast नियतमानसः one with subdued mind योगी Yogi निर्वाणपरमां that which culminates in Nirvâna (Moksha) मत्संस्थां residing in Me शान्तिं peace अधिगच्छति attains.

15. Thus always keeping the mind steadfast, the Yogi of subdued mind attains the peace residing in Me—the

11

peace which culminates in Nirvâna
(Moksha).

नात्यश्नतस्तु योगोऽस्ति न चैकान्तमनश्नतः ॥
न चातिस्वप्नशीलस्य जाग्रतो नैव चार्जुन ॥१६॥

अर्जुन O Arjuna अत्यश्नतः of one who eats too much
indeed न not योगः Yoga अस्ति is न not च and एकान्तं at all
अनश्नतः of one who does not eat न not च and अतिस्वप्न
शीलस्य of one who sleeps too much न not च and ए
verily जाग्रतः of the wakeful.

16. (Success in) Yoga is not for him
who eats too much or too little—nor
O Arjuna, for him who sleeps too much or too
little.

[The Yoga-shâstra prescribes : "Half (the
stomach) for food and condiments, the third (quarter)
for water, and the fourth should be reserved for free
motion of air."]

युक्ताहारविहारस्य युक्तचेष्टस्य कर्मसु ॥
युक्तस्वप्नावबोधस्य योगो भवति दुःखहा ॥१७॥

युक्ताहारविहारस्य Of one who is moderate in eating and
recreation (such as walking, etc.) कर्मसु in action
युक्तचेष्टस्य of one who is moderate in effort (for work)
युक्तस्वप्नावबोधस्य of one who is moderate in sleep and
wakefulness दुःखहा destructive of misery योगः Yoga
भवति becomes.

17. To him who is temperate in eating
and recreation, in his effort for work, and in

sleep and wakefulness, Yoga becomes the destroyer of misery.

यदा विनियतं चित्तमात्मन्येवावतिष्ठते ॥
निःस्पृहः सर्वकामेभ्यो युक्त इत्युच्यते तदा ॥१८॥

यदा When विनियतं completely controlled चित्तं mind
आत्मनि in the Self एव verily अवतिष्ठते rests तदा then
सर्वकामेभ्यः from all desires निःस्पृहः free from longing युक्तः
steadfast इति this उच्यते is said.

18. When the completely controlled
mind rests serenely in the Self alone, free from
longing after all desires, then is one called
steadfast (in the Self).

यथा दीपो निवातस्थो नेङ्गते सोपमा स्मृता ॥
योगिनो यतचित्तस्य युञ्जतो योगमात्मनः ॥१९॥

यथा As निवातस्थः placed in a windless spot दीपः lamp
न not इङ्गते flickers आत्मनः of the Self योगं concentration
युञ्जतः of the practising one यतचित्तस्य of one with subdued mind योगिनः of the Yogi सा that उपमा simile स्मृता
is thought.

19. "As a lamp in a spot sheltered
from the wind does not flicker"—even
such has been the simile used for a Yogi of
subdued mind, practising concentration in
the Self.

यत्रोपरमते चित्तं निरुद्धं योगसेवया ॥
यत्र चैवात्मनात्मानं पश्यन्नात्मनि तुष्यति ॥२०॥

सुखमात्यन्तिकं यत्तद्बुद्धिग्राह्यमतीन्द्रियम् ॥

वेत्ति यत्र न चैवायं स्थितश्चलति तत्त्वतः ॥२१॥

यं लब्ध्वा चापरं लाभं मन्यते नाधिकं ततः ॥

यस्मिन्स्थितो न दुःखेन गुरुणापि विचाल्यते ॥२२॥

तं विद्याद्दुःखसंयोगवियोगं योगसंज्ञितम् ॥

स निश्चयेन योक्तव्यो योगोऽनिर्विण्णचेतसा ॥२३॥

यत्र In which state योगसेवया by the practice of concentration निरुद्धं absolutely restrained चित्तं mind उपरमते
attains quietude यत्र in which state च and आत्मना by
self आत्मानं the Self पश्यन् seeing आत्मनि in the Self एव
alone तुष्यति is satisfied.

(यत्र Where) अयं this यत्तत् that which आत्यन्तिकं infinite
बुद्धिग्राह्य perceived by the intellect अतीन्द्रियं transcending
the senses सुखं bliss वेत्ति knows यत्र where च and स्थितः
established तत्त्वतः from one's real state न एव never
चलति departs.

यं Which च and लब्ध्वा having obtained ततः from
that अधिकं superior अपरं other लाभं acquisition न not
मन्यते regards यस्मिन् in which स्थितः established गुरुणा by
great दुःखेन sorrow अपि even न not विचाल्यते is moved.

तं That दुःखसंयोगवियोगं a state of severance from
the contact of pain योगसंज्ञितं called by the name of
Yoga विद्यात् should know अनिर्विण्णचेतसा with undepressed
heart सः that योगः Yoga निश्चयेन with perseverance योक्तव्य
should be practised.

20-23. When the mind, absolutely restrained by the practice of concentration, attains quietude, and when seeing the Self by the self, one is satisfied in his own Self ; when he feels that infinite bliss—which is perceived by the (purified) intellect and which transcends the senses, and established wherein he never departs from his real state ; and having obtained which, regards no other acquisition superior to that, and where established, he is not moved even by heavy sorrow ;—let that be known as the state, called by the name of Yoga—a state of severance from the contact of pain. This Yoga should be practised with perseverance, undisturbed by depression of heart.

[*Which is perceived...intellect :* Which the purified intellect can grasp independently of the senses. When in meditation the mind is deeply concentrated, the senses do not function and are resolved into their cause—that is, the mind ; and when the latter is steady, so that there is only the intellect functioning, or in other words, cognition only exists, the indescribable Self is realised.]

सङ्कल्पप्रभवान्कामांस्त्यक्त्वा सर्वानशेषतः ॥

मनसैवेन्द्रियग्रामं विनियम्य समन्ततः ॥२४॥

संकल्पप्रभवान् Born of Sankalpa सर्वान् all कामान् desires

अशेषतः without reserve त्यक्त्वा abandoning मनसा by the mind एव alone समन्ततः from all sides इन्द्रियग्रामं group of senses विनियम्य completely restraining.

24. Abandoning without reserve all desires born of Sankalpa, and completely restraining, by the mind alone, the whole group of senses from their objects in all directions ;

शनैः शनैरुपरमेद्बुद्ध्या धृतिगृहीतया ॥
आत्मसंस्थं मनः कृत्वा न किञ्चिदपि चिन्तयेत् ॥२५॥

धृतिगृहीतया Set in patience बुद्ध्या by the intellect मन mind आत्मसंस्थं placed in the Self कृत्वा making शनैः शनैः by degrees उपरमेत् should attain quietude न not किञ्चित् anything अपि even चिन्तयेत् should think.

25. With the intellect set in patience, with the mind fastened on the Self, let him attain quietude by degrees : let him not think of anything.

यतो यतो निश्चरति मनश्चञ्चलमस्थिरम् ॥
ततस्ततो नियम्यैतदात्मन्येव वशं नयेत् ॥२६॥

चञ्चलं Restless अस्थिरं unsteady मनः mind यतः यतः from whatever (reason) निश्चरति wanders away ततः ततः from that एतत् this (मनः mind) नियम्य curbing आत्मनि in the Self एव alone वशं subjugation नयेत् should bring.

26. Through whatever reason the rest-

less, unsteady mind wanders away, let him, curbing it from that, bring it under the sub- jugation of the Self alone.

प्रशान्तमनसं ह्येनं योगिनं सुखमुत्तमम् ॥
उपैति शान्तरजसं ब्रह्मभूतमकल्मषम् ॥२७॥

प्रशान्तमनसं One of perfectly tranquil mind शान्तरजसं one whose passions are quieted अकल्मषं one who is free from taint ब्रह्मभूतम् Brahman-become एनं this योगिनं Yogi हि verily उत्तमं supreme सुखं bliss उपैति comes.

27. Verily, the supreme bliss comes to that Yogi, of perfectly tranquil mind, with passions quieted, Brahman-become, and freed from taint.

[*Brahman-become,* i.e., one who has realised that all is Brahman.

Taint—of good and evil.]

युञ्जन्नेवं सदात्मानं योगी विगतकल्मषः ॥
सुखेन ब्रह्मसंस्पर्शमत्यन्तं सुखमश्नुते ॥२८॥

एवं Thus सदा constantly आत्मानं mind युञ्जन् engaging विगतकल्मषः free from taint योगी Yogi सुखेन easily ब्रह्मसंस्पर्शं generated by the contact with Brahman अत्यन्तं intense सुखं bliss अश्नुते attains.

28. The Yogi, freed from taint (of good and evil), constantly engaging the mind thus, with ease attains the infinite bliss of contact with Brahman.

सर्वभूतस्थमात्मानं सर्वभूतानि चात्मनि ॥

ईक्षते योगयुक्तात्मा सर्वत्र समदर्शनः ॥२६॥

योगयुक्तात्मा One whose heart is steadfast in Yoga
सर्वत्र everywhere समदर्शनः one who sees the same आत्मानं
Self सर्वभूतस्थं abiding in all beings सर्वभूतानि all beings च
and आत्मनि in the Self ईक्षते sees.

29. With the heart concentrated by
Yoga, with the eye of evenness for all things,
he beholds the Self in all beings and all beings
in the Self.

यो मां पश्यति सर्वत्र सर्वं च मयि पश्यति ॥

तस्याहं न प्रणश्यामि स च मे न प्रणश्यति ॥३०॥

यः Who मां Me सर्वत्र everywhere पश्यति sees मयि in Me
च and सर्वं everything पश्यति sees तस्य his (to him) अहं I
न not प्रणश्यामि vanish सः he च and मे My (to Me) न not
प्रणश्यति vanishes.

30. He who sees Me in all things, and
sees all things in Me, he never becomes
separated from Me, nor do I become separated
from him.

[*Separated,* i.e., by time, space, or anything
intervening.]

सर्वभूतस्थितं यो मां भजत्येकत्वमास्थितः ॥

सर्वथा वर्तमानोऽपि स योगी मयि वर्तते ॥३१॥

यः Who सर्वभूतस्थितं dwelling in all beings मां Me एकत्वम् unity आस्थितः established भजति worships सर्वथा in every way वर्तमानः remaining अपि even सः that योगी Yogi मयि in Me वर्तते abides.

31. He who being established in unity, worships Me, who am dwelling in all beings, whatever his mode of life, that Yogi abides in Me.

[*Worships Me* : Realises Me as the Self of all.
Established in unity, i.e., having resolved all duality in the underlying unity.]

आत्मौपम्येन सर्वत्र समं पश्यति योऽर्जुन ॥
सुखं वा यदि वा दुःखं स योगी परमो मतः ॥३२॥

अर्जुन O Arjuna यः who सर्वत्र everywhere सुखं pleasure वा or यदि if वा or दुःखं pain आत्मौपम्येन by comparison with himself समं the same पश्यति sees सः that योगी Yogi परमः highest मतः is regarded.

32. He who judges of pleasure or pain everywhere, by the same standard as he applies to himself, that Yogi, O Arjuna, is regarded as the highest.

[Seeing that whatever is pleasure or pain to himself, is alike pleasure or pain to all beings, he, the highest of Yogis, wishes good to all and evil to none—he is always harmless and compassionate to all creatures.]

अर्जुन उवाच ।

योऽयं योगस्त्वया प्रोक्तः साम्येन मधुसूदन ॥

एतस्याहं न पश्यामि चञ्चलत्वात् स्थितिं स्थिराम् ॥३३॥

अर्जुनः Arjuna उवाच said :
मधुसूदन O slayer of Madhu त्वया by Thee साम्येन by
unity or evenness यः which अयं this योगः Yoga प्रोक्तः said
एतस्य its स्थिरां lasting स्थितिं endurance चञ्चलत्वात् from
restlessness अहं I न not पश्यामि see.

Arjuna said :

33. This Yoga which has been taught
by Thee, O slayer of Madhu, as characterised
by evenness, I do not see (the possibility of)
its lasting endurance, owing to restlessness (of
the mind).

चञ्चलं हि मनः कृष्ण प्रमाथि बलवद्दृढम् ॥

तस्याहं निग्रहं मन्ये वायोरिव सुदुष्करम् ॥३४॥

कृष्ण O Krishna हि verily मनः mind चञ्चलं restless
प्रमाथि turbulent बलवत् strong दृढं unyielding अहं I तस्य of
that निग्रहं control वायोः of the wind इव like सुदुष्करं difficult to do मन्ये regard.

34. Verily, the mind, O Krishna, is
restless, turbulent, strong, and unyielding ; I
regard it quite as hard to achieve its control, as
that of the wind.

["*Krishna*", is derived from "Krish", to scrape:
Krishna is so called because He scrapes or draws
away all sins and other evils from His devotees.]

श्रीभगवानुवाच ।

असंशयं महाबाहो मनो दुर्निग्रहं चलम् ॥

अभ्यासेन तु कौन्तेय वैराग्येण च गृह्यते ॥३५॥

श्रीभगवान् The Blessed Lord उवाच said :
महाबाहो O mighty armed मनः mind दुर्निग्रहं difficult
of control चलं restless असंशयं undoubtedly तु but कौन्तेय
O son of Kunti अभ्यासेन by practice वैराग्येण by renunciation च and गृह्यते is restrained.

The Blessed Lord said :
35.   Without doubt, O mighty-armed, the
mind is restless, and difficult to control ; but
through practice and renunciation, O son of
Kunti, it may be governed.

[*Cf.* Patanjali I. 12.

Practice: Earnest and repeated attempt to make
the mind steady in its unmodified state of Pure
Intelligence, by means of constant meditation upon
the Chosen Ideal.

Renunciation: Freedom from desire for any
pleasures, seen or unseen, achieved by a constant
perception of evil in them.]

असंयतात्मना योगो दुष्प्राप इति मे मतिः ॥

वश्यात्मना तु यतता शक्योऽवाप्तुमुपायतः ॥३६॥

असंयतात्मना By a man of uncontrolled self योग: Yoga
दुष्प्राप: hard to attain इति this मे My मति: conviction
वश्यात्मना by the self-controlled one तु but उपायत: by
right means यतता by the striving one अवाप्तुं to obtain
शक्य: possible.

36. Yoga is hard to be attained by one
of uncontrolled self : such is My conviction ;
but the self-controlled, striving by right means,
can obtain it.

अर्जुन उवाच ।

अयति: श्रद्धयोपेतो योगाच्चलितमानस: ॥

अप्राप्य योगसंसिद्धिं कां गतिं कृष्ण गच्छति ॥३७॥

अर्जुन: Arjuna उवाच said:

कृष्ण O Krishna श्रद्धया by Shraddhâ उपेत: possessed
अयति: uncontrolled योगात् from Yoga चलितमानस: one
whose mind wanders away योगसंसिद्धिं perfection in
Yoga अप्राप्य not gaining कां which गतिं end गच्छति meets.

Arjuna said :
37. Though possessed of Shraddhâ but
unable to control himself, with the mind
wandering away from Yoga, what end does
one, failing to gain perfection in Yoga, meet,
O Krishna ?

कच्चिन्नोभयविभ्रष्टश्छिन्नाभ्रमिव नश्यति ॥

अप्रतिष्ठो महाबाहो विमूढो ब्रह्मण: पथि ॥३८॥

महाबाहो O mighty-armed ब्रह्मण: of Brahman पथि in
the path विमूढ: deluded अप्रतिष्ठ: supportless उभयविभ्रष्ट:
fallen from both छिन्न rent अभ्रं cloud इव like न not
नश्यति perishes कच्चित्—particle implying question.

38.   Does   he   not,   fallen   from   both,
perish,   without   support,   like   a   rent   cloud,
O   mighty-armed,   deluded   in   the   path   of
Brahman ?

[*Fallen from both:* That   is,   from   both   the
paths of knowledge and action.]

एतन्मे संशयं कृष्ण छेत्तुमर्हस्यशेषत: ॥

त्वदन्य: संशयस्यास्य छेत्ता न ह्युपपद्यते ॥३६॥

कृष्ण O Krishna मे my एतत् this संशयं doubt अशेषत:
completely छेत्तुं to dispel अर्हसि art justified त्वदन्य: but
Thee अस्य of this संशयस्य doubt छेत्ता dispeller न not हि
verily उपपद्यते is fit.

39.   This   doubt   of   mine,   O   Krishna,
Thou   shouldst   completely   dispel ;   for   it   is
not   possible   for   any   but   Thee   to   dispel   this
doubt.

[Since   there   can   be   no   better   teacher   than   the
Omniscient Lord.]

श्रीभगवानुवाच ।

पार्थ नैवेह नामुत्र विनाशस्तस्य विद्यते ॥

नहि कल्याणकृत्कश्चिद्दुर्गतिं तात गच्छति ॥४०॥

श्रीभगवान्The Blessed Lord उवाच Said:

पार्थ O son of Prithâ न not एव verily इह hereन not अमुत्र hereafter तस्य his विनाशः destruction विद्यते is तात O my son हि verily कल्याणकृत् doer of good कश्चित् any दुर्गतिं bad state, hence grief न not गच्छति goes.

The Blessed Lord said :

40. Verily, O son of Prithâ, there is destruction for him, neither here nor hereafter : for, the doer of good, O my son, never comes to grief.

[*Tâta*—son. A disciple is looked upon as a son; Arjuna is thus addressed having placed himself in the position of a disciple to Krishna.]

प्राप्य पुण्यकृतां लोकानुषित्वा शाश्वतीः समाः ॥

शुचीनां श्रीमतां गेहे योगभ्रष्टोऽभिजायते ॥४१॥

योगभ्रष्टः One fallen from Yoga पुण्यकृतां of the righteous लोकान् worlds प्राप्य having attained शाश्वतीः eternal समाः years उषित्वा having dwelt शुचीनां of the pure श्रीमतां of the prosperous गेहे in the home अभिजायते reincarnates.

41. Having attained to the worlds of the righteous, and dwelling there for ever-lasting years, one fallen from Yoga rein-carnates in the home of the pure and the prosperous.

[*Everlasting years*—meaning not absolutely, but a very long period.]

अथवा योगिनामेव कुले भवति धीमताम् ॥
एतद्धि दुर्लभतरं लोके जन्म यदीदृशम् ॥४२॥

अथवा Or धीमतां of the wise योगिनाम् of the Yogis एव
verily कुले in the family भवति is born ईदृशं such यत्
which जन्म birth एतत् this हि verily लोके in the world
दुर्लभतरं very rare to obtain.

42. Or else he is born into a family of
wise Yogis only ; verily, a birth such as that is
very rare to obtain in this world.

[*Very rare :* more difficult than the one mentioned in the preceding Shloka.]

तत्र तं बुद्धिसंयोगं लभते पौर्वदेहिकम् ॥
यतते च ततो भूयः संसिद्धौ कुरुनन्दन ॥४३॥

तत्र There पौर्वदेहिकं acquired in his former body त
that बुद्धिसंयोगं union with intelligence लभते gains कुरुनन्दन
O son of the Kurus च and ततः than that भूयः more
संसिद्धौ for perfection यतते strives.

43. There he is united with the intelligence acquired in his former body, and strives
more than before, for perfection, O son of the
Kurus.

[*Intelligence*—Samskâra : store of experience
in the shape of impressions and habits.

Strives..perfection : Strives more strenuously
to attain to higher planes of realisation than those
acquired in his former birth.]

पूर्वाभ्यासेन तेनैव ह्रियते ह्यवशोऽपि सः ॥
जिज्ञासुरपि योगस्य शब्दब्रह्मातिवर्तते ॥४४॥

तेन By that एव verily पूर्वाभ्यासेन previous practice
अवशः helpless अपि even सः he ह्रियते is borne योगस्य of
Yoga जिज्ञासुः enquirer अपि even शब्दब्रह्म Word-Brahman
अतिवर्तते goes beyond.

44. By that previous practice alone, he
is borne on in spite of himself. Even the
enquirer after Yoga rises superior to the per-
former of Vedic actions.

[*Borne on in spite of himself :* carried to the
goal of the course which he marked out for himself
in his last incarnation, by the force of his former
Samskâras, though he might be unconscious of them
—or even unwilling to pursue it, owing to the inter-
ference of some untoward Karma.

Rises, etc.: lit. goes beyond the Word-Brahman,
i.e., the Vedas.]

प्रयत्नाद्यतमानस्तु योगी संशुद्धकिल्बिषः ॥
अनेकजन्मसंसिद्धस्ततो याति परां गतिम् ॥४५॥

तु But प्रयत्नात् with assiduity यतमानः striving योगी Yogi
संशुद्धकिल्बिषः purified of taint अनेकजन्मसंसिद्धः perfected
through many births ततः then परां supreme गतिं goal
याति attains.

45. The Yogi, striving assiduously, purified of taint, gradually gaining perfection through many births, then reaches the highest goal.

तपस्विभ्योऽधिको योगी ज्ञानिभ्योऽपि मतोऽधिकः ॥
कर्मिभ्यश्चाधिको योगी तस्माद्योगी भवार्जुन ॥४६॥

योगी Yogi तपस्विभ्यः than ascetics अधिकः superior ज्ञानिभ्यः than the learned अपि even अधिकः superior कर्मिभ्य than the performers of action च and योगी Yogi अधिक superior मतः deemed तस्मात् therefore अर्जुन O Arjuna योगी Yogi भव be.

46. The Yogi is regarded as superior to those who practise asceticism, also to those who have obtained wisdom (through the Shâstras). He is also superior to the performers of action, (enjoined in the Vedas). Therefore, be thou a Yogi, O Arjuna !

[*Wisdom* : Knowledge from precepts, but not direct insight into the Divine Truth.]

योगिनामपि सर्वेषां मद्गतेनान्तरात्मना ॥
श्रद्धावान्भजते यो मां स मे युक्ततमो मतः ॥४७॥

यः Who श्रद्धावान् endued with Shraddhâ मद्गतेन absorbed in Me अन्तरात्मना with inner self मां Me भजते worships
12

सः he मे by Me सर्वेषां of all योगिनाम् Yogis अपि even युक्ततमः most steadfast मतः regarded.

47. And of all Yogis, he who with the inner self merged in Me, with Shraddhâ devotes himself to Me, is considered by Me the most steadfast.

[*Of all Yogis, etc.*:—Of all Yogis he who devotes himself to the All-pervading Infinite, is superior to those who devote themselves to the lesser ideals, or gods, such as Vasu, Rudra, Aditya, etc.]

इति ध्यानयोगो नाम षष्ठोऽध्यायः ॥

The end of the sixth chapter, designated, *The Way of Meditation.*

॥ सप्तमोऽध्यायः ॥

SEVENTH CHAPTER

श्रीभगवानुवाच ।

मय्यासक्तमनाः पार्थ योगं युञ्जन्मदाश्रयः ॥
असंशयं समग्रं मां यथा ज्ञास्यसि तच्छृणु ॥१॥

श्रीभगवान् The Blessed Lord उवाच said :

पार्थ O son of Prithâ मयि on Me आसक्तमनाः with mind intent मदाश्रयः taking refuge in Me योगं Yoga युञ्जन् practising समग्रं wholly मां Me असंशयं doubtless यथा how ज्ञास्यसि shalt know तत् that शृणु hear.

The Blessed Lord said :

1. With the mind intent on Me, O son of Prithâ, taking refuge in Me, and practising Yoga, how thou shalt without doubt know Me fully, that do thou hear.

[*Fully*, i.e., possessed of infinite greatness, strength, power, grace, and other infinite attributes.]

ज्ञानं तेऽहं सविज्ञानमिदं वक्ष्याम्यशेषतः ॥
यज्ज्ञात्वा नेह भूयोऽन्यज्ज्ञातव्यमवशिष्यते ॥२॥

अहं I ते to thee सविज्ञानं combined with realisation
इदं this ज्ञानं knowledge अशेषतः in full वक्ष्यामि shall tell यत्
which ज्ञात्वा having known इह here भूयः more अन्यत् anything else ज्ञातव्यं what ought to be known न not
अवशिष्यते remains.

2. I shall tell you in full, of knowledge, speculative and practical, knowing
which, nothing more here remains to be
known.

मनुष्याणां सहस्रेषु कश्चिद्यतति सिद्धये ॥
यततामपि सिद्धानां कश्चिन्मां वेत्ति तत्त्वतः ॥३॥

मनुष्याणां Of men सहस्रेषु among thousands कश्चित् some
one सिद्धये for perfection यतति strives यततां of the
striving ones सिद्धानां of the blessed ones अपि even कश्चित्
some one मां Me तत्त्वतः in reality वेत्ति knows.

3. One, perchance, in thousands of
men, strives for perfection ; and one perchance, among the blessed ones, striving
thus, knows Me in reality.

[*The Blessed :* Siddhânâm—this word literally
means the perfected ones—but here it means only
those who having acquired good Karma in a past
incarnation, strive for freedom in this life.]

भूमिरापोऽनलो वायुः खं मनो बुद्धिरेव च ॥
अहंकार इतीयं मे भिन्ना प्रकृतिरष्टधा ॥४॥

भूमिः Earth आपः water अनलः fire वायुः air खं ether मन
mind बुद्धिः intellect एव verily अहंकारः egoism च and इति
thus इयं this मे My अष्टधा eightfold भिन्ना divided प्रकृतिः
Prakriti, the Mâyâ belonging to the Ishvara.

4. Bhumi (earth), Ap (water), Anala
(fire), Vâyu (air), Kha (ether), mind, intellect, and egoism : thus is My Prakriti
divided eightfold.

[The *raison d'être* of this reduction of matter
into five elements is quite different from that conceived by modern science. Man has five senses only,
just five ways in which he can be affected by matter,
therefore his perception of matter cannot be divided
further. The five elements are of two kinds, subtle
and gross. The gross state is said to be formed by
taking half of a subtle element, and adding $\frac{1}{8}$th to it,
of each of the rest : e.g., gross Âkasha $= \frac{1}{2}$ subtle
Âkâsha $+ \frac{1}{8}$th subtle Vâyu $+ \frac{1}{8}$ subtle Tejas $+ \frac{1}{8}$th
subtle Ap $+ \frac{1}{8}$th subtle Bhumi. Then again, the
ether, air, light, water, and earth of modern science,
do not answer to the five elements of Hindu philosophy. Âkâsha is just the sound-producing agency.
From Akâsha rises Vâyu, having the properties of
sound and touch. From Vâyu springs Tejas, posses-
sing the property of visibility, as well as those of its
predecessors. From Tejas rises Ap, combining with
the above properties its distinctive feature—flavour.
Bhumi comes from Ap, bringing the additional property of smell to its inheritance.]

अपरेयमितस्त्वन्यां प्रकृतिं विद्धि मे पराम् ॥

जीवभूतां महाबाहो ययेदं धार्यते जगत् ॥५॥

तु But इयं this अपरा lower इतः from this अन्यां different जीवभूतां the very life-element मे My परां higher प्रकृतिं Prakriti विद्धि know महाबाहो O mighty-armed यया by which इदं this जगत् universe धार्यते is sustained.

5. This is the lower (Prakriti). But different from it, know thou, O mighty-armed, My higher Prakriti—the principle of self-consciousness, by which this universe is sustained.

एतद्योनीनि भूतानि सर्वाणीत्युपधारय ॥

अहं कृत्स्नस्य जगतः प्रभवः प्रलयस्तथा ॥६॥

सर्वाणि All भूतानि beings एतद्योनीनि those of which these two (Prakritis) are the womb इति this उपधारय know अहं I कृत्स्नस्य of the whole जगतः universe प्रभवः source तथा and also प्रलयं dissolution.

6. Know that these (two Prakritis) are the womb of all beings, I am the origin and dissolution of the whole universe.

[*I am the origin, etc.:* In Me the whole universe originates and dissolves, as everything springs from My Prakriti.]

मत्तः परतरं नान्यत्किश्चिदस्ति धनञ्जय ॥

मयि सर्वमिदं प्रोतं सूत्रे मणिगणा इव ॥७॥

धनञ्जय O Dhananjaya मत्तः than Me परतरं higher अन्यत् else किश्चित् aught न not अस्ति is सूत्रे on a thread मणिगणाः a row of jewels इव like इदं this सर्वं all मयि in Me प्रोतं is strung.

7. Beyond Me, O Dhananjaya, there is naught. All this is strung in Me, as a row of jewels on a thread.

[*Beyond Me*—there is no other cause of the universe but Me.]

रसोऽहमप्सु कौन्तेय प्रभास्मि शशिसूर्ययोः॥

प्रणवः सर्ववेदेषु शब्दः खे पौरुषं नृषु ॥८॥

कौन्तेय O son of Kunti अहम् I अप्सु in waters रसः sapidity शशिसूर्ययोः in the moon and the sun प्रभाः radiance सर्ववेदेषु in all the Vedas प्रणवः that syllable Om खे in Âkâsha शब्दः sound नृषु in men पौरुषं manhood अस्मि am.

8. I am the sapidity in waters, O son of Kunti ; I, the radiance in the moon and the sun ; I am the Om in all the Vedas, sound in Âkâsha, and manhood in men.

[In Me as essence, all these are woven, as being My manifestations.]

पुण्यो गन्धः पृथिव्यां च तेजश्चास्मि विभावसौ ॥

जीवनं सर्वभूतेषु तपश्चास्मि तपस्विषु ॥९॥

च And पृथिव्यां in earth पुण्यः sweet गन्धः fragrance च and विभावसौ in fire तेजः brilliancy अस्मि (I) am सर्वभूतेषु in all beings जीवनं life च and तपस्विषु in ascetics तपः austerity अस्मि (I) am.

9. I am the sweet fragrance in earth, and the brilliance in fire am I; the life in all beings, and the austerity am I in ascetics.

बीजं मां सर्वभूतानां विद्धि पार्थ सनातनम् ॥

बुद्धिर्बुद्धिमतामस्मि तेजस्तेजस्विनामहम् ॥१०॥

पार्थ O son of Prithâ मां Me सर्वभूतानां of all beings सनातनं eternal बीजं seed विद्धि know बुद्धिमतां of all the intelligent बुद्धिः intellect तेजस्विनां of the heroic तेजः heroism अहम् I अस्मि am.

10. Know Me, O son of Prithâ, as the eternal seed of all beings. I am the intellect of the intelligent, and the heroism of the heroic.

बलं बलवतामस्मि कामरागविवर्जितम् ॥

धर्माविरुद्धो भूतेषु कामोऽस्मि भरतर्षभ ॥११॥

भरतर्षभ O bull among the Bhâratas (अहं I) बलवताम् of the strong कामरागविवर्जितम् devoid of desire and attachment बलं strength अस्मि am भूतेषु in beings धर्माविरुद्ध unopposed to Dharma कामः desire अस्मि (I) am.

11. Of the strong, I am the strength devoid of desire and attachment. I am, O bull among he Bhâratas, desire in beings, unopposed to Dharma.

[*Desire—Kâma :* thirst for objects not present to the senses.

Attachment—Râga : for those presented to the senses.

Unopposed to Dharma : the desire which moves in harmony with the ordained duties of life.]

ये चैव सात्त्विका भावा राजसास्तामसाश्च ये ॥
मत्त एवेति तान्विद्धि न त्वहं तेषु ते मयि ॥१२॥

ये Whatever च and एव verily सात्त्विका: belonging to Sattva भावा: states च and ये whatever राजसा: belonging to Rajas तामसा: belonging to Tamas तान् them मत्त: proceeding from Me एव verily इति this विद्धि know तु but अहं I तेषु in them न not ते they मयि in Me.

12. And whatever states pertaining to Sattva, and those pertaining to Rajas, and to Tamas, know them to proceed from Me alone ; still I am not in them, but they are in Me.

[All things are in Him, yet not He in them. Logically, this can only happen in superimposition through illusion: as that of a ghost seen in the stump of a tree; the ghost is in the stump, from the point of view of the man in the dark, but the stump is never in the ghost. Similarly the universe is super-imposed on the Lord, seen in His place through Mâyâ, but He is not in it. The Lord returns to the same teaching in Chap. IX. 4, 5.]

त्रिभिर्गुणमयैर्भावैरेभिः सर्वमिदं जगत् ॥
मोहितं नाभिजानाति मामेभ्यः परमव्ययम् ॥१३॥

एभिः By these त्रिभिः three गुणमयैः composed of Gunas भावैः states मोहितं deluded इदं this सर्वं all जगत् world एभ्यः from them परं distinct अव्ययं immutable मां Me न not अभिजानाति knows.

13. Deluded by these states, the modi-fications of the three Gunas (of Prakriti), all this world does not know Me—beyond them, and immutable.

दैवी ह्येषा गुणमयी मम माया दुरत्यया ॥
मामेव ये प्रपद्यन्ते मायामेतां तरन्ति ते ॥१४॥

हि Verily एषा this गुणमयी constituted of Gunas दैवी divine मम My माया illusion दुरत्यया difficult to cross over ये who माम् एव Me only प्रपद्यन्ते take refuge (in) ते they एतां this मायां illusion तरन्ति get across.

14. Verily, this divine illusion of Mine constituted of the Gunas, is difficult to cross over ; those who devote themselves to Me alone cross over this illusion.

[*Divine :* transcending human perception.

Devotee . . . alone :   Abandoning all formal religion (Dharma) completely take refuge in Me, their own Self, the Lord of illusion.]

न मां दुष्कृतिनो मूढाः प्रपद्यन्ते नराधमाः ॥
माययाऽपहृतज्ञाना आसुरं भावमाश्रिताः ॥१६॥

दुष्कृतिनः Evil-doers मूढाः deluded नराधमाः the lowest of men माययां by Mâyâ अपहृतज्ञानाः deprived of discrimination आसुरं belonging to Asuras भावं way आश्रिताः having taken to मां Me न not प्रपद्यन्ते devote themselves.

15.   They do not devote themselves to Me—the evil-doers, the deluded, the lowest of men, deprived of discrimination by Mâyâ, and following the way of the Asuras.

[*Way of the Asuras,* i.e., cruelty, untruth, and the like.]

चतुर्विधा भजन्ते मां जनाः सुकृतिनोऽर्जुन ॥
आर्तो जिज्ञासुरर्थार्थी ज्ञानी च भरतर्षभ ॥१६॥

भरतर्षभ O bull among the Bhâratas अर्जुन O Arjuna चतुर्विधाः four kinds सुकृतिनः virtuous जनाः people आर्तः the distressed जिज्ञासुः the seeker of knowledge अर्थार्थी the seeker of enjoyment च and ज्ञानी the wise मां Me भजन्ते worship.

16. Four kinds of virtuous men worship Me, O Arjuna—the distressed, the seeker of knowledge, the seeker of enjoyment, and the wise, O bull among the Bhâratas.

[*Seeker of enjoyment :* One who wishes for objects of enjoyment, both here and hereafter.

The wise : One who has forsaken all desires, knowing them to arise from Mâyâ.]

तेषां ज्ञानी नित्ययुक्त एकभक्तिर्विशिष्यते ॥

प्रियो हि ज्ञानिनोऽत्यर्थमहं स च मम प्रियः ॥१७॥

तेषां Of them नित्ययुक्तः ever-steadfast एकभक्तिः whose devotion is to the one ज्ञानी the wise विशिष्यते excels हि verily अहम् I ज्ञानिनः of the wise अत्यर्थम् supremely प्रियः dear सःच he and मम My प्रियः dear.

17. Of them, the wise man, ever-steadfast, (and fired) with devotion to the One, excels ; for supremely dear am I to the wise, and he is dear to Me.

उदाराः सर्व एवैते ज्ञानी त्वात्मैव मे मतम् ॥

आस्थितः स हि युक्तात्मा मामेवानुत्तमां गतिम् ॥१८॥

एते These सर्वे all एव surely उदाराः noble तु but ज्ञानी the wise आत्मा Self एव very मे My मतं conviction हि verily युक्तात्मा steadfast-minded सः he अनुत्तमां the supreme गतिं goal मां Me एव verily आस्थितः is established.

18.   Noble indeed are they all, but the
wise man I regard as My very Self ; for with
the mind steadfast, he is established in Me
alone, as the supreme goal.

बहूनां जन्मनामन्ते ज्ञानवान्मां प्रपद्यते ॥
वासुदेवः सर्वमिति स महात्मा सुदुर्लभः ॥१९॥

बहूनां Of many जन्मनाम् (of) births अन्ते at the end
ज्ञानवान् the wise मां Me वासुदेवः Vâsudeva सर्व all इति thus
प्रपद्यते resorts सः that महात्मा the great soul सुदुर्लभः (is)
very rare.

19.   At the end of many births, the man
of wisdom takes refuge in Me, realising that
all this is Vâsudeva (the inner most Self).
Very rare is that great soul.

कामैस्तैस्तैर्हृतज्ञानाः प्रपद्यन्तेऽन्यदेवताः ॥
तं तं नियममास्थाय प्रकृत्या नियताः स्वया ॥२०॥

तैः तैः By this or that कामैः (by) desires हृतज्ञानाः those
deprived of discrimination तं तं this or that नियमं rite
आस्थाय having followed स्वया प्रकृत्या by their own nature
नियताः led अन्यदेवताः other gods प्रपद्यन्ते worship.

20.   Others again, deprived of discrimination by this or that desire, following this
or that rite, devote themselves to other gods,
led by their own natures.

[*Own natures :* Samskâras acquired in previous
lives.]

यो यो यां यां तनुं भक्तः श्रद्धयाऽर्चितुमिच्छति ॥

तस्य तस्याचलां श्रद्धां तामेव विदधाम्यहम् ॥२१॥

यः यः whatever भक्तः devotee यां यां whatsoever तनुं
form श्रद्धया with Shraddhâ अर्चितुं to worship इच्छति
desires तस्य तस्य of him तां that एव surely श्रद्धां Shraddhâ
अहम् I अचलाम् unflinching विदधामि make.

21.   Whatsoever form any devotee seeks
to worship with Shraddhâ—that Shraddhâ of
his do I make unwavering.

स तया श्रद्धया युक्तस्तस्याराधनमीहते ॥

लभते च ततः कामान्मयैव विहितान्हि तान् ॥२२॥

सः He तया with that श्रद्धया (by) Shraddhâ युक्तः
endued तस्य of it आराधनम् worship ईहते engages in च and
ततः from that मया by Me एव surely विहितान् dispensed
तान् those कामान् desires हि verily लभते gains.

22.   Endued with that Shraddhâ, he
engages in the worship of that, and from it,
gains his desires—these being verily dispensed
by Me alone.

अन्तवत्तु फलं तेषां तद्भवत्यल्पमेधसाम् ॥

देवान्देवयजो यान्ति मद्भक्ता यान्ति मामपि ॥२३॥

तु But अल्पमेधसां तेषां of those of little understanding
तत् that फलं fruit अन्तवत् limited भवति becomes देवयजः the
worshippers of the Devas देवान् the Devas यान्ति go to
मद्भक्ताः My devotees माम् Me अपि too यान्ति attain.

23.   But the fruit (accruing) to these men of little understanding is limited.   The worshippers of the Devas go to the Devas ; My devotees too come to me.

[*These men of little understanding :* Though the amount of exertion is the same (in the two kinds of worship), these people do not take refuge in Me, by doing which they may attain infinite results.]

अव्यक्तं व्यक्तिमापन्नं मन्यन्ते मामबुद्धयः ॥

परं भावमजानन्तो ममाव्ययमनुत्तमम् ॥२४॥

अबुद्धयः The foolish मम My अव्ययं immutable अनुत्तमं unsurpassed परं supreme भावं nature अजानन्तः not knowing अव्यक्तं the unmanifested मां Me व्यक्तिं manifestation आपन्नं come to मन्यन्ते regard.

24.   The foolish regard Me, the unmanifested, as come into manifestation, not knowing My supreme state—immutable and transcendental.

[The ignorant take Me as an ordinary mortal, assuming embodiment from the unmanifested state, like all other men, being impelled by the force of past Karma.   This is due to their ignorance of My real nature; hence they do not worship Me, the One without a second.]

नाहं प्रकाशः सर्वस्य योगमायासमावृतः ॥

मूढोऽयं नाभिजानाति लोको मामजमव्ययम् ॥२५॥

अहं I योगमायासमावृतः veiled by Yoga-Mâyâ, i.e., illusion born of Yoga or the union of the three Gunas सर्वस्य to all प्रकाशः manifest न not मूढः the deluded अयं this लोकः world अजं the Unborn अव्ययं the Immutable मां Me न not अभिजानाति knows.

25. Veiled by the illusion born of the congress of the Gunas, I am not manifest to all. This deluded world knows Me not—the Unborn, the Immutable.

[This Yoga-Mâyâ spread over the Lord, which veils the understanding of others in recognising Him, does not obscure His own knowledge, as it is His, and He is the wielder of it—just as the glamour (Mâyâ) caused by a juggler (Mâyâvi) does not obstruct his own knowledge. This illusion which binds others, cannot dim His vision.]

वेदाहं समतीतानि वर्तमानानि चार्जुन ॥

भविष्याणि च भूतानि मां तु वेद न कश्चन ॥२६॥

अर्जुन O Arjuna समतीतानि the past च and वर्तमानानि the present भविष्याणि the future च and भूतानि beings अहं I वेद know तु but मां Me कश्चन any one न not वेद knows.

26. I know, O Arjuna, the beings of the whole past, and the present, and the future, but Me none knoweth.

इच्छाद्वेषसमुत्थेन द्वन्द्वमोहेन भारत ॥

सर्वभूतानि संमोहं सर्गे यान्ति परन्तप ॥२७॥

परन्तप O scorcher of foes भारत O descendant of
Bharata सर्गे at birth इच्छाद्वेषसमुत्थेन arisen from desire
and aversion द्वन्द्वमोहेन by the delusion of the pairs of
opposites सर्वभूतानि all beings संमोहं delusion यान्ति go to.

27. By the delusion of the pairs of
opposites, arising from desire and aversion, O
descendant of Bharata, all beings fall into
delusion at birth, O scorcher of foes.

[To one whose mind is subject to the dualistic
delusion, caused by the passions of desire and aversion, there cannot indeed arise a knowledge of things
as they are, even of the external world; far less can
such an intellect grasp the transcendental knowledge
of the innermost Self.]

येषां त्वन्तगतं पापं जनानां पुण्यकर्मणाम् ॥

ते द्वन्द्वमोहनिर्मुक्ता भजन्ते मां दृढव्रताः ॥२८॥

तु But पुण्यकर्मणां of men of virtuous deeds येषां whose
जनानां of men पापं sin अन्तगतं is at an end द्वन्द्वमोहनिर्मुक्ताः
freed from the delusion of the pairs of opposites ते
they दृढव्रताः men of firm resolve मां Me भजन्ते worship.

28. Those men of virtuous deeds, whose
sin has come to an end—they, freed from the
delusion of the pairs of opposites, worship Me
with firm resolve.

जरामरणमोक्षाय मामाश्रित्य यतन्ति ये ॥

ते ब्रह्म तद्विदुः कृत्स्नमध्यात्मं कर्म चाखिलम् ॥२९॥

13

जरामरणमोक्षाय For freedom from old age and death मां in Me आश्रिय having taken refuge ये who यतन्ति strive ते they तत् that ब्रह्म Brahman कृत्स्नम् the whole अध्यात्मं Adhyâtma अखिलं the entire कर्म Karma च and विदु: know.

29. Those who strive for freedom from old age and death, taking refuge in Me—they know Brahman, the whole of Adhyâtma, and Karma in its entirety.

[(*They know*) *the whole of Adhyâtma :* They realise in full the Reality underlying the innermost individual Self.]

साधिभूतादिदैवं मां साधियज्ञं च ये विदु: ॥

प्रयाणकालेऽपि च मां ते विदुर्युक्तचेतस: ॥३०॥

ये Who च and मां Me साधिभूतं साधिदैवं साधियज्ञं च with Adhibhuta, Adhidaiva, and Adhiyajna विदु: know ते they युक्तचेतस: steadfast in mind प्रयाणकाले at the time of death अपि even मां Me विदु: know.

30. Those who know Me with the Adhibhuta, the Adhidaiva, and the Adhiyajna, (continue to) know Me even at the time of death, steadfast in mind.

[Their consciousness of Me continues as ever, unaffected by the change of approaching death.]

इति ज्ञानविज्ञानयोगो नाम सप्तमोऽध्याय: ॥

The end of the seventh chapter, designated, *The Way of Knowledge with Realisation.*

EIGHTH CHAPTER

अर्जुन उवाच ।

किं तद्ब्रह्म किमध्यात्मं किं कर्म पुरुषोत्तम ॥
अधिभूतं च किं प्रोक्तमधिदैवं किमुच्यते ॥१॥

अर्जुनः Arjuna उवाच said :

पुरुषोत्तम O best of Purushas तत् that ब्रह्म Brahman किं what [अध्यात्मं Adhyâtma किं what कर्म Karma (च and) किं what अधिभूतं Adhibhuta किं what प्रोक्तं called किं what च and अधिदैवं Adhidaiva उच्यते is said.

Arjuna said :

1. What is the Brahman, what is Adhyâtma, what is Karma, O best of Purushas ? What is called Adhibhuta, and what Adhidaiva ?

अधियज्ञः कथं कोऽत्र देहेऽस्मिन् मधुसूदन ॥
प्रयाणकाले च कथं ज्ञेयोऽसि नियतात्मभिः ॥२॥

मधुसूदन O destroyer of Madhu अत्र here अस्मिन् in this देहे body कः who कथं how अधियज्ञः Adhiyajna च and

प्रयाणकाले at the time of death नियतात्मभिः by the self-controlled कथं how ज्ञेयः knowable असि art.

2.   Who, and in what way, is Adhiyajna here in this body, O destroyer of Madhu ? And how art Thou known at the time of death, by the self-controlled ?

श्रीभगवानुवाच ।

अक्षरं ब्रह्म परमं स्वभावोऽध्यात्ममुच्यते ॥

भूतभावोद्भवकरो विसर्गः कर्मसंज्ञितः ॥३॥

श्रीभगवान् The Blessed Lord उवाच said :

अक्षरं The Imperishable परमं Supreme ब्रह्म Brahman स्वभावः (His) nature, the dwelling of Brahman in each individual body अध्यात्मं Adhyātma उच्यते is said भूतभावो-द्भवकरः that which causes the existence and genesis of beings विसर्गः offering (to gods) कर्मसंज्ञितः is called Karma.

The Blessed Lord said :

3.   The Imperishable is the Supreme Brahman. Its dwelling in each individual body is called Adhyâtma ; the offering in sacrifice which causes the genesis and support of beings, is called Karma.

[*Offering in sacrifice*—includes here all virtuous works.

Karma : Cf. III. 14, 15.]

अधिभूतं क्षरो भावः पुरुषश्चाधिदैवतम् ॥
अधियज्ञोऽहमेवात्र देहे देहभृतां वर ॥४॥

देहभृतां Of the embodied वर the best क्षरः perishable भावः existence अधिभूतं Adhibhuta पुरुषः Indweller अधिदैवतं Adhidaivata च and अत्र here देहे in the body अहं I एव verily अधियज्ञः Adhiyajna.

4. The perishable adjunct is the Adhibhuta, and the Indweller is the Adhidaivata ; I alone am the Adhiyajna here in this body, O best of the embodied.

[*Adhibhuta :* that perishable adjunct which is different from, and yet depends for its existence on the self-conscious principle, i.e., everything material, everything that has birth.

Adhidaivata : The universal Self in Its subtle aspect : the Centre from which all living beings have their sense-power.

Adhiyajna : the presiding deity of sacrifice— Vishnu.]

अन्तकाले च मामेव स्मरन्मुक्त्वा कलेबरम् ॥
यः प्रयाति स मद्भावं याति नास्त्यत्र संशयः ॥६॥

च And अन्तकाले at the time of death माम् Me एव only स्मरन् remembering कलेबरं body मुक्त्वा leaving यः who प्रयाति goes forth सः he मद्भावं My being याति attains अत्र here संशयः doubt न not अस्ति is.

5. And he who at the time of death
meditating on Me alone, goes forth, leaving the
body, attains My Being : there is no doubt
about this.

यं यं वापि स्मरन् भावं त्यजत्यन्ते कलेबरम् ॥
तं तमेवैति कौन्तेय सदा तद्भावभावितः ॥६॥

अन्ते At the end यं यं whatever भावं idea (object) वा
or अपि even स्मरन् remembering कलेबरं body त्यजति leaves
कौन्तेय O son of Kunti सदा constantly तद्भावभावितः devoted
to the thought of that object तं तं that एव alone एति
attains.

6. Remembering whatever object, at the
end, he leaves the body, that alone is reached
by him, O son of Kunti, (because) of his constant thought of that object.

[*Constant thought :* the idea is, that the most
prominent thought of one's life occupies the mind
at the time of death. One cannot get rid of it, even
as one cannot get rid of a disagreeable thought-image
in a dream ; so the character of the body to be next
attained by one is determined accordingly, i.e., by
the final thought.]

तस्मात् सर्वेषु कालेषु मामनुस्मर युध्य च ॥
मय्यर्पितमनोबुद्धिर्मामेवैष्यस्यसंशयः ॥७॥

तस्मात् Therefore सर्वेषु कालेषु at all times मां Me अनुस्मर
remember युध्य fight च and मय्यर्पितमनोबुद्धिः with mind

and intellect devoted to Me   असंशयः without doubt
मां Me एव verily एष्यसि shalt come to.

7. Therefore, at all times, constantly
remember Me, and fight. With mind and
intellect absorbed in Me, thou shalt doubtless
come to Me.

[*Remember Me and fight :* Do thou constantly
keep thy mind fixed on Me and at the same time perform thy Svadharma, as befits a Kshatriya ; and thus
thou shalt attain purification of the heart.]

अभ्यासयोगयुक्तेन चेतसा नान्यगामिना ॥

परमं पुरुषं दिव्यं याति पार्थानुचिन्तयन् ॥८॥

पार्थ O son of Prithâ अभ्यासयोगयुक्तेन (with the mind
made) steadfast by the method of habitual meditation नान्यगामिना not moving towards any other thing
चेतसा with mind परमं Supreme दिव्यं Resplendent पुरुषं
Purusha अनुचिन्तयन् meditating याति goes to.

8. With the mind not moving towards
anything else, made steadfast by the method of
habitual meditation, and dwelling on the
Supreme, Resplendent Purusha, O son of
Prithâ, one goes to Him.

[*Method*—Yoga.

Resplendent—the Being in the solar orb, same
as Adhidaivata, of the fourth shloka.]

कविं पुराणमनुशासितार-

मणोरणीयांसमनुस्मरेद्यः ॥

सर्वस्य धातारमचिन्त्यरूप-

मादित्यवर्णं तमसः परस्तात् ॥६॥

प्रयाणकाले मनसाऽचलेन

भक्त्या युक्तो योगबलेन चैव ॥

भ्रुवोर्मध्ये प्राणमावेश्य सम्यक्

स तं परं पुरुषमुपैति दिव्यम् ॥१०॥

कविं Omniscient पुराणं Ancient अनुशासितारं Overruler
अणोः than atom अणीयांसं minuter सर्वस्य of all धातारं Sustainer अचिन्त्यरूपं one whose form is inconceivable
आदित्यवर्णं self-luminous like the sun तमसः of the darkness (of ignorance) परस्तात् beyond प्रयाणकाले at the
time of death भक्त्या with devotion युक्तः endued अचलेन
unmoving मनसा with mind योगबलेन with the power of
Yoga च and एव verily भ्रुवोः of the two eye-brows मध्ये
betwixt प्राणं Prâna सम्यक् thoroughly आवेश्य placing यः
who अनुस्मरेत् remembers सः he तं that परं Supreme
दिव्यं Resplendent पुरुषं Purusha उपैति reaches.

9-10. The Omniscient, the Ancient, the
Overruler, minuter than an atom, the Sustainer
of all, of form inconceivable, self-luminous
like the sun, and beyond the darkness of Mâyâ
—he who meditates on Him thus, at the
time of death, full of devotion, with
the mind unmoving, and also by the power of

Yoga, fixing the whole Prâna betwixt the
eye-brows, he goes to that Supreme, Resplendent Purusha. *

[*Self-luminous :* Known by no agency like the
understanding, the mind or the senses, but by Self
alone.

Power of Yoga—which comes by the constant
practice of Samâdhi.

Prâna : the vital current.

Fixing the whole Prâna—means, concentrating
the whole will and self-consciousness.]

यदक्षरं वेदविदो वदन्ति
    विशन्ति यद्यतयो वीतरागाः ॥
यदिच्छन्तो ब्रह्मचर्यं चरन्ति
    तत्ते पदं संग्रहेण प्रवक्ष्ये ॥११॥

वेदविदः Knowers of the Veda यत् which अक्षरं imperishable वदन्ति speak वीतरागाः freed from attachment
यतयः self-controlled (Sannyâsis) यत् which विशन्ति enter
यत् which इच्छन्तः desiring ब्रह्मचर्यं Brahmacharya चरन्ति
practise ते to thee तत् that पदं state to be obtained
संग्रहेण in brief प्रवक्ष्ये (I) shall tell.

11.   What the knowers of the Veda speak
of as Imperishable, what the self-controlled
(Sannyâsis), freed from attachment enter, and
to gain which goal they live the life of a

Brahmachâri, that I shall declare unto thee in brief.

[*Brahmachâri*—a religious student who takes the vow of continence, etc.; every moment of this stage is one of hard discipline and asceticism.

Cf. Kathopanishad, II. 14.]

सर्वद्वाराणि संयम्य मनो हृदि निरुध्य च ॥

मूर्ध्न्याधायात्मनः प्राणमास्थितो योगधारणाम् ॥१२॥

ओमित्येकाक्षरं ब्रह्म व्याहरन्मामनुस्मरन् ॥

यः प्रयाति त्यजन्देहं स याति परमां गतिम् ॥१३॥

सर्वद्वाराणि All inlets (senses) संयम्य having controlled मनः mind हृदि in the heart निरुध्य having confined च and प्राणं Prâna मूर्ध्नि in the head आधाय having placed आत्मनः of one's self योगधारणां practice of concentration आस्थितः established (in) ओं Om इति this एकाक्षरं one-syllabled ब्रह्म Brahman व्याहरन् uttering मां Me अनुस्मरन् remembering देहं body त्यजन् leaving यः who प्रयाति departs सः he परमां Supreme गतिं Goal याति attains.

12-13. Controlling all the senses, confining the mind in the heart, drawing the Prâna into the head, occupied in the practice of concentration, uttering the one-syllabled "Om" —the Brahman, and meditating on Me ;—he who so departs, leaving the body, attains the Supreme Goal.

अनन्यचेताः सततं यो मां स्मरति नित्यशः ॥

तस्याहं सुलभः पार्थ नित्ययुक्तस्य योगिनः ॥१४॥

अनन्यचेताः with the mind not thinking of any other object यः who मां Me नित्यशः daily सततं constantly स्मरति remembers पार्थ O son of Prithâ अहं I तस्य of that नित्य-युक्तस्य ever-steadfast योगिनः Yogi सुलभः easily attainable.

14. I am easily attainable by that ever-steadfast Yogi who remembers Me constantly and daily, with a single mind, O son of Prithâ.

मामुपेत्य पुनर्जन्म दुःखालयमशाश्वतम् ॥

नाप्नुवन्ति महात्मानः संसिद्धिं परमां गताः ॥१५॥

परमां Highest संसिद्धिं perfection गताः reaching महात्मानः the great-souled ones माम् Me उपेत्य having attained दुःखालयं home of pain अशाश्वतं ephemeral (च and)पुनर्जन्म rebirth न not आप्नुवन्ति get.

15. Reaching the highest perfection and having attained Me, the great-souled ones are no more subject to rebirth—which is the home of pain, and ephemeral.

[*Ephemeral*: non-eternal, of an ever-changing nature.]

आब्रह्मभुवनाल्लोकाः पुनरावर्तिनोऽर्जुन ॥

मामुपेत्य तु कौन्तेय पुनर्जन्म न विद्यते ॥१६॥

अर्जुन O Arjuna आब्रह्मभुवनात् up to (i.e., including) the realm of Brahmâ लोका: worlds पुनरावर्तिन: subject to return तु but कौन्तेय O Kaunteya माम् Me उपेत्य having attained पुनर्जन्म rebirth न not विद्यते is.

16.   All the worlds, O Arjuna, including the realm of Brahmâ, are subject to return, but after attaining Me, O son of Kunti, there is no rebirth.

[*Subject to return*—because limited by time.]

सहस्रयुगपर्यन्तमहर्यद्ब्रह्मणो विदु: ॥
रात्रिं युगसहस्रान्तां तेऽहोरात्रविदो जना: ॥१७॥

सहस्रयुगपर्यन्तं Ending in a thousand Yugas ब्रह्मण: of Brahmâ यत् which अह: day युगसहस्रान्तां ending in a thousand Yugas रात्रिं night (ये who) विदु: know ते those जना: men अहोरात्रविद: knowers of day and night.

17.   They who know (the true measure of) day and night, know the day of Brahmâ, which ends in a thousand Yugas, and the night which (also) ends in a thousand Yugas.

[*Day and night*—mean evolution and involution of the whole universe respectively.]

अव्यक्ताद्व्यक्तय: सर्वा: प्रभवन्त्यहरागमे ॥
रात्र्यागमे प्रलीयन्ते तत्रैवाव्यक्तसंज्ञके ॥१८॥

अहरागमे At the approach of day अव्यक्तात् from the unmanifested सर्वाः all व्यक्तयः manifestations प्रभवन्ति proceed रात्रागमे at the approach of night तत्र into that एव verily अव्यक्तसंज्ञके in that which is called the unmanifested प्रलीयन्ते merge.

18. At the approach of (Brahmâ's) day, all manifestations proceed from the unmanifested state ; at the approach of night, they merge verily into that alone, which is called the unmanifested.

भूतग्रामः स एवायं भूत्वा भूत्वा प्रलीयते ॥

रात्र्यागमेऽवशः पार्थ प्रभवत्यहरागमे ॥१६॥

पार्थ O son of Prithâ सः that एव verily अयं this भूतग्रामः multitude of beings भूत्वा भूत्वा being born again and again रात्र्यागमे at the approach of night प्रलीयते merge अहरागमे at the approach of day अवशः helpless प्रभवति re-manifest.

19. The very same multitude of beings (that existed in the preceding day of Brahmâ), being born again and again, merge, in spite of themselves, O son of Prithâ, (into the unmanifested), at the approach of night, and re-manifest at the approach of day.

[*Being born . . . themselves*: They repeatedly come forth and dissolve, being forced by the effects of their own Karma.]

परस्तस्मात्तु भावोऽन्योऽव्यक्तोऽव्यक्तात्सनातनः ॥
यः स सर्वेषु भूतेषु नश्यत्सु न विनश्यति ॥२०॥

तस्मात् From that तु but अव्यक्तात् from the unmanifested पर: that which is beyond अन्य: another, distinct
अव्यक्त: Unmanifested सनातन: Eternal य: which भाव:
Existence स: That सर्वेषु भूतेषु all beings नश्यत्सु being
destroyed न not विनश्यति dies.

20. But beyond this unmanifested, there
is that other Unmanifested, Eternal Existence
—That which is not destroyed at the destruction of all beings.

[*This unmanifested*—which being the seed of
the manifested, is Avidyâ itself.]

अव्यक्तोऽक्षर इत्युक्तस्तमाहुः परमां गतिम् ॥
यं प्राप्य न निवर्तन्ते तद्धाम परमं मम ॥२१॥

अव्यक्त: Unmanifested अक्षर: Imperishable इति thus
उक्त: called तम् that परमां Supreme गतिम् Goal आहु: they
describe यं which प्राप्य having attained न not निवर्तन्ते
they return तत् that मम My परमं highest धाम state.

21. What has been called Unmanifested
and Imperishable, has been described as
the Goal Supreme. That is My highest
state, having attained which, there is no
return.

पुरुषः स परः पार्थं भक्त्या लभ्यस्त्वनन्यया ॥
यस्यान्तःस्थानि भूतानि येन सर्वमिदं ततम् ॥२२॥

पार्थ O son of Prithâ भूतानि beings यस्य of whom अन्तः-
स्थानि dwelling in येन by whom इदं this सर्वं all ततं pervaded तु also सः that परः Supreme पुरुषः Purusha अनन्यया
whole-souled भक्त्या by devotion लभ्यः is attainable.

22. And that Supreme Purusha is
attainable, O son of Prithâ, by whole-
souled devotion to Him alone, in Whom all
beings dwell, and by Whom all this is
pervaded.

यत्र काले त्वनावृत्तिमावृत्ति चैव योगिनः ॥
प्रयाता यान्ति तं कालं वक्ष्यामि भरतर्षभ ॥२३॥

भरतर्षभ O bull of the Bhâratas यत्र in which काले
time (path) तु but प्रयाता: travelling योगिनः Yogis अनावृत्तिम्
non-return आवृत्ति return च and एव again यान्ति go to
तं that कालं time (path) वक्ष्यामि (I) shall tell.

23. Now I shall tell thee, O bull of the
Bhâratas, of the time (path) travelling in which,
the Yogis return, (and again of that, taking
which) they do not return.

अग्निर्ज्योतिरहः शुक्लः षण्मासा उत्तरायणम् ॥
तत्र प्रयाता गच्छन्ति ब्रह्म ब्रह्मविदो जनाः ॥२४॥

अग्नि: Fire ज्योति: light अह: day-time शुक्र: the bright (fortnight) षण्मासा: the six months उत्तरायणं (of) the Northern passage of the sun तत्र in this (path) प्रयाता: departed ब्रह्मविद: the knowers of Brahman जना: people ब्रह्म Brahman गच्छन्ति go to.

24. Fire, flame, day-time, the bright fortnight, the six months of the Northern passage of the sun—taking this path, the knowers of Brahman go to Brahman.

धूमो रात्रिस्तथा कृष्ण: षण्मासा दक्षिणायनम् ॥
तत्र चान्द्रमसं ज्योतिर्योगी प्राप्य निवर्तते ॥२५॥

धूम: Smoke रात्रि: night-time तथा also कृष्ण: the dark (fortnight) षण्मासा: the six months दक्षिणायनम् (of) the Southern passage of the sun तत्र in this (path) योगी Yogi चन्द्रमसं lunar ज्योति: light प्राप्य attaining निवर्तते returns.

25. Smoke, night-time, the dark fortnight, the six months of the Southern passage of the sun—taking this path the Yogi, attaining the lunar light, returns.

[It is difficult to decide the true significance of these two verses (24 & 25). Some are inclined to think that each of the steps means a sphere; while others, a state of consciousness. Still others think, that the series beginning with fire means developing states of illumination and renunciation, and that beginning with smoke, increasing states of ignorance and attachment.

The two paths, Devayâna and Pitriyâna, by which the souls of the dead are supposed to travel to the other world according to their deserts are mentioned in the Upanishads, prominently in the Chhândogya, V. x. 1, 2. Bâdarâyana discusses these passages in the Brahma-Sutras, IV. ii. 18-21. But an interesting light has been thrown upon the question by the late Mr. Tilak's theory of the Arctic home of the ancestors of the Aryan race. He has also dealt with his subject specially, in a paper of great value which appeared in the *Prabuddha Bharata* (Vol. IX. p. 160). Considering the importance of the doctrine and the excellent way in which it has been elucidated by Mr. Tilak, we shall briefly note below the main heads of his argument.

The words Pitriyâna and Devayâna are used many times in the Rigveda. But the distinction made in the Upanishads about the soul's path, according as a man died during the dark or the bright half of the year, was unknown to the bards of the Rigveda, who held the view that the soul of a man always travelled by the Pitriyâna road, whatever the time of his death. It is therefore clear that the doctrine of the Upanishads was a later development, probably evolved after physical light and darkness had come to be connected with moral good and evil and the dual character of the world was established. Now, if along with this we consider that death during the Southern passage of the sun was regarded as inauspicious from the Arctic times, we can see

14

how the distinction arose between the paths of a man's soul according as he died in the dark or the bright part of the year.

As to the series of steps in each path, since Agni was believed to be the only leader of the soul on its path, and both paths ended with the passages of the sun, the starting and halting points thus settled, it was not difficult to fill in the intermediate steps. The dual character of the world is manifested in Agni as flame and smoke. The flame was therefore the starting point of one path and smoke, of the other. Day and night, increasing and decreasing moon, Northern and Southern passages of the sun came next in natural order. The number of steps can easily be increased, and as a matter of fact has been increased in Kaushitaki and some other Upanishads, on the same general principle.

Another point in this connection may be noted. There is nothing in the second or Pitriyâna path to correspond with Agni, in the first. We must therefore either reduce the number of steps in the first path by taking the words "fire" and "flame" in appositional relation and translate the same as "fire, that is flame", or increase the steps in the second by adding "fire" as one.]

शुक्लकृष्णे गती ह्येते जगतः शाश्वते मते ॥
एकया यात्यनावृत्तिमन्ययावर्तते पुनः ॥२६॥

हि Verily जगत: of the world शुक्लकृष्णे bright and dark
एते these गती two paths शाश्वते eternal मते are considered
एकया by one अनावृत्तिम् non-return याति goes to अन्यया
by the other पुन: again आवर्तते returns.

26. Truly are these bright and dark
paths of the world considered eternal : one
leads to non-return ; by the other, one
returns.

[The paths are eternal, because Samsâra is
eternal.]

नैते सृती पार्थ जानन् योगी मुह्यति कश्चन ॥

तस्मात्सर्वेषु कालेषु योगयुक्तो भवार्जुन ॥२७॥

पार्थ O son of Prithâ एते these सृती two paths जानन्
knowing कश्चन whosoever योगी Yogi न मुह्यति is not
deluded तस्मात् therefore अर्जुन O Arjuna सर्वेषु in all
कालेषु times योगयुक्त: steadfast in Yoga भव be (thou).

27. No Yogi, O son of Prithâ, is deluded
after knowing these paths. Therefore O
Arjuna, be thou steadfast in Yoga, at
all times.

[Knowing that one of the paths leads to
Samsâra and the other to Moksha, the Yogi takes
up the one leading to illumination and rejects
the other.]

वेदेषु यज्ञेषु तप:सु चैव

दानेषु यत्पुण्यफलं प्रदिष्टम् ॥

अत्येति तत्सर्वमिदं विदित्वा

योगी परं स्थानमुपैति चाद्यम् ॥२८॥

वेदेषु In the (study of the) Vedas यज्ञेषु in the (practice of) Yajnas तपःसु in the (practice of) austerities दानेषु in (giving) gifts च and एव also यत् whatever पुण्य- फलं meritorious effect प्रदिष्टम् is declared च and इदं this विदित्वा having known योगी a Yogi तत् it सर्वं all अत्येति rises above आद्यम् primeval परं supreme स्थानम् Abode उपैति goes to.

28. Whatever meritorious effect is declared (in the Scriptures) to accrue from (the study of) the Vedas, (the performance of) Yajnas, (the practice of) austerities and gifts—above all this rises the Yogi, having known this, and attains to the primeval, supreme Abode.

[*This*—the truth imparted by the Lord in answer to the question of Arjuna at the beginning of the present chapter.]

इति अक्षरब्रह्मयोगो नामाष्टमोऽध्यायः ॥

The end of the eighth chapter, designated, *The Way to the Imperishable Brahman.*

NINTH CHAPTER

श्रीभगवानुवाच ।

इदं तु ते गुह्यतमं प्रवक्ष्याम्यनसूयवे ॥
ज्ञानं विज्ञानसहितं यज्ज्ञात्वा मोक्ष्यसेऽशुभात् ॥१॥

श्रीभगवान् The Blessed Lord उवाच said :

इदं This गुह्यतमं most profound तु indeed विज्ञानसहितं united with realisation ज्ञानं knowledge अनसूयवे to one who does not carp ते to thee प्रवक्ष्यामि shall declare यत् which ज्ञात्वा having known अशुभात् from evil (Samsâra) मोक्ष्यसे (thou) shalt be free :

The Blessed Lord said :

1. To thee, who dost not carp, verily shall I now declare this, the most profound knowledge, united with realisation, having known which, thou shalt be free from evil (Samsâra).

राजविद्या राजगुह्यं पवित्रमिदमुत्तमम् ॥
प्रत्यक्षावगमं धर्म्यं सुसुखं कर्तुमव्ययम् ॥२॥

इदम् This राजविद्या the king of sciences (i.e., the highest science) राजगुह्य' kingly secret (i.e., the deepest of all profound truths) उत्तमम् supreme पवित्रम् purifier प्रत्यक्षावगमं realisable by direct perception धर्म्यं endowed with (immense) merit कर्तुं to perform सुसुखं very easy (च and) अव्ययम् of imperishable nature.

2. Of sciences, the highest; of profundities, the deepest; of purifiers, the supreme, is this; realisable by direct perception, endowed with (immense) merit, very easy to perform, and of an imperishable nature.

अश्रद्दधानाः पुरुषा धर्मस्यास्य परन्तप ॥

अप्राप्य मां निवर्तन्ते मृत्युसंसारवर्त्मनि ॥३॥

परन्तप O scorcher of foes अस्य of this धर्मस्य (of) Dharma अश्रद्दधानाः without Shraddhâ पुरुषाः persons मां Me अप्राप्य without attaining मृत्युसंसारवर्त्मनि in the path of rebirth fraught with death (मृत्युः death संसारः rebirth वर्त्मनि in the path) निवर्तन्ते return.

3. Persons without Shraddhâ for this Dharma, return, O scorcher of foes, without attaining Me, to the path of rebirth fraught with death.

[*Without . . . Dharma :* Who have no faith in this knowledge of the Self, regarding the physical body itself as the Self.]

मया ततमिदं सर्वं जगदव्यक्तमूर्तिना ॥

मत्स्थानि सर्वभूतानि न चाहं तेष्ववस्थितः ॥४॥

अव्यक्तमूर्तिना Of the unmanifested form मया by Me इदं this सर्वं all जगत् world ततम् pervaded सर्वभूतानि all beings मत्स्थानि exist in Me अहं I च and तेषु in them न not अवस्थितः dwelling.

4. All his world is pervaded by Me in My unmanifested form : all beings exist in Me, but I do not dwell in them.

[*Unmanifested :* being invisible to the senses.

Exist in Me—have an individual existence through Me, the Self, underlying them all.

Do not dwell in them—like corporeal things— in contact with them, or contained as though in a receptacle.]

न च मत्स्थानि भूतानि पश्य मे योगमैश्वरम् ॥

भूतभृन्न च भूतस्थो ममात्मा भूतभावनः ॥५॥

च And भूतानि beings न not मत्स्थानि dwelling in Me मे My ऐश्वरं Divine योगं Yoga पश्य behold मम My आत्मा Self भूतभृत् supporting the beings च and भूतभावनः bringing forth the beings न not भूतस्थः dwelling in the beings.

5. Nor do beings exist in Me (in reality), behold My Divine Yoga ! Bringing forth and supporting the beings, My Self does not dwell in them.

[Vide VII. 12.

Nor do, etc.—Because of the Self being un-
attached to or unconnected with any object.
"Devoid of attachment, He is never attached."—*Brih.
Upa.* III. ix. 26.]

यथाकाशस्थितो नित्यं वायुः सर्वत्रगो महान् ॥
तथा सर्वाणि भूतानि मत्स्थानीत्युपधारय ॥६॥

वायुः Wind नित्यं always सर्वत्रगः moving everywhere
महान् mighty यथा just as आकाशस्थितः rests in the Âkâsha
तथा so सर्वाणि all भूतानि beings मत्स्थानि dwell in Me इति thus
उपधारय know.

6. As the mighty wind, moving always
everywhere, rests ever in the Âkâsha, know
thou, that even so do all beings rest
in Me.

[*Rests ever in the Âkâsha*—without being attached to it.

The idea is that beings rest in the Lord without
contact with, and so without producing any effect on
Him.]

सर्वभूतानि कौन्तेय प्रकृतिं यान्ति मामिकाम् ॥
कल्पक्षये पुनस्तानि कल्पादौ विसृजाम्यहम् ॥७॥

कौन्तेय O son of Kunti सर्वभूतानि all beings कल्पक्षये at the
end of the Kalpa मामिकाम् My प्रकृतिं Prakriti यान्ति go to
पुनः again कल्पादौ at the beginning of the Kalpa तानि
them अहम् I विसृजामि send forth.

7. At the end of a Kalpa, O son of Kunti, all beings go back to My Prakriti : at the beginning of (another) Kalpa, I send them forth again.

[*Prakriti :* The inferior one composed of the three Gunas.

Kalpa—a period of cosmic manifestation.]

प्रकृतिं स्वामवष्टभ्य विसृजामि पुनः पुनः ॥

भूतग्राममिमं कृत्स्नमवशं प्रकृतेर्वशात् ॥८॥

स्वाम् My own प्रकृतिं Prakriti अवष्टभ्य having animated प्रकृतेः of Prakriti वशात् from the sway इमम् this कृत्स्नं whole अवशं helpless भूतग्रामम् multitude of beings पुनः पुनः again and again विसृजामि (I) send forth.

8. Animating My Prakriti, I project again and again this whole multitude of beings, helpless under the sway of Prakriti.

[*Animating My Prakriti*—invigorating and ferti-lising the Prakriti dependent on Him, which had gone to sleep at the universal dissolution, at the end of the Kalpa.]

न च मां तानि कर्माणि निबध्नन्ति धनञ्जय ॥

उदासीनवदासीनमसक्तं तेषु कर्मसु ॥६॥

धनञ्जय O Dhananjaya तानि these कर्माणि acts तेषु कर्मसु in those acts असक्तं unattached उदासीनवत् as one neutral or indifferent आसीनं sitting च and मां Me न निबध्नन्ति do not bind.

9. These acts do not bind Me, sitting as one neutral, unattached to them, O Dhananjaya.

[*These acts*—which involve the unequal creation and dissolution of the universe.

As in the case of Ishvara, so in the case of others also, the absence of the egotistic feeling of agency and attachment for results, is the cause of freedom (from Dharma and Adharma).]

मयाऽध्यक्षेण प्रकृतिः सूयते सचराचरम् ॥

हेतुनाऽनेन कौन्तेय जगद्विपरिवर्तते ॥१०॥

अध्यक्षेण By reason of proximity (lit. presiding over) मया by Me प्रकृतिः Prakriti सचराचरम् the moving and the unmoving सूयते produces कौन्तेय O son of Kunti अनेन through this हेतुना cause (इदं this) जगत् world विपरिवर्तते wheels round and round.

10. By reason of My proximity, Prakriti produces all this, the moving and the unmoving ; the world wheels round and round, O son of Kunti, because of this.

[In verses VII to X the Lord defines His position, following the Arundhati-Nyâya. When a bride is brought to her husband's house for the first time, he shows her a very tiny star, called Arundhati. To do this, he has to direct her gaze the right way, which he does by asking her to look at something near and something big, in the direction of the star, e.g., a branch of a tree. Next, he draws her attention to a large bright star observed beyond this branch, and so on, till by several steps, he succeeds in leading her eyes to the right thing. This method of leading to a subtle object through easy steps, is called Arundhati-Nyâya. The Lord begins by stating that He projects all beings at the beginning of evolution : Prakriti is only an instrument in His hands. Next, He says, He is not affected by that act, since He sits by, as one neutral, perfectly unattached. Lastly, He leads up to the final truth that really He does nothing, that it is Prakriti, who animated by His proximity produces all that is. It is His Light that lights up Prakriti, and makes her live and act. That is all the relation between Him and her.]

अवजानन्ति मां मूढा मानुषीं तनुमाश्रितम् ॥
परं भावमजानन्तो मम भूतमहेश्वरम् ॥११॥

भूतमहेश्वरम् Great Lord of beings मम My परं higher भावम् state or nature अजानन्तः unaware of मूढाः fools मानुषीं human तनुम् body or form आश्रितम् dwelling मां Me अवजानन्ति disregard.

11.   Unaware of My higher state, as the great Lord of beings, fools disregard Me, dwelling in the human form.

[*Great Lord*—Supreme Self.]

मोघाशा मोघकर्माणो मोघज्ञाना विचेतसः ॥
राक्षसीमासुरीं चैव प्रकृतिं मोहिनीं श्रिताः ॥१२॥

मोघाशा: Of vain hopes मोघकर्माण: of vain works मोघ-
ज्ञाना: of vain knowledge विचेतस: senseless मोहिनीं delusive राक्षसीम् of the nature of Râkshasas च and आसुरीं of
the nature of Asuras प्रकृतिं nature श्रिता: (are) possessed
of एव verily.

12. Of vain hopes, of vain works, of
vain knowledge, and senseless, they verily are
possessed of the delusive nature of Râkshasas
and Asuras.

[*Vain*—because they neglect their own Self. They
see no Self beyond the body.

They—refers to those described in the preceding
Shloka.

Râkshasas have Râjasika nature, Asuras,
Tâmasika.]

महात्मानस्तु मां पार्थ दैवीं प्रकृतिमाश्रिताः ॥
भजन्त्यनन्यमनसो ज्ञात्वा भूतादिमव्ययम् ॥१३॥

तु But पार्थ O son of Prithâ महात्मान: great-souled
ones दैवीं divine प्रकृतिं Prakriti आश्रिता: possessed of
अनन्यमनस: with a mind devoted to nothing else भूतादिम्
origin of beings अव्ययं immutable मां Me ज्ञात्वा knowing
भजन्ति worship.

13. But the great-souled ones, O son of

Prithâ, possessed of the Divine Prakriti, knowing Me to be the origin of beings and immutable, worship Me with a single mind.

सततं कीर्तयन्तो मां यतन्तश्च दृढव्रताः ॥
नमस्यन्तश्च मां भक्त्या नित्ययुक्ता उपासते ॥१४॥

सततं Always कीर्तयन्तः glorifying मां Me दृढव्रताः of
firm resolve यतन्तः striving च and भक्त्या with devotion
नमस्यन्तः bowing down च and नित्ययुक्ताः always steadfast
मां Me उपासते (they) worship.

14. Glorifying Me always and striving
with firm resolve, bowing down to Me in
devotion, always steadfast, they worship
Me.

ज्ञानयज्ञेन चाप्यन्ये यजन्तो मामुपासते ॥
एकत्वेन पृथक्त्वेन बहुधा विश्वतोमुखम् ॥१५॥

अन्ये Others अपि too च and ज्ञानयज्ञेन with the Yajna
of knowledge यजन्तः sacrificing माम् Me उपासते (they)
worship एकत्वेन as one पृथक्त्वेन as different विश्वतोमुखम् the
All-Formed बहुधा in various ways.

15. Others, too, sacrificing by the Yajna
of knowledge (i.e., seeing the Self in all),
worship Me the All-Formed, as one, as distinct,
as manifold.

[*All-Formed* : He who has assumed all the manifold forms in the universe.

As one—identifying himself with the All-Formed; —the Advaita view.

As distinct—making a distinction in essence between the Lord and himself :—the Dualistic view.

As manifold—as the various divinities, Brahmâ, Rudra, etc.]

अहं क्रतुरहं यज्ञः स्वधाहमहमौषधम् ॥
मन्त्रोऽहमहमेवाज्यमहमग्निरहं हुतम् ॥१६॥

अहं I क्रतुः the Kratu अहं I यज्ञः the Yajna अहम् I स्वधा the Svadhâ अहम् I औषधं the Aushadha अहम् I मन्त्रः the Mantra अहम् I आज्यम् the Âjya एव also अहम् I अग्निः the fire अहं I हुतम् the oblation.

16. I am the Kratu, I the Yajna, I the Svadhâ, I the Aushadha, I the Mantra, I the Âjya, I the fire, and I the oblation.

[*Kratu* is a particular Vedic rite.
Yajna : The worship enjoined in the Smriti.
Svadhâ : food offered to the manes (Pitris).
Aushadha : all vegetable food and medicinal herbs.

Mantra : the chant with which oblation is offered.
Âjya : articles of oblation.
The fire—into which the offering is poured.]

पिताहमस्य जगतो माता धाता पितामहः ॥

वेद्यं पवित्रमोङ्कार ऋक्‌ साम यजुरेव च ॥१७॥

गतिर्भर्ता प्रभुः साक्षी निवासः शरणं सुहृत् ॥

प्रभवः प्रलयः स्थानं निधानं बीजमव्ययम् ॥१८॥

अहम् I अस्य of this जगतः world पिता Father माता Mother धाता the Sustainer पितामहः the Grandfather वेद्यं the (one) thing to be known पवित्रम् the purifier ओंकारः (the syllable) 'Om' ऋक्‌ the Rik साम Sâman यजुः Yajus एव also च and.

गतिः The goal भर्ता Supporter प्रभुः Lord साक्षी the Witness निवासः Abode शरणं Refuge सुहृत् Friend प्रभवः Origin प्रलयः Dissolution स्थानं Substratum निधानं Storehouse बीजम् the Seed अव्ययम् immutable.

17. I am the Father of this world the Mother, the Sustainer, the Grandfather ; the Purifier, the (one) thing to be known, (the syllable) Om, and also the Rik, Sâman, and Yajus.

18. The Goal, the Supporter, the Lord, the Witness, the Abode, the Refuge, the Friend, the Origin, the Dissoluion, the Substratum, the Storehouse, the Seed immutable.

[Sustainer—by dispensing fruit of action.]

[*Seed :* cause of the origin of all things.

Immutable—because it endures so long as the Samsâra endures.]

तपाम्यहमहं वर्षं निगृह्णाम्युत्सृजामि च ॥
अमृतं चैव मृत्युश्च सदसच्चाहमर्जुन ॥१६॥

अर्जुन O Arjuna अहं I तपामि give heat अहं I वर्षं the rain उत्सृजामि send forth च and निगृह्णामि withhold अमृतं immortality च and एव also मृत्युः death च and अहं I सत् being च and असत् non-being.

19.   (As sun) I give heat : I withhold and send forth rain ; I am immortality and also death ; being and non-being am I, O Arjuna !

[*Being :* The manifested world of effects.

Non-being—means, the cause which is unmanifested only, and not non-existence, otherwise we have to conceive existence coming out of non-existence, which is absurd. The Shruti says, "How can existence come out of non-existence ?"— *Chhând. Upa.* VI. ii. 2.]

त्रैविद्या मां सोमपाः पूतपापा
यज्ञैरिष्ट्वा स्वर्गतिं प्रार्थयन्ते ॥
ते पुण्यमासाद्य सुरेन्द्रलोक-
मश्नन्ति दिव्यान्दिवि देवभोगान् ॥२०॥

त्रैविद्याः The knowers of the three Vedas यज्ञैः by

Yajnas मां Me इष्ट्वा worshipping सोमपाः the drinkers of Soma पूतपापाः purified from sin स्वर्गतिं passage to heaven प्रार्थयन्ते pray ते they पुण्यं holy सुरेन्द्रलोकम् the world of the Lord of the Devas आसाद्य reaching दिवि in heaven दिव्यान् divine देवभोगान् the pleasures of the Devas अश्नन्ति enjoy.

20. The knowers of the three Vedas, worshipping Me by Yajna, drinking the Soma, and (thus) being purified from sin, pray for passage to heaven; reaching the holy world of the Lord of the Devas, they enjoy in heaven the divine pleasures of the Devas.

[*Lord of the Devas*—Indra, who is called Shata-kratu, because he had performed a hundred sacrifices.]

ते तं भुक्त्वा स्वर्गलोकं विशालं

क्षीणे पुण्ये मर्त्यलोकं विशन्ति ॥

एवं त्रयीधर्ममनुप्रपन्ना

गतागतं कामकामा लभन्ते ॥२१॥

ते They तं that विशालं vast स्वर्गलोकं the Svarga-world भुक्त्वा having enjoyed पुण्ये merit क्षीणे at the exhaustion of मर्त्यलोकं the mortal world विशन्ति enter एवं thus त्रयीधर्मम् njunctions of the three (Vedas) अनुप्रपन्नाः abiding by कामकामाः desiring desires गतागतं the state of going and hat of coming लभन्ते attain to.

15

21. Having enjoyed the vast Svarga-world, they enter the mortal world, on the exhaustion of their merit : Thus, abiding by the injunctions of the three (Vedas), desir-ing desires, they (constantly) come and go.

[*Injunctions*—Ritualistic, the Karma-Kânda.]

अनन्याश्चिन्तयन्तो मां ये जनाः पर्युपासते ॥
तेषां नित्याभियुक्तानां योगक्षेमं वहाम्यहम् ॥२२॥

अनन्याः Non-separate मां Me चिन्तयन्तः meditating who जनाः persons पर्युपासते worship (Me) in all thing नित्याभियुक्तानां ever zealously engaged तेषां to them अहम् योगक्षेमं the supply of what is lacking and the preserv ation of what is already possessed वहामि carry.

22. Persons who, meditating on Me a non-separate, worship Me in all beings, t them thus ever zealously engaged, I carry wha they lack and preserve what they alread have.

[*Ananyâh*—as non-separate, i.e., looking upo the Supreme Being as not separate from their ow self. Or Ananyâh may mean, without any oth (thought). Then the translation of the Shloka shoul be—persons who worship Me in all beings, nev harbouring any other thought, to them, etc.

I carry, etc.—Because while other devotees wo for their own gain and safety, those who do not s

anything as separate from themselves, do not do so ;
they even do not cherish a desire for life ; so the Lord
secures to them gain and safety.]

येऽप्यन्यदेवता भक्ता यजन्ते श्रद्धयाऽन्विताः ॥
तेऽपि मामेव कौन्तेय यजन्त्यविधिपूर्वकम् ॥२३॥

कौन्तेय O son of Kunti श्रद्धया with Shraddhâ अन्विताः
endued (with) भक्ताः devotees ये who अन्यदेवताः other
gods अपि even यजन्ते worship ते they अपि too अविधिपूर्वकम्
by the wrong method माम् Me एव alone यजन्ति worship.

23. Even those devotees, who endued
with Shraddhâ, worship other gods, they too
worship Me alone, O son of Kunti, (but) by
the wrong method.

[*Wrong method*—ignorantly, not in the way by
which they can get Moksha.]

अहं हि सर्वयज्ञानां भोक्ता च प्रभुरेव च ॥
न तु मामभिजानन्ति तत्त्वेनातश्च्यवन्ति ते ॥२४॥

हि Indeed सर्वयज्ञानाम् of all Yajnas अहं I एव alone
भोक्ता enjoyer च and प्रभुः Lord च and ते they तु but मां Me
तत्त्वेन in reality न अभिजानन्ति do not know अतः hence
च्यवन्ति (they) all return.

24. For I alone am the Enjoyer, and
Lord of all Yajnas ; but because they do not
know Me in reality, they return, (to the mortal
world).

[*They return*—by worshipping other gods they attain no doubt to the spheres of their sacrifice, but after the exhaustion of this merit, they fall from those spheres and return to the mortal world.]

यान्ति देवव्रता देवान् पितॄन्यान्ति पितृव्रताः ॥

भूतानि यान्ति भूतेज्या यान्ति मद्याजिनोऽपि माम् ॥२५॥

देवव्रताः Votaries of the Devas देवान् the Devas यान्ति go to पितृव्रताः the votaries of the Pitris पितॄन् the Pitris यान्ति go to भूतेज्याः the worshippers of Bhutas भूतानि Bhutas यान्ति go to मद्याजिनः My votaries अपि too माम् Me यान्ति go to.

25.   Votaries of the Devas go to the Devas ; to the Pitris, go their votaries ; to the Bhutas, go the Bhuta worshippers ; My votaries too come unto Me.

[*Bhutas*—beings lower than the Devas, but higher than human beings.

Me—The Imperishable.]

पत्रं पुष्पं फलं तोयं यो मे भक्त्या प्रयच्छति ॥

तदहं भक्त्युपहृतमश्नामि प्रयतात्मनः ॥२६॥

यः Whoever मे to Me भक्त्या with devotion पत्रं a leaf पुष्पं a flower फलं a fruit तोयं water प्रयच्छति offers अहं प्रयतात्मनः of the pure-minded भक्त्युपहृतम् the devout gift तत् that अश्नामि accept.

26. Whoever with devotion offers Me a leaf, a flower, a fruit, or water, that I accept—the devout gift of the pure-minded.

[Not only does the single-minded devotion to the Supreme lead to imperishable result, but it is also so easy and simple to perform—says Krishna in this Shloka.]

यत्करोषि यदश्नासि यज्जुहोषि ददासि यत् ॥
यत्तपस्यसि कौन्तेय तत्कुरुष्व मदर्पणम् ॥२७॥

कौन्तेय O son of Kunti यत् whatever करोषि thou doest यत् whatever अश्नासि thou eatest यत् whatever जुहोषि thou offerest in sacrifice यत् whatever ददासि thou givest away यत् whatever तपस्यसि thou practisest as austerity तत् that मदर्पणं offering unto Me कुरुष्व do.

27. Whatever thou doest, whatever thou eatest, whatever thou offerest in sacrifice, whatever thou givest away, whatever austerity thou practisest, O son of Kunti, do that as an offering unto Me.

शुभाशुभफलैरेवं मोक्ष्यसे कर्मबन्धनैः ॥
संन्यासयोगयुक्तात्मा विमुक्तो मामुपैष्यसि ॥२८॥

एवं Thus शुभाशुभफलैः from good and evil results कर्मबन्धनैः from the bondages of actions मोक्ष्यसे (thou) shalt be freed विमुक्तः liberated संन्यासयोगयुक्तात्मा with the heart

steadfast in the Yoga of renunciation मां unto Me
उपैष्यसि (thou) shalt come.

28.   Thus shalt thou be freed from the
bondages of actions, bearing good and evil
results : with the heart steadfast in the Yoga of
renunciation, and liberated thou shalt come
unto Me.

[*The Yoga of renunciation*—This way of purification of the heart by offering everything to the
Lord.

Liberated, etc.—thou shalt be liberated while in
the body, and at its death, become Me.]

समोऽहं सर्वभूतेषु न मे द्वेष्योऽस्ति न प्रियः ॥
ये भजन्ति तु मां भक्त्या मयि ते तेषु चाप्यहम् ॥२६॥

अहं I सर्वभूतेषु to all beings समः the same मे to Me न
not द्वेष्यः hateful न not प्रियः dear अस्ति is ये those तु but
मां Me भक्त्या with devotion भजन्ति worship ते they मयि in
Me च and अहम् I अपि too तेषु in them.

29.   I am the same to all beings : to Me
there is none hateful or dear.   But those who
worship Me with devotion, are in Me, and I
too am in them.

[I am like fire.   As fire gives heat to those who
draw near to it, and not to those who move away
from it, even so do I.   My grace falls upon My

devotees, but not owing to any attachment on My part. As the sun's light, though pervading everywhere, is reflected in a clean mirror, so also I, the Supreme Lord, present as a matter of course everywhere, manifest Myself in these persons only, from whose minds all the dirt of ignorance has been removed by devotion.]

अपि चेत् सुदुराचारो भजते मामनन्यभाक् ॥
साधुरेव स मन्तव्यः सम्यग्व्यवसितो हि सः ॥३०॥

सुदुराचारः A very wicked person अपि even चेत् if अनन्यभाक् with devotion to none else माम् Me भजते worships सः he साधुः good एव verily मन्तव्यः should be regarded हि indeed सः he सम्यक् rightly व्यवसितः resolved.

30. If even a very wicked person worships Me, with devotion to none else, he should be regarded as good, for he has rightly resolved. .

[*He has rightly resolved*—He is one who has formed a holy resolution, to abandon the evil ways of his life.]

क्षिप्रं भवति धर्मात्मा शश्वच्छान्तिं निगच्छति ॥
कौन्तेय प्रतिजानीहि न मे भक्तः प्रणश्यति ॥३१॥

क्षिप्रं Soon धर्मात्मा righteous भवति (he) becomes शश्वत् eternal शान्तिं peace निगच्छति attains to कौन्तेय O son of

Kunti मे My भक्त: devotee न प्रणश्यति is never destroyed (इति this) प्रतिजानीहि know (do thou proclaim boldly).

31. Soon does he become righteous, and attain eternal Peace, O son of Kunti ; boldly canst thou proclaim, that My devotee is never destroyed.

मां हि पार्थ व्यपाश्रित्य येऽपि स्यु: पापयोनय: ॥
स्त्रियो वैश्यास्तथा शूद्रास्तेऽपि यान्ति परां गतिम् ॥३२॥

पार्थ O son of Pritha ये who अपि also पापयोनय: of inferior birth स्यु: might be स्त्रिय: women वैश्या: Vaishyas तथा as well as शूद्रा: Shudras ते they अपि even मां Me व्यपाश्रित्य taking refuge in परां the Supreme गतिम् Goal हि indeed यान्ति attain.

32. For, taking refuge in Me, they also, O son of Pritha, who might be of inferior birth—women, Vaishyas, as well as Shudras—even they attain to the Supreme Goal.

[*Of inferior birth . . . Shudras*—Because by birth, the Vaishyas are engaged only in agriculture, etc., and the women and Shudras are debarred from the study of the Vedas.]

किं पुनर्ब्राह्मणा: पुण्या भक्ता राजर्षयस्तथा ॥
अनित्यमसुखं लोकमिमं प्राप्य भजस्व माम् ॥३३॥

पुण्या: Holy ब्राह्मणा: Brâhmanas तथा also भक्ता: devoted राजर्षय: Râjarshis किं पुन: how much more अनित्यम् transient असुखं joyless इमं this लोकम् world प्राप्य having attained भजस्व do thou worship माम् Me.

33. What need to mention holy Brâhmanas, and devoted Râjarshis! Having obtained this transient, joyless world, worship thou Me.

[*Râjarshis*—kings who have attained to sainthood (Rishihood).

What need, etc.: How much more easily then do the holy Brâhmanas and the devoted royal saints attain that Goal!

Having ... world—Being born in this human body which is hard to get, one should exert oneself immediately for perfection, without depending on the future, as everything in this world is transient, and without seeking for happiness, as this world is joyless.]

मन्मना भव मद्भक्तो मद्याजी मां नमस्कुरु ।
मामेवैष्यसि युक्त्वैवमात्मानं मत्परायण: ॥३४॥

मन्मना: With mind filld with Me मद्भक्त: My devotee मद्याजी sacrificer unto Me भव be thou मां to Me नमस्कुरु bow down एवं thus मत्परायण: taking Me as the Supreme Goal आत्मानं heart युक्त्वा having made steadfast मां Me एव alone एष्यसि thou shalt come to.

34. Fill thy mind with Me, be My devotee, sacrifice unto Me, bow down to Me ; thus having made thy heart steadfast in Me, taking Me as the Supreme Goal, thou shalt come to Me.

इति राजविद्याराजगुह्ययोगो नाम नवमोऽध्याय: ॥

The end of the ninth chapter, designated, *The Way of the Kingly Knowledge and the Kingly Secret.*

॥ दशमोऽध्यायः ॥

TENTH CHAPTER

श्रीभगवानुवाच ।

भूय एव महाबाहो शृणु मे परमं वचः ॥
यत्तेऽहं प्रीयमाणाय वक्ष्यामि हितकाम्यया ॥१॥

श्रीभगवान् The Blessed Lord उवाच said :

महाबाहो O mighty-armed भूयः again एव verily मे My परमं supreme वचः word शृणु hear (thou) यत् which प्रीयमाणाय who art delighted (to hear) ते to thee अहं I हितकाम्यया wishing (thy) welfare वक्ष्यामि will tell.

The Blessed Lord said :

1. Again, O mighty-armed, do thou listen to My supreme word, which I, wishing thy welfare, will tell thee who art delighted (to hear Me).

[*Supreme*—as revealing the unsurpassed truth.]

न मे विदुः सुरगणाः प्रभवं न महर्षयः ॥
अहमादिर्हि देवानां महर्षीणां च सर्वशः ॥२॥

न Not सुरगणाः the hosts of Devas न nor महर्षयः the great Rishis मे My प्रभवं origin विदुः do know हि for अहम्

I देवानां of the Devas महर्षीणां of the great Rishis च and सर्वशः in every way आदिः source.

2. Neither the hosts of Devas, nor the great Rishis, know My origin, for in every way I am the source of all the Devas and the great Rishis.

[*Prabhavam*—higher origin (birth) ;—though birthless, yet taking various manifestations of power. Or it may mean, great Lordly power.

In every way : not only as their producer, but also as their efficient cause, and the guide of their intellect, etc.]

यो मामजमनादिं च वेत्ति लोकमहेश्वरम् ॥
असंमूढः स मर्त्येषु सर्वपापैः प्रमुच्यते ॥३॥

यः Who माम् Me अनादिं beginningless अजम् birthless च and लोकमहेश्वरम् the great Lord of worlds वेत्ति knows सः he मर्त्येषु among mortals असंमूढः undeluded सर्वपापैः from all sins प्रमुच्यते is freed.

3. He who knows Me, birthless and beginningless, the great Lord of worlds—he, among mortals, is undeluded, he is freed from all sins.

[*All sins*—consciously or unconsciously incurred.]

बुद्धिर्ज्ञानमसंमोहः क्षमा सत्यं दमः शमः ॥
सुखं दुःखं भवोऽभावो भयं चाभयमेव च ॥४॥

अहिंसा समता तुष्टिस्तपो दानं यशोऽयशः ॥

भवन्ति भावा भूतानां मत्त एव पृथग्विधाः ॥५॥

बुद्धि: Intellect ज्ञानं knowledge असंमोह: non-delusion क्षमा forbearance सत्यं truth दम: restraint of the external senses शम: calmness of the heart सुखं happiness दुःखं misery भव: birth अभाव: death भयं fear च and एव even अभयं fearlessness च as well as अहिंसा non-injury समता evenness तुष्टि: contentment तप: austerity दानं benevolence यश: good name अयश: ill-fame भूतानां of beings पृथग्विधा: of different kinds भावा: qualities मत्त: from Me एव alone भवन्ति arise.

4-5. Intellect, knowledge, non-delusion, forbearance, truth, restraint of the external senses, calmness of heart, happiness, misery, birth, death, fear, as well as fearlessness, non-injury, evenness, contentment, austerity, benevolence, good name, (as well as) ill-fame ;— (these) different kinds of qualities of beings arise from Me alone.

[*Arise, etc.*—according to their respective Karma.]

महर्षयः सप्त पूर्वे चत्वारो मनवस्तथा ॥

मद्भावा मानसा जाता येषां लोक इमाः प्रजाः ॥६॥

सप्त Seven महर्षय: great Rishis पूर्वे ancient चत्वार: four तथा as well as मनव: Manus मद्भावा: possessed of powers like Me मानसा: from mind जाता: born लोके in this world इमा: these येषाम् from whom प्रजा: creatures.

6. The seven great Rishis as well as the four ancient Manus, possessed of powers like Me (due to their thoughts being fixed on Me), were born of (My) mind ; from them are these creatures in the world.

[*The four ancient Manus :* The four Manus of the past ages known as Savarnas.]

एतां विभूतिं योगं च मम यो वेत्ति तत्त्वतः ॥
सोऽविकम्पेन योगेन युज्यते नात्र संशयः ॥७॥

य: Who मम Mine एतां these विभूतिं manifold manifestations of (My) being योगं Yoga power च and तत्त्वतः in reality वेत्ति knows स: he अविकम्पेन unshakable योगेन in Yoga युज्यते becomes established अत्र here न संशयः no doubt.

7. He who in reality knows these manifold manifestations of My being and (this) Yoga power of Mine, becomes established in the unshakable Yoga ; there is no doubt about it.

[*This Yoga power*—i.e., the fact that the great Rishis and the Manus possessed their power and wisdom, as partaking of a very small portion of the Lord's infinite power and wisdom.

Unshakable Yoga : Samâdhi, the state of steadiness in right realisation.]

अहं सर्वस्य प्रभवो मत्तः सर्वं प्रवर्तते ॥
इति मत्वा भजन्ते मां बुधा भावसमन्विताः ॥८॥

अहं I सर्वस्य of all प्रभवः the origin मत्तः from Me सर्वं everything प्रवर्तते evolves इति thus मत्वा thinking बुधाः the wise भावसमन्विताः with loving consciousness मां Me भजन्ते worship.

8.   I am the origin of all, from Me everything evolves ;—thus thinking, the wise worship Me with loving consciousness.

[*Loving consciousness*—of the One Self in all.]

मच्चित्ता मद्गतप्राणा बोधयन्तः परस्परम् ॥
कथयन्तश्च मां नित्यं तुष्यन्ति च रमन्ति च ॥६॥

मच्चित्ताः With (their) minds wholly in Me मद्गतप्राणाः with (their) senses absorbed in Me परस्परं mutually बोधयन्तः enlightening च and नित्यं always कथयन्तः speaking of च and तुष्यन्ति (they)are satisfied रमन्ति(they) are delighted च and.

9.   With their minds wholly in Me, with their senses absorbed in Me, enlightening one another, and always speaking of Me, they are satisfied and delighted.

[*Satisfied :* when there is cessation of all thirst.

Says the Purâna : All the pleasures of the senses
in the world, and also all the great happiness in the
divine spheres, are not worth a sixteenth part of that
which comes from the cessation of all desires.]

तेषां सततयुक्तानां भजतां प्रीतिपूर्वकम् ॥

ददामि बुद्धियोगं तं येन मामुपयान्ति ते ॥१०॥

सततयुक्तानां Ever steadfast प्रीतिपूर्वकम् with affection
भजतां serving तेषाम् to them तं that बुद्धियोगं Buddhi-
Yoga ददामि (I) give येन by which ते they मां Me उपयान्ति
come unto.

10.   To them, ever steadfast and serving
Me with affection, I give that Buddhi-Yoga by
which they come unto Me.

[Buddhi-Yoga—Devotion of right knowledge,
through Dhyâna, of My essential nature as devoid
of all limitations.

See II. 39.]

तेषामेवानुकम्पार्थमहमज्ञानजं तमः ॥

नाशयाम्यात्मभावस्थो ज्ञानदीपेन भास्वता ॥११॥

तेषां For them अनुकम्पार्थम् out of compassion एव mere
अहम् I आत्मभावस्थः abiding in (their) hearts भास्वता luminous ज्ञानदीपेन by the lamp of knowledge अज्ञानजं born of
ignorance तमः the darkness (of their mind) नाशयामि
(I) destroy.

11.   Out of mere compassion for them,

I, abiding in their hearts, destroy the darkness
(in them) born of ignorance, by the luminous
lamp of knowledge.

[*Luminous lamp of knowledge*—characterised by
discrimination ; fed by the oil of contentment due to
Bhakti ; fanned by the wind of absorbing meditation
on Me ; furnished with wick of pure consciousness
evolved by the constant cultivation of Brahmacharya and other pious virtues ; held in the reservoir
of the heart devoid of worldliness ; placed in the wind-
sheltered recess of the mind, withdrawn from the
sense-objects, and untainted by attachment and
aversion ; shining with the light of right knowledge,
engendered by incessant practice of concentration.—
Shankara.]

अर्जुन उवाच ।

परं ब्रह्म परं धाम पवित्रं परमं भवान् ॥

पुरुषं शाश्वतं दिव्यमादिदेवमजं विभुम् ॥१२॥

आहुस्त्वामृषयः सर्वे देवर्षिर्नारदस्तथा ॥

असितो देवलो व्यासः स्वयं चैव ब्रवीषि मे ॥१३॥

अर्जुनः Arjuna उवाच said :
भवान् Thou परं Supreme ब्रह्म Brahman परं Supreme
धाम Abode परमं Supreme पवित्रं Purifier (च and) सर्वे all
ऋषयः the Rishis देवर्षिः Deva-Rishi नारदः Nârada तथा as
well as असितः Asita देवलः Devala व्यासः Vyâsa त्वां Thee
शाश्वतं the eternal पुरुषं Purusha दिव्यम् Self-luminous आदि-
देवम् the first Deva अजं Birthless विभं the All-pervading

16

आहुः (they) declared स्वयं Thyself च and एव also मे to me ब्रवीषि (Thou) sayest.

Arjuna said :

12-13. The Supreme Brahman, the Supreme Abode, the Supreme Purifier, art Thou. All the Rishis, the Deva-Rishi Nârada as well as Asita, Devala, and Vyâsa have declared Thee as the Eternal, the Self-luminous Purusha, the first Deva, Birthless, and All-pervading. So also Thou Thyself sayest to me.

सर्वमेतदृतं मन्ये यन्मां वदसि केशव ॥

न हि ते भगवन् व्यक्तिं विदुर्देवा न दानवाः ॥१४॥

केशव O Keshava मां to me यत् what वदसि (Thou) sayest एतत् that सर्वम् all ऋतं true मन्ये (I) regard हि verily भगवन् O Bhagavân ते Thy व्यक्तिं manifestation न neither देवाः Devas न nor दानवाः Dânavas विदुः do know.

14. I regard all this that Thou sayest to me as true, O Keshava. Verily, O Bhagavân, neither the Devas nor the Dânavas know Thy manifestation.

[Bhagavân—is he in whom ever exist in their fulness, all powers, all Dharma, all glory, all success, all renunciation, and all freedom. Also he that knows the origin and dissolution and the future of all beings, as well as knowledge and ignorance, is called Bhagavân.]

स्वयमेवात्मनात्मानं वेत्थ त्वं पुरुषोत्तम ॥

भूतभावन भूतेश देवदेव जगत्पते ॥१५॥

पुरुषोत्तम O Purusha Supreme भूतभावन O Source of
beings भुतेश O Lord of beings देवदेव O Deva of Devas
जगत्पते O Ruler of the world त्वं Thou स्वयम् Thyself एव
verily आत्मना by Thyself आत्मानं Thyself वेत्थ (Thou)
knowest.

15. Verily, Thou Thyself knowest Thyself by Thyself, O Purusha Supreme, O Source
of beings, O Lord of beings, O Deva of Devas,
O Ruler of the World.

वक्तुमर्हस्यशेषेण दिव्या ह्यात्मविभूतयः ॥

याभिर्विभूतिभिर्लोकानिमांस्त्वं व्याप्य तिष्ठसि ॥१६॥

याभिः By which विभूतिभिः (divine) attributes त्वं
Thou इमान् all these लोकान् worlds व्याप्य having filled
तिष्ठसि existest दिव्याः divine आत्मविभूतयः Thy attributes हि
indeed अशेषेण without reserve वक्तुम् to speak of अर्हसि
(Thou) shouldst.

16. Thou shouldst indeed speak, without reserve, of Thy divine attributes by
which, filling all these worlds, Thou
existest.

[Since none else can do so.]

कथं विद्यामहं योगिंस्त्वां सदा परिचिन्तयन् ॥

केषु केषु च भावेषु चिन्त्योऽसि भगवन्मया ॥१७॥

योगिन् O Yogi सदा ever परिचिन्तयन् meditating कथं how त्वां Thee अहं I विद्याम् shall know भगवन् O Bhagavân मया by me केषु केषु in what and what भावेषु aspects, things च and चिन्त्य: to be thought of असि (Thou) art.

17. How shall I, O Yogi, meditate ever to know Thee ? In what things, O Bhagavân, art Thou to be thought of by me ?

[*In what things, etc.:* In order that the mind even thinking of external objects, may be enabled to contemplate Thee in Thy particular manifestations in them.]

विस्तरेणात्मनो योगं विभूतिं च जनार्दन ॥
भूय: कथय तृप्तिर्हि श्रृण्वतो नास्ति मेऽमृतम् ॥१८॥

जनार्दन O Janârdana आत्मन: Thy योगं Yoga-powers विभूतिं attributes च and विस्तरेण in detail भूय: again कथय speak of हि for अमृतम् ambrosia श्रृण्वत: to (me) who am hearing मे to me तृप्ति: satiety न अस्ति there is not.

18. Speak to me again in detail, O Janârdana, of Thy Yoga-powers and attributes ; for I am never satiated in hearing the ambrosia (of Thy speech).

[*Janârdana*—to whom all pray for prosperity and salvation.]

श्रीभगवानुवाच ।

हन्त ते कथयिष्यामि दिव्या ह्यात्मविभूतयः ॥

प्राधान्यतः कुरुश्रेष्ठ नास्त्यन्तो विस्तरस्य मे ॥१९॥

श्रीभगवान् The Blessed Lord उवाच said :

हन्त O कुरुश्रेष्ठ best of the Kurus दिव्याः divine आत्म-
विभूतयः My attributes प्राधान्यतः according to their prominence ते to thee कथयिष्यामि (I) shall speak of हि for मे
My विस्तरस्य particulars अन्तः end नास्ति there is not.

The Blessed Lord said :

19. I shall speak to thee now, O best
of the Kurus, of my divine attributes,
according to their prominence ; there is
no end to the particulars of My manifestation.

[*According to their prominence, i.e.,* only where
they are severally the most prominent.]

अहमात्मा गुडाकेश सर्वभूताशयस्थितः ॥

अहमादिश्च मध्यं च भूतानामन्त एव च ॥२०॥

गुडाकेश O Gudâkesha सर्वभूताशयस्थितः existent in the
heart of all beings आत्मा the Self च and अहम् I भूतानां of
(all) beings आदिः the beginning च and मध्यं the middle
अन्तः the end च and अहम् I एव also.

20. I am the Self, O Gudâkesha, existent in the heart of all beings ; I am the

beginning, the middle, and also the end of all beings.

[*Gudâkesha*—conqueror of sleep.

Beginning, etc.—That is, the birth, the life, and the death of all beings.]

आदित्यानामहं विष्णुर्ज्योतिषां रविरंशुमान् ॥

मरीचिर्मरुतामस्मि नक्षत्राणामहं शशी ॥२१॥

अहं I आदित्यानाम् of the (twelve) Âdityas विष्णु: Vishnu ज्योतिषां of luminaries अंशुमान् the radiant रवि: the Sun मरुतां of the winds (forty-nine wind-gods) मरीचि: Marichi अस्मि (I) am नक्षत्राणाम् of the asterisms अहं I शशी the Moon.

21. Of the Âdityas, I am Vishnu ; of luminaries, the radiant Sun, of the winds, I am Marichi ; of the asterisms, the Moon.

वेदानां सामवेदोऽस्मि देवानामस्मि वासव: ॥

इन्द्रियाणां मनश्चास्मि भूतानामस्मि चेतना ॥२२॥

वेदानां Of the Vedas सामवेद: Sâma-Veda अस्मि (I) am देवानाम् of the gods वासव: Vâsava अस्मि (I) am इन्द्रियाणां of the senses मन: Manas च and अस्मि (I) am भूतानाम् in living beings चेतना intelligence अस्मि (I) am.

22. I am the Sâma-Veda of the Vedas, and Vâsava (Indra) of the gods ; of the senses I am Manas, and intelligence in living beings am I.

रुद्राणां शङ्करश्चास्मि वित्तेशो यक्षरक्षसाम् ॥

वसूनां पावकश्चास्मि मेरुः शिखरिणामहम् ॥२३॥

रुद्राणां Of the Rudras शङ्करः Shankara च and अस्मि (I)
am यक्षरक्षसाम् of the Yakshas and the Râkshasas वित्तेशः
the Lord of wealth (Kuvera) (अस्मि I am) (वसूनां of the
Vasus पावकः Pâvaka च and अस्मि (I) am शिखरिणाम् of
mountains मेरुः Meru अहम् I (अस्मि am).

23.   And of the Rudras I am Shankara ;
of the Yakshas and Râkshasas, the Lord of
wealth (Kuvera); of the Vasus I am Pâvaka ;
and of mountains, Meru am I.

पुरोधसां च मुख्यं मां विद्धि पार्थ बृहस्पतिम् ॥

सेनानीनामहं स्कन्दः सरसामस्मि सागरः ॥२४॥

पार्थ O son of Prithâ मां Me पुरोधसां of the priests
मुख्यं the chief बृहस्पतिम् Brihaspati च and विद्धि know अहं
I सेनानीनाम् of generals स्कन्दः Skanda सरसाम् of bodies of
water सागरः the ocean अस्मि (I) am.

24.   And of priests, O son of Prithâ,
know Me the chief, Brihaspati ; of generals,
I am Skanda ; of bodies of water, I am the
ocean.

महर्षीणां भृगुरहं गिरामस्म्येकमक्षरम् ॥

यज्ञानां जपयज्ञोऽस्मि स्थावराणां हिमालयः ॥२५॥

अहं I महर्षीणां of the great Rishis भृगु: Bhrigu गिराम्
of words एकं one अक्षरम् the syllable "Om" अस्मि (I) am
यज्ञानां of Yajnas जपयज्ञ: the Yajna of Japa (silent
repetition) स्थावराणां of immovable things हिमालय: the
Himâlaya अस्मि (I) am.

25. Of the great Rishis I am Bhrigu ;
of words I am the one syllable "Om"; of
Yajnas I am the Yajna of Japa (silent
repetition);   of   immovable   things   the
Himâlaya.

[*Yajna of Japa*—because there is no injury or
loss of life involved in it, it is the best of all Yajnas.]

अश्वत्थ: सर्ववृक्षाणां देवर्षीणां च नारद: ॥
गन्धर्वाणां चित्ररथ: सिद्धानां कपिलो मुनि: ॥२६॥

सर्ववृक्षाणां Of all trees अश्वत्थ: the Ashvattha देवर्षीणां
of the Deva-Rishis च and नारद: Nârada गन्धर्वाणां of
Gandharvas चित्ररथ: Chitraratha सिद्धानां of the perfected
ones कपिल: Kapila मुनि: the Muni.

26. Of all trees (I am) the Ashvattha,
and Nârada of Deva-Rishis ; Chitraratha of
Gandharvas am I, and the Muni Kapila of the
perfected ones.

उच्चै:श्रवसमश्वानां विद्धि माममृतोद्भवम् ॥
ऐरावतं गजेन्द्राणां नराणां च नराधिपम् ॥२७॥

अश्वानां Among horses अमृतोद्भवम् Amrita-born उच्चै :श्रवसम्
Uchchaisshravas गजेन्द्राणां of lordly elephants ऐरावतं
Airâvata नराणां of men नराधिपम् the king च and मां Me
विद्धि know.

27. Know Me among horses as Uchchaisshravas, Amrita-born ; of lordly elephants
Airâvata, and of men the king.

[*Amrita-born :* Brought forth from the ocean
when it was churned for the nectar.]

आयुधानामहं वज्रं धेनूनामस्मि कामधुक्॥
प्रजनश्चास्मि कन्दर्पः सर्पाणामस्मि वासुकिः ॥२८॥

आयुधानाम् Of weapons अहं I वज्रं the thunderbolt
धेनूनाम् of cows कामधुक् Kâmadhuk (Surabhi, the heavenly
cow yielding all desires) अस्मि (I) am (अहं I) प्रजनः
cause of offspring कन्दर्पः Kandarpa च and अस्मि (I) am
सर्पाणाम् of serpents वासुकिः Vâsuki अस्मि (I) am.

28. Of weapons I am the thunderbolt,
of cows I am Kâmadhuk ; I am the Kandarpa,
the cause of offspring ; of serpents I am
Vâsuki.

अनन्तश्चास्मि नागानां वरुणो यादसामहम्॥
पितृणामर्यमा चास्मि यमः संयमतामहम् ॥२९॥

नागानां Of snakes अनन्तः Ananta च and अस्मि (I) am
यादसाम् of water-beings अहम् I वरुणः Varuna (अस्मि I am)

पितृणाम् of Pitris अर्यमा Aryaman च and अस्मि (I) am संयमतां
of controllers अहम् I यम: Yama (अस्मि I am).

29. And Ananta of snakes I am, I am
Varuna of water-beings ; and Aryaman of
Pitris I am, I am Yama of controllers.

प्रह्लादश्चास्मि दैत्यानां काल: कलयतामहम् ॥
मृगाणां च मृगेन्द्रोऽहं वैनतेयश्च पक्षिणाम् ॥३०॥

दैत्यानां Of Diti's progeny च and प्रह्लाद: Prahlâda
अस्मि (I) am कलयताम् of measurers अहम् I काल: Time (अस्मि
I am) मृगाणां of beasts अहं I च and मृगेन्द्र: the lord of
beasts (lion) पक्षिणाम् of birds वैनतेय: son of Vinatâ,
Garuda च and.

30. And Prahlâda am I of Diti's
progeny, of measurers I am Time ; and of
beasts I am the lord of beasts, and Garuda of
birds.

पवन: पवतामस्मि राम: शस्त्रभृतामहम् ॥
झषाणां मकरश्चास्मि स्रोतसामस्मि जाह्नवी ॥३१॥

पवताम् Of purifiers पवन: the wind अस्मि (I) am
शस्त्रभृताम् of wielders of weapons (warriors) अहम् I राम:
Râma (अस्मि I am) झषाणां of fishes मकर: Makara (shark)
च and अस्मि (I) am स्रोतसाम् of streams जाह्नवी Jâhnavi,
Ganges अस्मि (I) am.

31. Of purifiers I am the wind, Râma

of warriors am I ; of fishes I am the shark, of
streams I am Jâhnavi (the Ganges).

सर्गाणामादिरन्तश्च मध्यं चैवाहमर्जुन ॥

अध्यात्मविद्या विद्यानां वादः प्रवदतामहम् ॥३२॥

अर्जुन O Arjuna सर्गाणाम् of manifestations आदिः the
beginning च and अन्तः the end मध्यं the middle च and
अहम् I एव also विद्यानां of all knowledges अध्यात्मविद्या the
knowledge of the Self प्रवदतां of disputants (च and)
अहम् I वादः Vâda.

32. Of manifestations I am the beginning, the middle and also the end ; of all
knowledges I am the knowledge of the Self,
and Vâda of disputants.

[*Vâda.* Discussion is classified under three heads :
1. Vâda ; 2. Vitandâ ; 3. Jalpa.

In the first, the object is to arrive at truth ; in
the second, idle carping at the arguments of another,
without trying to establish the opposite side of the
question ; and in the third, the assertion of one's
own opinion, and the attempt to refute that of the
adversary by overbearing reply or wrangling rejoinder.]

अक्षराणामकारोऽस्मि द्वन्द्वः सामासिकस्य च ॥

अहमेवाक्षयः कालो धाताहं विश्वतोमुखः ॥३३॥

अक्षराणां Of letters अकारः the letter A अस्मि (I) am
सामासिकस्य of all compounds च and द्वन्द्वः (that called in

Sanskrit) Dvandva, the copulative अहम् I एव alone अक्षय: the inexhaustible काल: Time अहं I विश्वतोमुख: the All-formed धाता the Sustainer (by distributing fruits of actions).

33. Of letters the letter A am I, and Dvandva of all compounds ; I alone am the inexhaustible Time, I the Sustainer (by dispensing fruits of actions) All-formed.

[*Inexhaustible Time,* i.e., Eternity. Kâla spoken of before is finite time.]

मृत्यु: सर्वहरश्चाहमुद्भवश्च भविष्यताम् ॥

कीर्ति: श्रीर्वाक् च नारीणां स्मृतिर्मेधा धृति: क्षमा ॥३४॥

अहम् I सर्वहर: the all-seizing मृत्यु: Death च and भविष्यतां of those who are to be prosperous उद्भव: the prosperity च and नारीणां of the feminine कीर्ति: Fame श्री: Prosperity (or beauty) वाक् Inspiration (lit. speech) स्मृति: Memory मेधा Intelligence धृति: Constancy क्षमा Forbearance च and (अहम् I).

34. And I am the all-seizing Death, and the prosperity of those who are to be prosperous ; of the feminine qualities (I am) Fame, Prosperity (or beauty), Inspiration, Memory, Intelligence, Constancy and Forbearance.

बृहत्साम तथा साम्नां गायत्री छन्दसामहम् ॥

मासानां मार्गशीर्षोऽहमृतूनां कुसुमाकर: ॥३५॥

अहम् I तथा also साम्नां of Sâma hymns बृहत्साम Brihat-
Sâma छन्दसाम् of metres अहम् I गायत्री Gâyatri मासानां of
months मार्गशीर्ष: Mârgashirsha ऋतूनां of seasons कुसुमाकर:
the flowery season.

35. Of Sâmas also I am the Brihat-
Sâma, of metres Gâyatri am I ; of months
I am Mârgashirsha, of seasons the flowery
season.

[*Mârgashirsha*—month including parts of No-
vember and December.

Flowery season—Spring.]

द्यूतं छलयतामस्मि तेजस्तेजस्विनामहम् ॥
जयोऽस्मि व्यवसायोऽस्मि सत्त्वं सत्त्ववतामहम् ॥३६॥

अहम् I छल्यताम् of the fraudulent द्यूतं the gambling
तेजस्विनाम् of the powerful तेज: power अस्मि (I) am अहम् I
जय: victory अस्मि (I) am व्यवसाय: effort अस्मि (I) am सत्त्ववताम्
of the Sâttvika सत्त्वं the Sattva (अस्मि I am).

36. I am the gambling of the fraudulent, I am the power of the powerful ; I
am victory, I am effort, I am Sattva of the
Sâttvika.

[*I am victory, I am effort* : I am victory of the
victorious, I am the effort of those who make an
effort.]

वृष्णीनां वासुदेवोऽस्मि पाण्डवानां धनञ्जय: ॥
मुनीनामप्यहं व्यास: कवीनामुशना कवि: ॥३७॥

अहं I वृष्णीनां of the Vrishnis वासुदेव: Vâsudeva पाण्डवानां of the Pândavas धनञ्जय: Dhananjaya अपि also मुनीनाम् of the Munis व्यास: Vyâsa कवीनाम् of the sages उशना Ushanas कवि: the sage अस्मि (I) am.

37. Of the Vrishnis I am Vâsudeva ; of the Pândavas, Dhananjaya ; and also of the Munis I am Vyâsa ; of the sages, Ushanas the sage.

दण्डो दमयतामस्मि नीतिरस्मि जिगीषताम् ॥
मौनं चैवास्मि गुह्यानां ज्ञानं ज्ञानवतामहम् ॥३८॥

अहम् I दमयताम् of punishers दण्ड: the sceptre अस्मि am जिगीषताम् of those who seek to conquer नीति: statesmanship अस्मि (I) am गुह्यानां of things secret मौनं silence च and also अस्मि (I) am ज्ञानवताम् of knowers ज्ञानं the knowledge.

38. Of punishers I am the sceptre ; of those who seek to conquer, I am states-manship ; and also of things secret I am silence, and the knowledge of knowers am I.

यच्चापि सर्वभूतानां बीजं तदहमर्जुन ॥
न तदस्ति विना यत्स्यान्मया भूतं चराचरम् ॥३९॥

अर्जुन O Arjuna यत् what च and सर्वभूतानां of all beings बीजं the seed तत् that अहम् I अपि also मया विना without

Me यत् what स्यात् can exist तत् that चराचरम् moving or unmoving भूतं being न अस्ति there is not.

39.　And whatsoever is the seed of all beings, that also am I, O Arjuna. There is no being, whether moving or unmoving, that can exist without Me.

नान्तोऽस्ति मम दिव्यानां विभूतीनां परन्तप ॥
एष तूद्देशतः प्रोक्तो विभूतेर्विस्तरो मया ॥४०॥

परन्तप O scorcher of foes मम My दिव्यानां of divine विभूतीनां attributes अन्तः end न not अस्ति is एषः this तु only विभूतेः of attributes विस्तरः particulars मया by Me उद्देशतः brief statement प्रोक्तः has been stated.

40.　There is no end of My divine attributes, O scorcher of foes ; but this is a brief statement by Me of the particulars of My divine attributes.

यद्यद्विभूतिमत्सत्त्वं श्रीमदूर्जितमेव वा ॥
तत्तदेवावगच्छ त्वं मम तेजोंऽशसम्भवम् ॥४१॥

विभूतिमत् Great श्रीमत् prosperous वा or एव also ऊर्जितम् powerful यत् यत् whatever सत्त्वं being तत् तत् that एव also मम My तेजोंऽशसम्भवम् a product of a part of splendour त्वं thou अवगच्छ know.

41.　Whatever being there is great,

prosperous, or powerful, that know thou to be
a product of a part of My splendour.

अथवा बहुनैतेन किं ज्ञातेन तवार्जुन ॥
विष्टभ्याहमिदं कृत्स्नमेकांशेन स्थितो जगत् ॥४२॥

अथवा Or अर्जुन O Arjuna एतेनby this बहुना(by) many
ज्ञातेन to know तव thy किं what (avails) अहम् I इदं this
कृत्स्नम् whole जगत् world एकांशेन by a portion विष्टभ्य
supporting स्थितः exist.

42.   Or what avails thee to know all this
diversity, O Arjuna?   (Know thou this, that)
I exist, supporting this whole world by a
portion of Myself.

इति विभूतियोगो नाम दशमोऽध्यायः ॥

The end of the tenth chapter, designated,
Glimpses of the Divine Glory.

।। एकादशोऽध्यायः ।।

ELEVENTH CHAPTER

अर्जुन उवाच ।

मदनुग्रहाय परमं गुह्यमध्यात्मसंज्ञितम् ।।
यत्त्वयोक्तं वचस्तेन मोहोऽयं विगतो मम ।।१।।

अर्जुनः Arjuna उवाच said :
मदनुग्रहाय Out of compassion towards me परमं supremely गुह्य profound अध्यात्मसंज्ञितम् that which treats of the discrimination of Self and non-Self यत् that वचः words त्वया by Thee उक्तं spoken तेन by that मम my अयं this मोहः delusion विगतः is gone.

Arjuna said :

1. By the supremely profound words, on the discrimination of Self, that have been spoken by Thee out of compassion towards me, this my delusion is gone.

भवाप्ययौ हि भूतानां श्रुतौ विस्तरशो मया ।।
त्वत्तः कमलपत्राक्ष माहात्म्यमपि चाव्ययम् ।।२।।

कमलपत्राक्ष O Thou with eyes like the lotus-leaf त्वत्तः of Thee भूतानां of beings भवाप्ययौ the origin and

17

dissolution मया by me विस्तरशः at length हि indeed श्रुतौ
have been heard अव्ययं inexhaustible माहात्म्य greatness
अपि च and also.

2. Of Thee, O lotus-eyed, I have
heard at length, of the origin and dissolution of beings, as also Thy inexhaustible
greatness.

एवमेतद्यथात्थ त्वमात्मानं परमेश्वर ॥
द्रष्टुमिच्छामि ते रूपमैश्वरं पुरुषोत्तम ॥३॥

परमेश्वर O Supreme Lord यथा as त्वं Thou आत्मानं
Thyself आत्थ hast declared एतत् it एवम् so पुरुषोत्तम O
Purusha Supreme ते Thy ऐश्वरं रूपम् Ishvara-Form द्रष्टुम्
to see इच्छामि (I) desire.

3. So it is, O Lord Supreme ! as Thou
hast declared Thyself. (Still) I desire
to see Thy Ishvara-Form, O Purusha
Supreme.

[*Thy Ishvara-Form*—as possessed of omnipotence,
omnipresence, infinite wisdom, strength, virtue, and
splendour.]

मन्यसे यदि तच्छक्यं मया द्रष्टुमिति प्रभो ॥
योगेश्वर ततो मे त्वं दर्शयात्मानमव्ययम् ॥४॥

प्रभो O Lord यदि if तत् that मया by me द्रष्टुम् to   see

शक्यं capable इति as मन्यसे Thou thinkest ततः then योगेश्वर
O Lord of Yogisत्व' Thou मे me अव्ययं immutable आत्मानम्
Self दर्शय show.

4. If, O Lord, Thou thinkest me
capable of seeing it, then, O Lord of Yogis,
show me Thy immutable Self.

श्रीभगवानुवाच ।

पश्य मे पार्थ रूपाणि शतशोऽथ सहस्रशः ॥

नानाविधानि दिव्यानि नानावर्णाकृतीनि च ॥५॥

श्रीभगवान् The Blessed Lord उवाच said :
पार्थ O son of Prithâ मे My दिव्यानि celestial नानाविधानि
different in kind नानावर्णाकृतीनि of various colours and
shapes च and शतशः by the hundred अथ and सहस्रशः by
the thousand रूपाणि forms पश्य behold.

The Blessed Lord said :

5. Behold, O son of Prithâ, by
hundreds and thousands, My different
forms celestial, of various colours and
shapes.

पश्यादित्यान्वसून् रुद्रानश्विनौ मरुतस्तथा ॥

बहून्यदृष्टपूर्वाणि पश्याश्चर्याणि भारत ॥६॥

भारत O descendant of Bharata आदित्यान् the (twelve)
Âdityas वसून् the (eight) Vasus रुद्रान् the (eleven)
Rudras अश्विनौ the twin Ashvins तथा also मरुतः the

Maruts (the forty-nine wind-gods) पश्य behold बहूनि
many अदृष्टपूर्वाणि never seen before आश्चर्याणि wonders
पश्य behold.

6. Behold the Âdityas, the Vasus, the
Rudras, the twin Ashvins, and the Maruts;
behold, O descendant of Bharata, many
wonders never seen before.

इहैकस्थं जगत्कृत्स्नं पश्याद्य सचराचरम् ॥

मम देहे गुडाकेश यच्चान्यद्द्रष्टुमिच्छसि ॥७॥

गुडाकेश O Gudâkesha (Arjuna) इह in this मम My देहे
(in) body एकस्थं centred in one कृत्स्नं whole सचराचरं with
the moving and the unmoving जगत् universe अन्यत्
else च and यत् that द्रष्टुम् to see इच्छसि (thou) desirest अद्य
now पश्य see.

7. See now, O Gudâkesha, in this My
body, the whole universe centred in one—
including the moving and the unmoving—
and all else that thou desirest to see.

[Centred in one—as part of My body.

All else—e.g., your success or defeat in the war
about which you entertain a doubt (II. 6).]

न तु मां शक्यसे द्रष्टुमनेनैव स्वचक्षुषा ॥

दिव्यं ददामि ते चक्षुः पश्य मे योगमैश्वरम् ॥८॥

अनेनैव With this स्वचक्षुषा with eye of thine तु but मां
Me द्रष्टुम् to see न शक्यसे thou canst not ते (to) thee दिव्यं

divine, supersensuous चक्षुः sight ददामि (I) give मे My
ऐश्वरं Supreme योगम् Yoga Power पश्य behold.

8. But thou canst not see Me with these
eyes of thine ; I give thee supersensuous sight ;
behold My Yoga Power Supreme.

[Me—in My Universal Form.]

सञ्जय उवाच

एवमुक्त्वा ततो राजन् महायोगेश्वरो हरिः ॥
दर्शयामास पार्थाय परमं रूपमैश्वरम् ॥६॥

सञ्जयः Sanjaya उवाच said :
राजन् O King (Dhritarâshtra) महायोगेश्वरः the Great
Lord of Yoga हरिः Hari एवम् thus उक्त्वा having spoken
ततः then पार्थाय unto the son of Prithâ परमं Supreme
ऐश्वरं रूपम् Ishvara-Form दर्शयामास showed.

Sanjaya said :
9. Having thus spoken, O King, Hari,
the Great Lord of Yoga, showed unto the
son of Prithâ, His Supreme Ishvara-
Form—

अनेकवक्त्रनयनमनेकाद्भुतदर्शनम् ॥
अनेकदिव्याभरणं दिव्यानेकोद्यतायुधम् ॥१०॥

अनेकवक्त्रनयनम् With numerous mouths and eyes अनेका-
द्भुतदर्शनम् with numerous wondrous sight अनेकदिव्याभरणं
with numerous celestial ornaments दिव्यानेकोद्यतायुधम् with
numerous celestial weapons uplifted.

10. With numerous mouths and eyes, with numerous wondrous sights, with numerous celestial ornaments, with numerous celestial weapons uplifted ;

दिव्यमाल्याम्बरधरं दिव्यगन्धानुलेपनम् ॥
सर्वाश्चर्यमयं देवमनन्तं विश्वतोमुखम् ॥११॥

दिव्यमाल्याम्बरधरं Wearing celestial garlands and apparel दिव्यगन्धानुलेपनम् anointed with celestial-scented unguents सर्वाश्चर्यमयं the All-wonderful देवम् Resplendent अनन्तं Boundless विश्वतोमुखम् All-formed.

11. Wearing celestial garlands and apparel, anointed with celestial-scented unguents, the All-wonderful Resplendent, Boundless, and All-formed.

दिवि सूर्यसहस्रस्य भवेद्युगपदुत्थिता ॥
यदि भाः सदृशी सा स्याद्भासस्तस्य महात्मनः ॥१२॥

दिवि In the sky यदि if सूर्यसहस्रस्य of a thousand suns भाः splendour युगपत् at once उत्थिता भवेत् were to rise up सा that तस्य of that महात्मनः of the Mighty Being भासः splendour सदृशी like स्यात् would be.

12. If the splendour of a thousand suns were to rise up at once in the sky, that would be like the splendour of that Mighty Being.

[*Mighty Being :* The Universal Form.
The splendour of the Universal Form excels all others ; it is indeed beyond compare.]

तत्रैकस्थं जगत्कृत्स्नं प्रविभक्तमनेकधा ॥
अपश्यद्देवदेवस्य शरीरे पाण्डवस्तदा ॥१३॥

तदा Then पाण्डवः the son of Pându तत्र there देवदेवस्य of the God of gods शरीरे in the body अनेकधा in manifold ways प्रविभक्तम् divided कृत्स्नं whole जगत् universe एकस्थं resting in one अपश्यत् saw.

13.   There in the body of the God of gods, the son of Pându then saw the whole universe resting in one, with its manifold divisions.

ततः स विस्मयाविष्टो हृष्टरोमा धनञ्जयः ॥
प्रणम्य शिरसा देवं कृताञ्जलिरभाषत ॥१४॥

ततः Then सः he धनञ्जयः Dhananjaya विस्मयाविष्टः filled with wonder हृष्टरोमा with hair standing on end देवं to the Deva शिरसा with (his) head प्रणम्य bending कृताञ्जलिः with joined palms अभाषत spoke.

14.   Then Dhananjaya, filled with wonder, with his hair standing on end, bending down his head to the Deva in adoration, spoke with joined palms.

[*Deva :* God, in His Universal Form.]

अर्जुन उवाच ।
पश्यामि देवांस्तव देव देहे
सर्वांस्तथा भूतविशेषसङ्घान् ॥
ब्रह्माणमीशं कमलासनस्थ-
मृषींश्च सर्वानुरगांश्च दिव्यान् ॥१५॥

अर्जुन: Arjuna उवाच said :

देव O Deva तव Thy देहे in the body सर्वान् all देवान् the Devas तथा and भूतविशेषसङ्घान् hosts of all grades of beings ईशं the Lord कमलासनस्थम् seated on the lotus ब्रह्माणम् Brahmâ ऋषीन् Rishis च and सर्वान् all दिव्यान् celestial उरगान् serpents च and पश्यामि (I) see.

Arjuna said :

15. I see all the Devas, O Deva, in Thy body, and hosts of all grades of beings ; Brahmâ, the Lord, seated on the lotus, and all the Rishis and celestial serpents.

अनेकबाहूदरवक्त्रनेत्रं
पश्यामि त्वां सर्वतोऽनन्तरूपम् ॥
नान्तं न मध्यं न पुनस्तवादिं
पश्यामि विश्वेश्वर विश्वरूप ॥१६॥

विश्वेश्वर O Lord of the universe विश्वरूप O Universal Form अनेकबाहूदरवक्त्रनेत्रं with manifold arms, stomachs, mouths, and eyes अनन्तरूपं of boundless form त्वां Thee सर्वतः on every side पश्यामि (I) see तव of Thee पुन: also न

neither अन्तं the end न nor मध्यं the middle न nor आदिं
the beginning पश्यामि do (I) see.

16. I see Thee of boundless form on
every side with manifold arms, stomachs,
mouths, and eyes; neither the end nor the
middle, nor also the beginning of Thee do
I see, O Lord of the universe, O Universal
Form.

किरीटिनं गदिनं चक्रिणं च
तेजोराशिं सर्वतोदीप्तिमन्तम् ॥
पश्यामि त्वां दुर्निरीक्ष्यं समन्ताद्-
दीप्तानलार्कद्युतिमप्रमेयम् ॥१७॥

किरीटिनं One with diadem गदिनं with club चक्रिणं
with discus च and सर्वतः everywhere दीप्तिमन्तम् shining
तेजोराशिं a mass of radiance दुर्निरीक्ष्यं very hard to look at
दीप्तानलार्कद्युतिम् blazing like burning fire and sun अप्रमेयम्
immeasurable त्वां Thee समन्तात् all around पश्यामि (I) see.

17. I see Thee with diadem, club, and
discus; a mass of radiance shining everywhere, very hard to look at, all around
blazing like burning fire and sun, and immeasurable.

त्वमक्षरं परमं वेदितव्यं
त्वमस्य विश्वस्य परं निधानम् ॥

त्वमव्ययः शाश्वतधर्मगोप्ता

सनातनस्त्वं पुरुषो मतो मे ॥१८॥

त्वं Thou अक्षरं the Imperishable परमं the Supreme
Being वेदितव्यं the one thing to be known त्वं Thou अस्य
विश्वस्य of this universe परं the great निधानम् Refuge त्वम्
Thou अव्ययः the undying शाश्वतधर्मगोप्ता Guardian of the
Eternal Dharma त्वं Thou सनातनः the Ancient पुरुषः
Purusha मे मतः I ween.

18. Thou art the Imperishable, the
Supreme Being, the one thing to be known.
Thou art the great Refuge of this universe ;
Thou art the undying Guardian of the
Eternal Dharma, Thou art the Ancient
Purusha, I ween.

अनादिमध्यान्तमनन्तवीर्य-

मनन्तबाहुं शशिसूर्यनेत्रम् ॥

पश्यामि त्वां दीप्तहुताशवक्त्रं

स्वतेजसा विश्वमिदं तपन्तम् ॥१९॥

अनादिमध्यान्तम् Without beginning, middle, or end
अनन्तवीर्यम् infinite in power अनन्तबाहुं of manifold arms
शशिसूर्यनेत्रम् the sun and the moon (Thy) eyes दीप्तहुताशवक्त्रं
the burning fire (Thy) mouth स्वतेजसा with Thy
radiance इदं this विश्वम् universe तपन्तम् heating त्वां Thee
पश्यामि (I) see.

19. I see Thee without beginning, middle, or end, infinite in power, of manifold arms ; the sun and the moon Thine eyes, the burning fire Thy mouth ; heating the whole universe with Thy radiance.

द्यावापृथिव्योरिदमन्तरं हि

व्याप्तं त्वयैकेन दिशश्च सर्वाः ॥

दृष्ट्वाऽद्भुतं रूपमुग्रं तवेदं

लोकत्रयं प्रव्यथितं महात्मन् ॥२० ॥

महात्मन् O Great-souled One द्यावापृथिव्योः (of) heaven and earth इदम् the अन्तरं space betwixt एकेन alone त्वया by Thee हि indeed व्याप्तं are filled सर्वाः all दिशः quarters च and तव Thy अद्भुतं wonderful इदं this उग्रं awful रूपम् form दृष्ट्वा having seen लोकत्रयं the three worlds प्रव्यथितं are trembling (with fear).

20. The space betwixt heaven and earth and all the quarters are filled by Thee alone ; having seen this, Thy marvellous and awful Form, the three worlds are trembling with fear, O Great-souled One.

अमी हि त्वां सुरसङ्घा विशन्ति ॥

केचिद्भीताः प्राञ्जलयो गृणन्ति ॥

स्वस्तीत्युक्त्वा महर्षिसिद्धसङ्घाः

स्तुवन्ति त्वां स्तुतिभिः पुष्कलाभिः ॥२१॥

अमी These सुरसङ्घाः hosts of Devas हि verily त्वां Thee विशन्ति enter केचित् some भीताः in fear प्राञ्जलयः with joined palms गृणन्ति extol महर्षिसिद्धसङ्घाः bands of great Rishis and Siddhas "स्वस्ति" "May it be well" इति thus उक्त्वा saying पुष्कलाभिः splendid स्तुतिभिः with hymns त्वां Thee स्तुवन्ति praise.

21. Verily, into Thee enter these hosts of Devas ; some extol Thee in fear with joined palms ; "May it be well !" thus saying, bands of great Rishis and Siddhas praise Thee with splendid hymns.

रुद्रादित्या वसवो ये च साध्या
विश्वेऽश्विनौ मरुतश्चोष्मपाश्च ॥
गन्धर्वयक्षासुरसिद्धसङ्घा
वीक्षन्ते त्वां विस्मिताश्चैव सर्वे ॥२२॥

रुद्रादित्याः The Rudras and Âdityas वसवः Vasus ये those that च and साध्याः Sâdhyas विश्वे Vishva-Devas अश्विनौ the two Ashvins मरुतः Maruts च and उष्मपाः Ushmapâs च and गन्धर्वयक्षासुरसिद्धसङ्घाः hosts of Gandharvas, Yakshas, Asuras, and Siddhas सर्वे all विस्मिता quite astounded त्वां Thee च and वीक्षन्ते are looking at.

22. The Rudras, Âdityas, Vasus, Sâdhyas, Vishva-Devas, the two Ashvins, Maruts, Ushmapâs, and hosts of Gandharvas, Yakshas, Asuras, and Siddhas—all

these are looking at Thee, all quite
astounded.

[*Ushmapâs*—The Pitris.]

रूपं महत्ते बहुवक्त्रनेत्रं
महाबाहो बहुबाहूरुपादम् ॥
बहूदरं बहुदंष्ट्राकरालं
दृष्ट्वा लोकाः प्रव्यथितास्तथाहम् ॥२३॥

महाबाहो O mighty-armed बहुवक्त्रनेत्रं with many
mouths and eyes बहुबाहूरुपादम् with many arms, thighs,
and feet बहूदरं with many stomachs बहुदंष्ट्राकरालं fearful
with many tusks ते Thy महत् immeasurable रूपं Form
दृष्ट्वा having seen लोकाः worlds प्रव्यथिताः are terrified अहम् I
तथा so also.

23. Having seen Thy immeasurable
Form—with many mouths and eyes, O
mighty-armed, with many arms, thighs,
and feet, with many stomachs, and fearful
with many tusks—the worlds are terrified,
and so am I.

नभःस्पृशं दीप्तमनेकवर्णं
व्यात्ताननं दीप्तविशालनेत्रम् ॥
दृष्ट्वा हि त्वां प्रव्यथितान्तरात्मा
धृतिं न विन्दामि शमं च विष्णो ॥२४॥

विष्णो O Vishnu नभःस्पृशं touching the sky दीप्तं shining

अनेकवर्ण in many a colour व्यात्ताननं with mouths wide
open दीप्तविशालनेत्रम् with large fiery eyes त्वां Thee हि
indeed दृष्ट्वा on seeing प्रव्यथितान्तरात्मा terrified at heart
(अहं I) धृतिं patience, courage शमं peace च and न not
विन्दामि find.

24. On seeing Thee touching the sky,
shining in many a colour, with mouths
wide open, with large fiery eyes, I am terrified
at heart, and find no courage nor peace, O
Vishnu.

दंष्ट्राकरालानि च ते मुखानि

दृष्ट्वैव कालानलसन्निभानि ॥

दिशो न जाने न लभे च शर्म

प्रसीद देवेश जगन्निवास ॥२५॥

देवेश O Lord of Devas दंष्ट्राकरालानि fearful with tusks
कालानलसन्निभानि (blazing) like Pralaya-fires च and ते Thy
मुखानि mouths दृष्ट्वा एव having seen दिशः the four quarters
न जाने I know not शर्म peace न च nor लभे do (I) find
जगन्निवास O Abode of the universe प्रसीद have mercy.

25. Having seen Thy mouths, fearful
with tusks, (blazing) like Pralaya-fires, I
know not the four quarters, nor do I find peace;
have mercy, O Lord of the Devas, O Abode of
the universe.

[*Pralaya-fires :* The fires which consume the

worlds at the time of the final dissolution (Pralaya)
of the universe.

I know....quarters: I cannot distinguish the
East from the West, nor the North from the South.]

अमी च त्वां धृतराष्ट्रस्य पुत्राः
सर्वे सहैवावनिपालसङ्घैः ॥

भीष्मो द्रोणः सूतपुत्रस्तथासौ
सहास्मदीयैरपि योधमुख्यैः ॥२६॥

वक्त्राणि ते त्वरमाणा विशन्ति
दंष्ट्राकरालानि भयानकानि ॥

केचिद्विलग्ना दशनान्तरेषु
संदृश्यन्ते चूर्णितैरुत्तमाङ्गैः ॥२३॥

अवनिपालसङ्घैः Hosts of kings of the earth सहैव with
अमी these च and धृतराष्ट्रस्य of Dhritarâshtra सर्वे all पुत्राः
sons तथा and भीष्मः Bhishma द्रोणः Drona असौ this सूतपुत्रः
Sutaputra अस्मदीयैः (with those) of ours अपि also योधमुख्यैः
(with) warrior chiefs सह with त्वरमाणाः precipitately ते
Thy दंष्ट्राकरालानि terrible with tusks भयानकानि fearful to
behold वक्त्राणि mouths त्वां Thee विशन्ति enter केचित् some
चूर्णितैः crushed to powder उत्तमाङ्गैः with (their) heads
दशनान्तरेषु in the gaps betwixt the teeth विलग्नाः sticking
संदृश्यन्ते are found.

26-27. All these sons of Dhritarâshtra,
with hosts of monarchs, Bhishma, Drona,

and Sutaputra, with the warrior chiefs of ours, enter precipitately into Thy mouth, terrible with tusks and fearful to behold. Some are found sticking in the interstices of Thy teeth, with their heads crushed to powder.

[*Sutaputra*: The son of a charioteer, Karna.]

यथा नदीनां बहवोऽम्बुवेगाः
समुद्रमेवाभिमुखा द्रवन्ति ॥
तथा तवामी नरलोकवीरा
विशन्ति वक्त्राण्यभिविज्वलन्ति ॥२८॥

यथा As नदीनां of rivers बहवः many अम्बुवेगाः water-currents अभिमुखाः towards समुद्रम् the ocean एव verily द्रवन्ति flow तथा so अमी these नरलोकवीराः heroes in the world of men अभिविज्वलन्ति fiercely flaming तव Thy वक्त्राणि mouths विशन्ति enter.

28. Verily, as the many torrents of rivers flow towards the ocean, so do these heroes in the world of men enter Thy fiercely flaming mouths.

यथा प्रदीप्तं ज्वलनं पतङ्गा
विशन्ति नाशाय समृद्धवेगाः ॥
तथैव नाशाय विशन्ति लोका-
स्तवापि वक्त्राणि समृद्धवेगाः ॥२९॥

यथा As पतङ्गाः moths समृद्धवेगाः with precipitous speed नाशाय to perish प्रदीसं blazing ज्वलनं fire विशन्ति rush into तथा just so समृद्धवेगाः with precipitous speed लोकाः crea- tures अपि also नाशाय to perish एव only तव Thy वक्त्राणि mouths विशन्ति rush into.

29. As moths precipitately rush into a blazing fire only to perish, even so do these creatures also precipitately rush into Thy mouths only to perish.

[28 and 29.—The two similes vividly illustrate how the assembled warriors rush to destruction, out of their uncontrollable nature, with or without discrimination.]

लेलिह्यसे ग्रसमानः समन्ता-

ल्लोकान्समग्रान्वदनैर्ज्वलद्भिः ॥

तेजोभिरापूर्य जगत्समग्रं

भासस्तवोग्राः प्रतपन्ति विष्णो ॥३०॥

ज्वलद्भिः Flaming वदनैः with mouths समग्रान् all लोकान् the worlds ग्रसमानः swallowing समन्तात् on every side लेलिह्यसे Thou art licking Thy lips विष्णो O Vishnu तव Thy उग्राः fierce भासः rays तेजोभिः with radiance समग्रं the whole जगत् world आपूर्य filling प्रतपन्ति are burning.

30. Swallowing all the worlds on every side with Thy flaming mouths, Thou art licking Thy lips. Thy fierce rays, filling the

18

whole world with radiance, are burning,
O Vishnu !

[*Licking Thy lips :* consuming entirely, enjoying
it, as it were.]

आख्याहि मे को भवानुग्ररूपो

नमोऽस्तु ते देववर प्रसीद ॥

विज्ञातुमिच्छामि भवन्तमाद्यं

न हि प्रजानामि तव प्रवृत्तिम् ॥३१॥

उग्ररूप: Fierce in form भवान् Thou क: who (art) मे me
आख्याहि tell ते to Thee नम: salutation अस्तु be देववर O Deva
Supreme प्रसीद have mercy आद्य the Primeval One भवन्तम्
Thee विज्ञातुम् to know इच्छामि (I) desire हि indeed तव Thy
प्रवृत्ति purpose न not प्रजानामि (I) know.

31. Tell me who Thou art, fierce in
form. Salutation to Thee, O Deva Sup-
preme ; have mercy. I desire to know Thee,
O Primeval One. I know not indeed Thy
purpose.

श्रीभगवानुवाच ।

कालोऽस्मि लोकक्षयकृत्प्रवृद्धो

लोकान्समाहर्तुमिह प्रवृत्त: ॥

ऋतेऽपि त्वां न भविष्यन्ति सर्वे

येऽवस्थिता: प्रत्यनीकेषु योधा: ॥३२॥

श्रीभगवान् The Blessed Lord उवाच said :

लोक्षयकृत् World-destroying प्रवृद्ध: mighty काल: Time
अस्मि (I) am लोकान् world समाहर्तुम् to infold इह here प्रवृत्त:
engaged त्वां thee ऋते without अपि even प्रत्यनीकेषु in hostile
armies ये these योधा: warriors अवस्थिता: arrayed सर्वे न
none भविष्यन्ति shall live.

The Blessed Lord said :

32. I am the mighty world-destroying
Time, here made manifest for the purpose of
infolding the world.   Even without thee, none
of the warriors arrayed in the hostile armies
shall live.

[*Even without thee, etc.*—Even without thy instrumentality, i.e., even if, thou, O Arjuna, wouldst not
fight, the end of all these warriors is inevitable,
because I as the all-destroying Time have already
killed them ; so thy instrumentality in that work is
insignificant.]

तस्मात्त्वमुत्तिष्ठ यशो लभस्व

जित्वा शत्रून् भुङ्क्ष्व राज्यं समृद्धम् ॥

मयैवैते निहता: पूर्वमेव

निमित्तमात्रं भव सव्यसाचिन् ॥३३॥

तस्मात् Therefore त्वम् thou उत्तिष्ठ do arise यश: fame
लभस्व acquire शत्रून् enemies जित्वा after conquering समृद्धम्
the unrivalled राज्यं dominion भुङ्क्ष्व enjoy मया by Myself
एव verily एते they पूर्वम् already एव even निहता: have been

slain सव्यसाचिन् O Savyasâchi (त्वं thou) निमित्तमात्रं an
apparent cause भव be.

33.   Therefore do thou arise and acquire
fame.   Conquer the enemies, and enjoy
the   unrivalled   dominion.   Verily   by
Myself have they been already slain ; be
thou merely an apparent cause, O Savyasâchi
(Arjuna).

[*Be thou . . . cause.*—People will think thee
as the vanquisher of thy enemies, whom even the
Devas cannot kill, and thus thou wilt gain glory ; but
thou art only an instrument in My hand.

Savyasâchi—one who could shoot arrows even
with his left hand.]

द्रोणश्च भीष्मश्च जयद्रथश्च
कर्णं तथान्यानपि योधवीरान् ॥
मया हतांस्त्वं जहि मा व्यथिष्ठा
युध्यस्व जेतासि रणे सपत्नान् ॥३४॥

द्रोणं Drona च and भीष्मं Bhishma च and जयद्रथं
Jayadratha च and कर्णं Karna तथा as well as अन्यान् others
योधवीरान् brave warriors अपि already मया by Me हतान्
killed त्वं thou जहि do kill मा not व्यथिष्ठाः be distressed
with fear रणे in battle सपत्नान् the enemies जेतासि shalt
conquer युध्यस्व fight.

34.   Drona, Bhishma, Jayadratha, Karna,
as well as other brave warriors—these already

killed by Me, do thou kill. Be not distressed
with fear ; fight, and thou shalt conquer thy
enemies in battle.

[*Already killed by me :*—so do not be afraid of
incurring sin by killing Drona, Bhishma, and others
though they are venerable to you as your Guru,
grandsire, etc.

Distressed with fear—as regards success because
these great warriors are regarded as invincible.]

सञ्जय उवाच ।

एतच्छ्रुत्वा वचनं केशवस्य

कृताञ्जलिर्वेपमानः किरीटी ॥

नमस्कृत्वा भूय एवाह कृष्णं

सगद्गदं भीतभीतः प्रणम्य ॥३५॥

सञ्जयः Sanjaya उवाच said :
केशवस्य Of Keshava एतत् that वचनं speech श्रुत्वा having
heard वेपमानः trembling किरीटी the diademed one
कृताञ्जलिः with joined palms नमस्कृत्वा prostrating (himself)
भीतभीतः overwhelmed with fear प्रणम्य bowing down भूयः
एव again सगद्गदं in a choked voice कृष्णं to Krishna आह
addressed.

Sanjaya said :
35.   Having heard that speech of Keshava,
the diademed one (Arjuna), with joined
palms, trembling, prostrated himself, and
again addressed Krishna in a choked

voice, bowing down, overwhelmed with fear.

अर्जुन उवाच ।

स्थाने हृषीकेश तव प्रकीर्त्या

जगत् प्रहृष्यत्यनुरज्यते च ॥

रक्षांसि भीतानि दिशो द्रवन्ति

सर्वे नमस्यन्ति च सिद्धसङ्घाः ॥३६॥

अर्जुनः Arjuna उवाच said :

हृषीकेश O Hrishikesha तव Thy प्रकीर्त्या in praise जगत् the world प्रहृष्यति is delighted अनुरज्यते rejoices च and रक्षांसि Rākshasas भीतानि in fear दिशः to all quarters द्रवन्ति fly सर्वे all सिद्धसङ्घाः the hosts of Siddhas च and नमस्यन्ति bow (to Thee) स्थाने it is meet.

Arjuna said :

36. It is meet, O Hrishikesha, that the world is delighted and rejoices in Thy praise, that Râkshasas fly in fear to all quarters and all the hosts of Siddhas bow down to Thee in adoration.

कस्माच्च ते न नमेरन्महात्मन्

गरीयसे ब्रह्मणोऽप्यादिकर्त्रे ॥

अनन्त देवेश जगन्निवास

त्वमक्षरं सदसत्तत्परं यत् ॥३७॥

महात्मन् O Great-souled One अनन्त O Infinite देवेश O

Lord of the Devas जगन्निवास O Abode of the universe ब्रह्मणः of Brahmâ अपि even गरीयसे greater आदिकर्त्रे the Primal Cause च and ते to Thee कस्मात् why न not नमेरन् they should bow सत् the Being असत् the non-Being परं Beyond (them) यत् which अक्षरं the Imperishable तत् That च and त्वम् Thou (art).

37. And why should they not, O Great-souled One, bow to Thee, greater than, and the Primal Cause of even Brahmâ, O Infinite Being, O Lord of the Devas, O Abode of the universe? Thou art the Imperishable, the Being and the non-Being, (as well as) That which is Beyond (them).

[*Brahmâ* : the Hiranyagarbha.

The Being and the non-Being, etc.—The Sat (manifested) and the Asat (unmanifested), which form the Upâdhis (adjuncts) of the Akshara (Imperishable); as such He is spoken of as the Sat and the Asat. In reality, the Imperishable transcends the Sat and the Asat.]

त्वमादिदेवः पुरुषः पुराण-
स्त्वमस्य विश्वस्य परं निधानम् ॥
वेत्तांसि वेद्यं च परं च धाम
त्वया ततं विश्वमनन्तरूप ॥३८॥

अनन्तरूप O boundless Form त्वम् Thou आदिदेवः the

Primal Deva पुराण: the Ancient पुरुष: Purusha त्वम् Thou अस्य विश्वस्य of this universe परं the Supreme निधानम् Refuge वेत्ता the Knower च and वेद्य the One Thing to be known च and परं the Supreme धाम Goal असि (Thou) art त्वया by Thee विश्वम् the universe ततं is pervaded.

38. Thou art the Primal Deva, the Ancient Purusha ; Thou art the Supreme Refuge of this universe, Thou art the Knower, and the One Thing to be known ; Thou art the Supreme Goal. By Thee is the universe pervaded, O boundless Form.

वायुर्यमोऽग्निर्वरुणः शशाङ्कः

प्रजापतिस्त्वं प्रपितामहश्च ॥

नमो नमस्तेऽस्तु सहस्रकृत्वः

पुनश्च भूयोऽपि नमो नमस्ते ॥३९॥

त्वं Thou (art) वायुः Vâyu यमः Yama अग्निः Agni वरुणः Varuna शशाङ्कः the Moon प्रजापतिः Prajâpati प्रपितामहः the Great-Grandfather च and ते to Thee नमः नमः salutation, salutation अस्तु be सहस्रकृत्वः a thousand times पुनः again च and भूयः अपि and again ते to Thee नमः नमः salutation, salutation.

39. Thou art Vâyu, Yama, Agni, Varuna, the Moon, Prajâpati, and the Great-Grand-father. Salutation, salutation to Thee, a

thousand times, and again and again salutation,
salutation to Thee !

[*Vâyu ... Moon :* The gods of wind, death, fire,
waters, and the moon.

The Great-Grandfather—The creator even of
Brahmâ who is known as the Grandfather.]

नमः पुरस्तादथ पृष्ठतस्ते

नमोऽस्तु ते सर्वत एव सर्व ॥

अनन्तवीर्यामितविक्रमस्त्वं

सर्वं समाप्नोषि ततोऽसि सर्वः ॥४०॥

सर्व O All ते to Thee पुरस्तात् before अथ and पृष्ठतः
behind नमः saluation ते to Thee सर्वतः एव on every side
नमः salutation अस्तु be अनन्तवीर्यः infinite in power
अमितविक्रमः infinite in prowess त्वं Thou सर्व all समाप्नोषि
pervadest ततः wherefore सर्वः all असि Thou art.

40. Salutation to Thee before and behind, salutation to Thee on every side, O All !
Thou, infinite in power and infinite in
prowess, pervadest all ; wherefore Thou art
All.

[*On every side :* As Thou art present everywhere.

Pervadest : by thy One Self.]

सखेति मत्वा प्रसभं यदुक्तं

हे कृष्ण हे यादव हे सखेति ॥

अजानता महिमानं तवेदं
मया प्रमादात्प्रणयेन वापि ॥४१॥
यच्चावहासार्थमसत्कृतोऽसि
विहारशय्यासनभोजनेषु ॥
एकोऽथवाप्यच्युत तत्समक्षं
तत्क्षामये त्वामहमप्रमेयम् ॥४२॥

तव Thy महिमानं greatness इदं this च and अजानता
unconscious of मया by me प्रमादात् from carelessness
प्रणयेन due to love वा or अपि merely सखा friend इति as
मत्वा regarding हे कृष्ण O Krishna हे यादव O Yâdava हे सखे
O friend इति as प्रसभं presumptuously यत् whatever उक्तं
said अच्युत O Achyuta विहारशय्यासनभोजनेषु while walking,
reposing, sitting, or at meals एकः when alone अथवा or
अपि even तत्समक्षं in company अवहासार्थम् for the sake of
fun यत् in whatever way असत्कृतः disrespectfully treated
असि Thou art अहम् I अप्रमेयम् immeasurable त्वाम् Thee तत्
that क्षामये implore to forgive.

41-42. Whatever I have presumptuously
said from carelessness or love, addressing
Thee as "O Krishna, O Yâdava, O friend,"
regarding Thee merely as a friend, unconscious
of this Thy greatness—in whatever way
I may have been disrespectful to Thee
in fun, while walking, reposing, sitting,
or at meals, when alone (with Thee),
O Achyuta, or in company—I implore

Thee, Immeasurable One, to forgive all
this.

[*Love* : Confidence born of affection.
In company : in the presence of others.]

पितासि लोकस्य चराचरस्य

त्वमस्य पूज्यश्च गुरुर्गरीयान् ॥

न त्वत्समोऽस्त्यभ्यधिकः कुतोऽन्यो

लोकत्रयेऽप्यप्रतिमप्रभाव ॥४३॥

अप्रतिमप्रभाव Of power incomparable त्वं Thou चराचरस्य
moving and unmoving लोकस्य of the world पिता Father
असि (Thou) art पूज्यः the object of worship अस्य its च
and गुरुर्गरीयान् greater than the great लोकत्रये in the
three worlds अपि even त्वत्समः equal to Thee न not अस्ति
is अभ्यधिकः surpassing अन्यः any other कुतः whence.

43. Thou art the Father of the world,
moving and unmoving ; the object of its
worship ; greater than the great. None there
exists who is equal to Thee in he three worlds ;
who then can excel Thee, O Thou of power
incomparable ?

[*None . . . to Thee*—There cannot be two or
more Ishvaras; if there were, the world could not
get on as it does. When one Ishvara desires to create,
another may desire to destroy. Who knows that all
the different Ishvaras would be of one mind, as they
would all be independent of each other ?]

तस्मात्प्रणम्य प्रणिधाय कायं

प्रसादये त्वामहमीशमीड्यम् ॥

पितेव पुत्रस्य सखेव सख्युः

प्रियः प्रियायार्हसि देव सोढुम् ॥४४॥

देव O Deva तस्मात् so अहम् I कायं (my) body प्रणिधाय having prostrated प्रणम्य saluting ईड्यम् adorable ईशं Lord त्वाम् Thee प्रसादये crave forgiveness पुत्रस्य of the son पिता a father इव as सख्युः of a dear friend सखा a friend इव as प्रियायाः of one's love प्रियः a beloved one (इव as) सोढुम् to forgive अर्हसि Thou shouldst.

44. So prostrating my body in adoration, I crave Thy forgiveness, Lord adorable ! As a father forgiveth his son, friend a dear friend, a beloved one his love, even so shouldst Thou forgive me, O Deva.

अदृष्टपूर्वं हृषितोऽस्मि दृष्ट्वा

भयेन च प्रव्यथितं मनो मे ॥

तदेव मे दर्शय देव रूपं

प्रसीद देवेश जगन्निवास ॥४५॥

देव O Deva अदृष्टपूर्वं what was never seen before दृष्ट्वा having seen हृषितः overjoyed अस्मि I am भयेन with terror च yet मे my मनः mind प्रव्यथितं is distracted तत् that रूपं Form एव only मे me दर्शय show देवेश O Lord of Devas जगन्निवास O Abode of the universe प्रसीद have mercy.

45. Overjoyed am I to have seen what I
saw never before ; yet my mind is distracted
with terror. Show me, O Deva, only that
Form of Thine.   Have mercy, O Lord of Devas,
O Abode of the universe.

किरीटिनं गदिनं चक्रहस्त-
मिच्छामि त्वां द्रष्टुमहं तथैव ॥
तेनैव रूपेण चतुर्भुजेन
सहस्रबाहो भव विश्वमूर्ते ॥४६॥

अहं I तथा एव as before त्वां Thee किरीटिनं diademed
गदिनं bearing a mace चक्रहस्तम् with a discus in the hand
द्रष्टुम् to see इच्छामि I desire सहस्रबाहो O (Thou) of thousand
arms विश्वमूर्ते of universal Form तेनैव that same चतुर्भुजेन
four-armed रूपेण of Form भव be.

46. Diademed, bearing a mace and a
discus, Thee I desire to see as before. Assume
that same four-armed Form, O Thou of thousand arms, of universal Form.

श्रीभगवानुवाच ।
मया प्रसन्नेन तवार्जुनेदं
रूपं परं दर्शितमात्मयोगात् ॥
तेजोमयं विश्वमनन्तमाद्यं
यन्मे त्वदन्येन न दृष्टपूर्वम् ॥४७॥

श्रीभगवान् The Blessed Lord उवाच said :

अर्जुन O Arjuna प्रसन्नेन gracious मया by Me आत्मयोगात्
by My own Yoga power तव to thee इदं this तेजोमयं
resplendent अनन्तम् infinite आद्यं‍ primeval मे of Mine परं
supreme विश्वम् universal रूपं Form दर्शितम् has been shown
यत् which त्वदन्येन by any other than thyself न not दृष्टपूर्वं
hath been seen before.

The Blessed Lord said :

47. Graciously have I shown to thee,
O Arjuna, this Form supreme, by My own
Yoga power, this resplendent, primeval,
infinite, universal Form of Mine, which
hath not been seen before by anyone
else.

न वेदयज्ञाध्ययनैर्नं दानै-
        नं च क्रियाभिर्नं तपोभिरुग्रैः ॥
एवंरूपः शक्य अहं नृलोके
        द्रष्टुं त्वदन्येन कुरुप्रवीर ॥४८॥

कुरुप्रवीर O great hero of the Kurus न neither वेदयज्ञा-
ध्ययनैः by the study of the Veda and of Yajna न nor
दानैः by gifts न च nor क्रियाभिः by rituals न nor उग्रैः severe
तपोभिः by austerities एवंरूपः in such Form अहं I त्वदन्येन
by any other than thee नृलोके in the world of men द्रष्टुं
to be seen शक्यः possible.

48. Neither by the study of the Veda and
Yajna, nor by gifts, nor by rituals, nor by severe

austerities, am I in such Form seen, in the world of men, by any other than thee, O great hero of the Kurus.

मा ते व्यथा मा च विमूढभावो
दृष्ट्वा रूपं घोरमीदृङ्ममेदम् ॥
व्यपेतभीः प्रीतमनाः पुनस्त्वं
तदेव मे रूपमिदं प्रपश्य ॥४९॥

ईदृक् So घोरम् terrible मम of Mine इदं this रूपं Form दृष्ट्वा having seen मा not ते thine व्यथा fear विमूढभावः bewildered state (अस्तु be) मा च nor व्यपेतभीः with (thy) fears dispelled प्रीतमनाः with gladdened heart च and पुनः again त्वं thou मे of Mine तत् इदं this former रूपम् एव Form प्रपश्य see (now).

49.   Be not afraid nor bewildered, having beheld this Form of Mine, so terrific. With thy fears dispelled and with gladdened heart, now see again this former Form of Mine.

सञ्जय उवाच ।
इत्यर्जुनं वासुदेवस्तथोक्त्वा
स्वकं रूपं दर्शयामास भूयः ॥
आश्वासयामास च भीतमेनं
भूत्वा पुनः सौम्यवपुर्महात्मा ॥५०॥

सञ्जयः Sanjaya उवाच said :

वासुदेवः Vâsudeva अर्जुनं to Arjuna इति thus उक्त्वा having spoken भूयः again तथा so खकं His own रूपं Form दर्शयामास showed महात्मा the Great-souled One सौम्यवपुः of gentle Form भूत्वा being पुनः again भीतम् who was terrified एनं him आश्वासयामास pacified च and.

Sanjaya said :
50. So Vâsudeva, having thus spoken to Arjuna, showed again His own Form ; and the Great-souled One, assuming His gentle Form, pacified him who was terrified

अर्जुन उवाच ।

दृष्ट्वेदं मानुषं रूपं तव सौम्यं जनार्दन ॥

इदानीमस्मि संवृत्तः सचेताः प्रकृतिं गतः ॥५१॥

अर्जुनः Arjuna उवाच said :
जनार्दन O Janârdana तव Thy इदं this सौम्यं gentle मानुषं human रूपं Form दृष्ट्वा having seen इदानीम् now अहं I सचेताः with thoughts संवृत्तः composed अस्मि am प्रकृतिं (my) nature गतः restored.

Arjuna said :
51. Having seen this Thy gentle human Form, O Janârdana, my thoughts are now composed, and I am restored to my nature.

श्रीभगवानुवाच ।

सुदुर्दर्शमिदं रूपं दृष्टवानसि यन्मम ॥

देवा अप्यस्य रूपस्य नित्यं दर्शनकांक्षिणः ॥५२॥

श्रीभगवान् The Blessed Lord उवाच said :

मम Mine इदं this सुदुर्दर्शम् very hard to see यत् which
रूपं Form दृष्टवान् असि thou hast seen देवाः Devas अपि
even अस्य रूपस्य of this Form नित्यं ever दर्शनकांक्षिणः (are)
desirous to behold.

The Blessed Lord said :

52. Very hard indeed it is to see this
Form of Mine which thou hast seen. Even
the Devas ever long to behold this Form.

नाहं वेदैन तपसा न दानेन न चेज्यया ॥

शक्य एवंविधो द्रष्टुं दृष्टवानसि मां यथा ॥५३॥

यथा As मां Me दृष्टवान् असि (thou) hast seen एवंविधः
like this अहं I न neither वेदैः by the Vedas न nor तपसा
by austerity न nor दानेन by gifts न nor इज्यया by sacrifice
च and also द्रष्टुं to be seen शक्यः (am) possible.

53. Neither by the Vedas, nor by austerity, nor by gifts, nor by sacrifice can I be seen
as thou hast seen Me.

भक्त्या त्वनन्यया शक्य अहमेवंविधोऽर्जुन ॥

ज्ञातुं द्रष्टुंच तत्त्वेन प्रवेष्टुं च परन्तप ॥५४॥

19

परन्तप O scorcher of foes अर्जुन Arjuna अनन्यया single-minded भक्त्या by devotion तु but एवंविधः in this Form अहम् I तत्त्वेन in reality ज्ञातुं to be known द्रष्टुं to be seen च and प्रवेष्टुं to be entered into च and also शक्यः (am) possible.

54. But by single-minded devotion I may in this form, be known, O Arjuna, and seen in reality, and also entered into, O scorcher of foes.

[*Single-minded devotion :* That devotion which never seeks any other object but the Lord alone, and consequently cognises no other object but the Lord.]

मत्कर्मकृन्मत्परमो मद्भक्तः सङ्गवर्जितः ॥
निर्वैरः सर्वभूतेषु यः स मामेति पाण्डव ॥५५॥

पाण्डव O Pândava यः who मत्कर्मकृत् does work for Me मत्परमः has Me for his goal मद्भक्तः is devoted to Me सङ्गवर्जितः is freed from attachment सर्वभूतेषु towards all creatures निर्वैरः bearing no enmity च and सः he माम् Me एति enters into.

55. He who does work for Me alone and has Me for his goal, is devoted to Me, is freed from attachment, and bears enmity towards no creature—he entereth into Me, O Pândava.

[*Does work for me alone :*   Serves Me alone in all forms and manner of ways, with his whole heart and soul, and thus does not become attached to them.

He alone, whose devotion takes the forms as described in this Shloka, can know and realise Him as He is in reality, and subsequently become one with Him.]

इति विश्वरूपदर्शनं नाम एकादशोऽध्यायः ॥

The end of the eleventh chapter, designated, *The Vision of the Universal Form.*

॥ द्वादशोऽध्यायः ॥

TWELFTH CHAPTER

अर्जुन उवाच ।

एवं सततयुक्ता ये भक्तास्त्वां पर्युपासते ॥
ये चाप्यक्षरमव्यक्तं तेषां के योगवित्तमाः ॥१॥

अर्जुनः Arjuna उवाच said :

एवं Thus सततयुक्ताः ever-steadfast ये those भक्ताः devotees त्वां Thee पर्युपासते worship ये those च and अपि also अव्यक्तं the Unmanifested अक्षरं the Imperishable तेषां of them के which योगवित्तमाः better versed in Yoga.

Arjuna said :

1. Those devotees who, ever-steadfast, thus worship Thee, and those also who worship the Imperishable, the Unmanifested —which of them are better versed in Yoga ?

[*Thus :* as declared in the last verse of the preceding chapter (XI. 55).

The Unmanifested : Avyakta—i.e., That which is incomprehensible to the senses, as devoid of all Upâdhis.]

श्रीभगवानुवाच ।

मय्यावेश्य मनो ये मां नित्ययुक्ता उपासते ॥

श्रद्धया परयोपेतास्ते मे युक्ततमा मताः ॥२॥

श्रीभगवान् The Blessed Lord उवाच said :
मयि On Me मनः mind आवेश्य fixing नित्ययुक्ताः ever-
steadfast परया supreme श्रद्धया with Shraddhâ उपेताः endowed ये who मां Me उपासते worship ते those युक्ततमाः the
best versed in Yoga मे मताः are in My opinion.

The Blessed Lord said :

2. Those who, fixing their mind on Me,
worship Me, ever-steadfast, and endowed with
supreme Shraddhâ, they in My opinion are the
best versed in Yoga.

ये त्वक्षरमनिर्देश्यमव्यक्तं पर्युपासते ॥

सर्वत्रगमचिन्त्यं च कूटस्थमचलं ध्रुवम् ॥३॥

संनियम्येन्द्रियग्रामं सर्वत्र समबुद्धयः ॥

ते प्राप्नुवन्ति मामेव सर्वभूतहिते रताः ॥४॥

सर्वत्र Everywhere समबुद्धयः even-minded ये who तु but
च also इन्द्रियग्रामं the aggregate of the senses संनियम्य
having subdued अनिर्देश्यं the Indefinable अव्यक्तं the
Unmanifested सर्वत्रगं the Omnipresent अचिन्त्यं the Unthinkable कूटस्थं the Unchangeable अचलं the Immovable
ध्रुवं the Eternal अक्षरं the Unchangeable पर्युपासते worship

सर्वभूतहिते in the welfare of all beings रताः engaged ते they मां Myself एव only प्राप्नुवन्ति reach.

3-4. But those also, who worship the Imperishable, the Indefinable, the Unmanifested, the Omnipresent, the Unthinkable, the Unchangeable, the Immovable, the Eternal— having subdued all the senses, even-minded everywhere, engaged in the welfare of all beings—verily, they reach only Myself.

[*Worship*—Upâsanâ : is approaching the object of worship by way of meditating on it, in accordance with the teachings of the Shâstras and the Guru, and dwelling steadily in the current of that one thought, even as a thread of oil poured from one vessel to another.

Unchangeable—Kutastha : lit., remaining like a mass. He who is seated in Mâyâ as its Witness.]

क्लेशोऽधिकतरस्तेषामव्यक्तासक्तचेतसाम् ॥

अव्यक्ता हि गतिर्दुःखं देहवद्भिरवाप्यते ॥५॥

तेषां Of those अव्यक्तासक्तचेतसां whose mind is set on the Unmanifested अधिकतरः (is) greater क्लेशः trouble हि for देहवद्भिः for the embodied अव्यक्ता the Unmanifested गतिः the goal दुःखं with hard toil अवाप्यते is reached.

5. Greater is their trouble whose minds are set on the Unmanifested ; for the goal of the Unmanifested is very hard for the embodied to reach.

[*The embodied :* Those who are attached to, or have identified themselves with, their bodies.

No comparison between the worshippers of the conditioned and unconditioned Brahman is meant here—since by the context, both reach the same goal. The path of the conditioned Brahman is described as superior only because it is easier. The path of the unconditioned Brahman is harder, because of the necessity of having to abandon all attachment to the body, from the very beginning of the practice.]

ये तु सर्वाणि कर्माणि मयि संन्यस्य मत्परा: ॥

अनन्येनैव योगेन मां ध्यायन्त उपासते ॥६॥

तेषामहं समुद्धर्ता मृत्युसंसारसागरात् ॥

भवामि न चिरात्पार्थं मय्यावेशितचेतसाम् ॥७॥

ये Who तु but सर्वाणि all कर्माणि actions मयि in Me संन्यस्य resigning मत्परा: regarding Me as the Supreme Goal अनन्येन single-minded योगेन with Yoga एव verily मां Me ध्यायन्त: meditating उपासते worship पार्थं O son of Prithâ अहं I मयि on Me आवेशितचेतसाम् of those whose mind is set तेषाम् for them मृत्युसंसारसागरात् out of the ocean of the mortal Samsâra न चिरात् ere long समुद्धर्ता the Saviour भवामि I become.

6-7. But those who worship Me, resigning all actions in Me, regarding Me as the Supreme Goal, meditating on Me with single-minded Yoga—to these whose mind is

set on Me, verily, I become ere long, O son
of Prithâ, the Saviour out of the ocean of the
mortal Samsâra.

[*Mortal Samsâra :* The round of birth and death.]

मय्येव मन आधत्स्व मयि बुद्धिं निवेशय ॥
निवसिष्यसि मय्येव अत ऊर्ध्वं न संशयः ॥८॥

मयि On Me एव only मनः (thy) mind आधत्स्व fix मयि
in Me बुद्धिं (thy) intellect निवेशय place अतः ऊर्ध्वं hereafter
मयि in Me एव alone निवसिष्यसि thou shalt live न no संशयः
doubt.

8. Fix thy mind on Me only, place thy
intellect in Me : (then) thou shalt no doubt
live in Me hereafter.

[*Mind*—Manas : purpose and thought.

Intellect : the faculty which resolves and determines.

Live in Me : as My Self.]

अथ चित्तं समाधातुं न शक्नोषि मयि स्थिरम् ॥
अभ्यासयोगेन ततो मामिच्छाप्तुं धनञ्जय ॥९॥

धनञ्जय O Dhananjaya अथ if मयि on Me चित्तं (thy)
mind स्थिरं steadily समाधातुं to fix न शक्नोषि (thou) art
unable ततः then अभ्यासयोगेन by Abhyâsa-Yoga माम् Me
आप्तुं to reach इच्छ do (thou) seek.

9. If thou art unable to fix thy mind

steadily on Me, then by Abhyâsa-Yoga do thou
seek to reach Me, O Dhananjaya.

[*Abhyâsa-Yoga* : the practice of repeatedly with-
drawing the mind from the objects to which it
wanders, and trying to fix it on one thing.]

अभ्यासेऽप्यसमर्थोऽसि मत्कर्मपरमो भव ॥
मदर्थमपि कर्माणि कुर्वन्सिद्धिमवाप्स्यसि ॥१०॥

अभ्यासे (In) Abhyâsa अपि also असमर्थः unable to
practise असि (if) thou art मत्कर्मपरमः intent on doing
actions for My sake भव be thou मदर्थम् for My sake कर्माणि
actions कुर्वन् by doing अपि even सिद्धिम् perfection अवाप्स्यसि
thou shalt attain.

10. If also thou art unable to practise
Abhyâsa, be thou intent on doing actions for
My sake. Even by doing actions for My sake,
thou shalt attain perfection.

अथैतदप्यसक्तोऽसि कर्तुं मद्योगमाश्रितः ॥
सर्वकर्मफलत्यागं ततः कुरु यतात्मवान् ॥११॥

अथ If अपि even एतत् this कर्तुं to do अशक्तः unable असि
thou art ततः then मद्योगम् refuge in Me आश्रितः taking
यतात्मवान् self-controlled सर्वकर्मफलत्यागं the renunciation of
the fruit of all action कुरु do.

11. If thou art unable to do even this,

then taking refuge in Me, abandon the fruit of
all action, self-controlled.

[In the preceding Shlokas—first, the concentration of the mind on the Lord is enjoined ; in case
of inability to do that, Abhyasa-Yoga is advised ; if
one finds that to be too hard, the performance of
actions for the sake of the Lord alone, has been
taught. Those who cannot do this even, who want
to do things impelled by personal or other desires,
are directed to give up the fruits of those actions
to the Lord—i.e., not to anticipate, dwell, or build
on, or care for, the results, knowing them to be dependent upon the Lord. Those who cannot control
their desire for work are taught to practise indifference
to the effects thereof.]

श्रेयो हि ज्ञानमभ्यासात् ज्ञानाद्ध्यानं विशिष्यते ॥
ध्यानात्कर्मफलत्यागस्त्यागाच्छान्तिरनन्तरम् ॥१२॥

अभ्यासात् Than (blind) Abhyâsa ज्ञानम् knowledge हि
indeed श्रेयः better ज्ञानात् than (mere) knowledge ध्यानं
meditation (with knowledge) विशिष्यते is more esteemed
ध्यानात् than meditation कर्मफलत्यागः the renunciation of
the fruit of action त्यागात् from renunciation अनन्तरं
immediately शान्तिः peace (भवति follows).

12. Better indeed is knowledge than
(blind) Abhyâsa ; meditation (with knowledge)
is more esteemed than (mere) knowledge ;
than meditation the renunciation of the fruit

of action ; peace immediately follows renunciation.

[Renunciation of the fruit of all action, as a means to the attainment of Bliss, is merely extolled here by the declaration of the superiority of one over another. Wherefore ? Because it constitutes a common factor which immediately precedes Peace, both in the case of the man of wisdom who is steadily engaged in devout contemplation, and also of the ignorant one who, unable to tread the paths taught before, takes it up as the easiest means of Bliss.]

अद्वेष्टा सर्वभूतानां मैत्रः करुण एव च ॥

निर्ममो निरहङ्कारः समदुःखसुखः क्षमी ॥१३॥

सन्तुष्टः सततं योगी यतात्मा दृढनिश्चयः ॥

मय्यर्पितमनोबुद्धिर्यो मद्भक्तः स मे प्रियः ॥१४॥

सर्वभूतानां Of (to) all creatures अद्वेष्टा free from hatred or malevolence मैत्रः friendly करुणः compassionate च and एव even निर्ममः who is free from the idea of "mineness" निरहङ्कारः free from egoism, from the notion of "I" समदुःखसुखः even-minded in pain and pleasure क्षम forbearing सततं ever सन्तुष्टः content योगी steady in contemplation यतात्मा self-controlled दृढनिश्चयः possessed of firm conviction मयि in Me अर्पितमनोबुद्धिः with mind and intellect fixed यः who मद्भक्तः devoted to Me सः he मे to Me प्रियः (is) dear.

13-14.   He who hates no creature, and
is friendly and compassionate towards all,
who is free from the feelings of "I and mine",
even-minded in pain and pleasure, forbearing, ever content, steady in meditation,
self-controlled, and possessed of firm conviction, with mind and intellect fixed on
Me—he who is thus devoted to Me, is dear to
Me.

यस्मान्नोद्विजते लोको लोकान्नोद्विजते च यः ॥
हर्षामर्षभयोद्वेगैर्मुक्तो यः स च मे प्रियः ॥१५॥

यस्मात् From whom लोकः the world न not उद्विजते
is agitated, afflicted यः who च and लोकात् from the
world न not उद्विजते is agitated यः who च and हर्षामर्षभयो-
द्वेगैः by (from) joy, envy, fear, and anxiety मुक्तः freed
सः he मे to Me प्रियः (is) dear.

15.   He by whom the world is not agitated and who cannot be agitated by the world,
who is freed from joy, envy, fear, and anxiety
—he is dear to Me.

अनपेक्षः शुचिर्दक्ष उदासीनो गतव्यथः ॥
सर्वारम्भपरित्यागी यो मद्भक्तः स मे प्रियः ॥१६॥

अनपेक्षः (who is) free from dependence शुचिः who is
pure दक्षः prompt उदासीनः unconcerned गतव्यथः untroubled सर्वारम्भपरित्यागी renouncing every undertaking
यः who मद्भक्तः devoted to Me सः he मे to Me प्रियः (is) dear.

16. He who is free from dependence, who is pure, prompt, unconcerned, untroubled, renouncing every undertaking— he who is thus devoted to Me, is dear to Me.

[*Free from dependence :* on the body, the senses, the sense-objects, and their mutual connections.

Prompt : able to decide rightly and immediately in matters demanding prompt action.

Every undertaking : calculated to secure objects of desire, whether of this world or of the next.]

यो न हृष्यति न द्वेष्टि न शोचति न कांक्षति ॥
शुभाशुभपरित्यागी भक्तिमान् यः स मे प्रियः ॥१७॥

यः Who न neither हृष्यति rejoices न nor द्वेष्टि hates न nor शोचति grieves न nor कांक्षति desires शुभाशुभपरित्यागी renouncing good and evil यः who भक्तिमान् full of devotion सः he मे to Me प्रियः (is) dear.

17. He who neither rejoices, nor hates, nor grieves, nor desires, renouncing good and evil, full of devotion, he is dear to Me.

[*Hates :* Frets at receiving anything undesirable.

Grieves : at parting with a beloved object.
Desires : the unattained.]

समः शत्रौ च मित्रे च तथा मानापमानयोः ॥

शीतोष्णसुखदुःखेषु समः सङ्गविवर्जितः ॥१८॥

तुल्यनिन्दास्तुतिर्मौनी सन्तुष्टो येनकेनचित् ॥

अनिकेतः स्थिरमतिर्भक्तिमान्मे प्रियो नरः ॥१९॥

शत्रौ To foe मित्रे to friend च and तथा also च and
मानापमानयोः in honour and dishonour समः (who is) the
same शीतोष्णसुखदुःखेषु in cold and heat, in pleasure and
pain समः the same सङ्गविवर्जितः free from attachment
तुल्यनिन्दास्तुतिः to whom censure and praise are equal मौनी
who is silent येनकेनचित् with anything सन्तुष्टः content
अनिकेतः homeless स्थिरमतिः steady-minded भक्तिमान् full of
devotion नरः (that) man मे to Me प्रियः (is) dear.

18-19.   He who is the same to friend and
foe, and also in honour and dishonour ; who
is the same in heat and cold, and in pleasure
and pain ; who is free from attachment ; to
whom censure and praise are equal ; who is
silent, content with anything, homeless, steady-
minded, full of devotion—that man is dear to
Me.

[*Content with anything, homeless :*   content with
the bare means of bodily sustenance.   Says the
Mahâbhârata :

येनकेनचिदाच्छन्नो येनकेनचिदाशितः ।

यत्र क्वचनशायी स्यात्तन्देवा ब्राह्मणं विदुः ॥

"Who is clad with anything, who is fed on any food, who lies down anywhere, him the gods call a Brâhmana."—*Shânti-Parva.*]

ये तु धर्म्यामृतमिदं यथोक्तं पर्युपासते ॥

श्रद्दधाना मत्परमा भक्तास्तेऽतीव मे प्रियाः ॥२०॥

ये Who तु indeed यथोक्तं as declared (above) इदं this धर्म्यामृतम् Immortal Dharma पर्युपासते follow श्रद्दधानाः endued with Shraddhâ मत्परमाः regarding Me as the Supreme Goal भक्ताः devoted ते they अतीव exceedingly मे to Me प्रियाः (are) dear.

20. And they who follow this Immortal Dharma, as described above, endued with Shraddhâ, regarding Me as the Supreme Goal, and devoted—they are exceedingly dear to Me.

इति भक्तियोगो नाम द्वादशोऽध्यायः ॥

The end of the twelfth chapter, designated, *The Way of Devotion.*

|| त्रयोदशोऽध्यायः ||

THIRTEENTH CHAPTER

अर्जुन उवाच।

प्रकृतिं पुरुषं चैव क्षेत्रं क्षेत्रज्ञमेव च ॥
एतद्वेदितुमिच्छामि ज्ञानं ज्ञेयं च केशव ॥

अर्जुनः Arjuna उवाच said :
केशव O Keshava प्रकृतिं the Prakriti पुरुषं Purusha
च and एव also क्षेत्रं Kshetra क्षेत्रज्ञम् the knower of the
Kshetra च and एव also ज्ञानं knowledge ज्ञेयं what ought
to be known च and एतत् this वेदितुम् to know इच्छामि (I)
desire.

Arjuna said :

Prakriti and Purusha, also the Kshetra and
the knower of the Kshetra, knowledge, and that
which ought to be known—these, O Keshava,
I desire to learn.

[This verse is omitted in many editions.]

श्रीभगवानुवाच।

इदं शरीरं कौन्तेय क्षेत्रमित्यभिधीयते ॥
एतद्यो वेत्ति तं प्राहुः क्षेत्रज्ञ इति तद्विदः ॥१॥

श्रीभगवान् The Blessed Lord उवाच said :

कौन्तेय O son of Kunti इदं this शरीरं body क्षेत्रम्
Kshetra इति Thus अभिधीयते is called यः who एतत् this वेत्ति
knows तद्विदः who know of them तं him क्षेत्रज्ञः the
knower of the Kshetra इति as प्राहुः they call.

The Blessed Lord said :

1. This body, O son of Kunti, is called
Kshetra, and he who knows it is called Kshe-
trajna by those who know of them (Kshetra and
Kshetrajna).

[*Kshetra :* Literally, field ; the body is so
called because the fruits of action are reaped in it as
in a field.]

क्षेत्रज्ञं चापि मां विद्धि सर्वक्षेत्रेषु भारत ॥
क्षेत्रक्षेत्रज्ञयोर्ज्ञानं यत्तज्ज्ञानं मतं मम ॥२॥

भारत O descendant of Bharata सर्वक्षेत्रेषु in all Kshetras अपि also मां Me च and क्षेत्रज्ञं the Kshetrajna विद्धि
do thou know क्षेत्रक्षेत्रज्ञयोः of Kshetra and Kshetrajna
यत् which ज्ञानं knowledge तत् that ज्ञानं knowledge मम
by Me मतं is considered to be.

2. Me do thou also know, O descendant
of Bharata, to be Kshetrajna in all
Kshetras. The knowledge of Kshetra and
Kshetrajna is considered by Me to be *the*
knowledge.

तत्क्षेत्रं यच्च याहक् च यद्विकारि यतश्च यत् ॥
स च यो यत्प्रभावश्च तत्समासेन मे शृणु ॥३॥

तत् The क्षेत्रं Kshetra यत् what (is) च and याहक् what
its properties च and यद्विकारि what its modifications
यतः from what (causes) च and यत् what (effects arise)
सः he (is) च and यः who यत्प्रभावः what its powers च and
तत् that समासेन in brief मे from Me शृणु hear.

3. What the Kshetra is, what its properties are, what are its modifications, what effects
arise from what causes, and also who He is and
what His powers are, that hear from Me in
brief.

[*That* : the true nature of Kshetra and Kshetrajna in all these specific aspects.]

ऋषिभिर्बहुधा गीतं छन्दोभिर्विविधैः पृथक् ॥
ब्रह्मसूत्रपदैश्चैव हेतुमद्भिर्विनिश्चितैः ॥४॥

ऋषिभिः By Rishis विविधैः various छन्दोभिः in chants
पृथक् distinctive बहुधा in many ways गीतं has been sung
विनिश्चितैः convincing हेतुमद्भिः full of reasoning ब्रह्मसूत्रपदै
in phrases indicative of Brahman च and एव also.

4. (This truth) has been sung by Rishi
in many ways, in various distinctive chants, ir
passages indicative of Brahman, full of reason
ing, and convincing.

महाभूतान्यहङ्कारो बुद्धिरव्यक्तमेव च ॥

इन्द्रियाणि दशैकं च पञ्च चेन्द्रियगोचराः ॥५॥

इच्छा द्वेषः सुखं दुःखं सङ्घातश्चेतना धृतिः ॥

एतत्क्षेत्रं समासेन सविकारमुदाहृतम् ॥६॥

महाभूतानि The great Elements अहङ्कारः Egoism बुद्धिः Intellect अव्यक्तम् the Unmanifested (Mulâ Prakriti) च and एव also दश ten इन्द्रियाणि the senses एकं the one (mind) च and पञ्च five इन्द्रियगोचराः objects of the senses च and इच्छा desire द्वेषः hatred सुखं pleasure दुःखं pain सङ्घातः the aggregate, the body चेतना intelligence धृतिः fortitude एतत् this सविकारम् with its modifications क्षेत्रं Kshetra समासेन briefly उदाहृतं has been described.

5-6. The great Elements, Egoism, Intellect, as also the Unmanifested (Mulâ Prakriti), the ten senses and the one (mind), and the five objects of the senses ; desire, hatred, pleasure, pain, the aggregate, intelligence, fortitude—the Kshetra has been thus briefly described with its modifications.

[The Sânkhyas speak of those mentioned in the fifth Shloka as the twenty-four Tattvas or Principles.

The great Elements—Mahâbhutas : pervade all Vikâras, modifications of matter.

Aggregate—Samghâta : combination of the body and the senses.

Desire and other qualities which the Vaisheshikas speak of as inherent attributes of the Âtman, are spoken of in the sixth Shloka as merely the attributes of Kshetra, and not the attributes of Kshetrajna. Desire and other qualities mentioned here, stand for all the qualities of the Antah-Karana or inner sense—as mere mental states. Each of them, being knowable, is Kshetra.

The Kshetra, of which the various modifications in their totality are spoken of as "this body" in the first Shloka, has been here dwelt upon in all its different forms, from "The great Elements" to "fortitude".]

अमानित्वमदम्भित्वमहिंसा क्षान्तिरार्जवम् ॥
आचार्योपासनं शौचं स्थैर्यमात्मविनिग्रहः ॥७॥

अमानित्वम् Humility अदम्भित्वम् unpretentiousness अहिंसा non-injury क्षान्तिः forbearance आर्जवम् uprightness आचार्यो-पासनं service to the teacher शौचं purity स्थैर्यम् steadiness आत्मविनिग्रहः self-control.

7. Humility, unpretentiousness, non-injury, forbearance, uprightness, service to the teacher, purity, steadiness, self-control ;

[*Âchârya* : one who teaches the means of attaining Moksha.

Purity : external and internal. The former consists in washing away the dirt from the body by means of water, etc.; and the latter—the purity of mind—consists in the removal from it of the dirt of attachment and other passions, by the recognition of evil in all objects of the senses.]

इन्द्रियार्थेषु वैराग्यमनहङ्कार एव च ॥
जन्ममृत्युजराव्याधिदुःखदोषानुदर्शनम् ॥८॥

इन्द्रियार्थेषु Of sense-objects वैराग्यम् renunciation अनहङ्कारः absence of egoism एव also च and जन्ममृत्युजराव्याधिदुःखदोषानु- दर्शनम् reflection on the evils of birth, death, old age, sickness, and pain.

8. The renunciation of sense-objects, and also absence of egoism ; reflection on the evils of birth, death, old age, sickness, and pain ;

[*Sense-objects :* such as sound, touch, etc., of pleasures seen or unseen.

Pain : whether Âdhyâtmika, i.e., arising in one's own person; or Âdhibhautika, i.e., produced by external agents, or Âdhidaivika, i.e., produced by supernatural beings.

Reflection...pain : or the passage may be inter- preted as—reflection on the evils and miseries of birth, death, old age, and sickness. Birth, etc., are all miseries, not that they are miseries in them- selves, but because they produce misery. From such reflection arises indifference to sense- pleasures, and the senses turn towards the Innermost Self for knowledge.]

असक्तिरनभिष्वङ्गः पुत्रदारगृहादिषु ॥

नित्यं च समचित्तत्वमिष्टानिष्टोपपत्तिषु ॥६॥

असक्तिः Non-attachment पुत्रदारगृहादिषु with son, wife, home, and the rest   अनभिष्वङ्गः non-identification of self इष्टानिष्टोपपत्तिषु in the occurrence of the desirable and the undesirable नित्यं constant समचित्तत्वं even-mindedness च and.

9.   Non-attachment, non-identification of self with son, wife, home, and the rest, and constant even-mindedness in the occurrence of the desirable and the undesirable ;

[*Identification of self:* as in the case of a person who feels happy or miserable when another to whom he is attached, is happy or miserable, and who feels himself alive or dead when his beloved one is alive or dead.]

मयि चानन्ययोगेन भक्तिरव्यभिचारिणी ॥

विविक्तदेशसेवित्वमरतिर्जनसंसदि ॥१०॥

मयि To Me अनन्ययोगेन by the Yoga of non-separation अव्यभिचारिणी unswerving भक्तिः devotion च and विविक्तदेश-सेवित्वम् resort to sequestered places जनसंसदि for the society of men अरतिः distaste ;

10.   Unswerving devotion to Me by the Yoga of non-separation, resort to sequestered places, distaste for the society of men ;

[*Resort...places :* favourable to equanimity of mind, so that uninterrupted meditation on the Self, and the like, may be possible.

Society of men : of the unenlightened and un-disciplined people, not of the pure and holy, because association with the latter leads to Jnâna.]

अध्यात्मज्ञाननित्यत्वं तत्त्वज्ञानार्थदर्शनम् ॥

एतज्ज्ञानमिति प्रोक्तमज्ञानं यदतोऽन्यथा ॥११॥

अध्यात्मज्ञाननित्यत्वं Constant application to spiritual knowledge   तत्त्वज्ञानार्थदर्शनम् understanding of the end of true knowledge एतत् this ज्ञानम् knowledge इति thus प्रोक्तम् is declared यत् what अतः to it अन्यथा opposed अज्ञानं ignorance.

11. Constant application to spiritual knowledge, understanding of the end of true knowledge : this is declared to be knowledge, and what is opposed to it is ignorance.

[These attributes—from "Humility" to "Under-standing of the end of true knowledge"—are declared to be knowledge, because they are the means con-ducive to knowledge.]

ज्ञेयं यत्तत्प्रवक्ष्यामि यज्ज्ञात्वाऽमृतमश्नुते ॥

अनादिमत्परं ब्रह्म न सत्तन्नासदुच्यते ॥१२॥

यत् Which ज्ञेयं has to be known तत् that प्रवक्ष्यामि I shall describe यत् which ज्ञात्वा knowing अमृतम् Immortality अश्नुते (one) attains to तत् it अनादिमत् the beginningless परम्

Supreme ब्रह्म Brahman न neither सत् being न nor असत् non-being उच्यते is called.

12. I shall describe that which has to be known, knowing which one attains to immortality, the beginningless Supreme Brahman. It is called neither being nor non-being.

सर्वतः पाणिपादं तत्सर्वतोक्षिशिरोमुखम् ॥
सर्वतःश्रुतिमल्लोके सर्वमावृत्य तिष्ठति ॥१३॥

सर्वतः Everywhere पाणिपादं with hands and feet सर्वतः everywhere अक्षिशिरोमुखम् with eyes, heads, and mouths सर्वतः everywhere श्रुतिमत् with ears तत् That लोके in the universe सर्वम् all आवृत्य pervading तिष्ठति exists.

13. With hands and feet everywhere, with eyes, heads, and mouths everywhere, with ears everywhere in the universe—That exists pervading all.

सर्वेन्द्रियगुणाभासं सर्वेन्द्रियविवर्जितम् ॥
असक्तं सर्वभृच्चैव निर्गुणं गुणभोक्तृ च ॥१४॥

सर्वेन्द्रियगुणाभासं Shining by the functions of all the senses सर्वेन्द्रियविवर्जितम् (yet) without the senses असक्तं devoid of all attachment or relativity, Absolute सर्वभृत् sustaining all चैव yet निर्गुणं devoid of Gunas गुणभोक्तृ experiencer of the Gunas च and.

14. Shining by the functions of all the

senses, yet without the senses ; Absolute, yet sustaining all ; devoid of Gunas, yet their experiencer.

बहिरन्तश्च भूतानामचरं चरमेव च ॥

सूक्ष्मत्वात्तदविज्ञेयं दूरस्थं चान्तिके च तत् ॥१५॥

भूतानाम् (Of all) beings बहि: without च and अन्त: within अचरं the unmoving चरम् the moving एव also च and सूक्ष्मत्वात् because of its subtlety तत् It अविज्ञेयं (is) incomprehensible दूरस्थं is far च and अन्तिके near च and तत् It.

15. Without and within (all) beings ; the unmoving and also the moving ; because of Its subtlety incomprehensible ; It is far and near.

[*Incomprehensible :* to the unillumined, though knowable in Itself.

Far : when unknown.

Near : to the illumined, because It is their own Self.]

अविभक्तं च भूतेषु विभक्तमिव च स्थितम् ॥

भूतभर्तृ च तज्ज्ञेयं ग्रसिष्णु प्रभविष्णु च ॥१६॥

भूतेषु In beings च and अविभक्तं impartible विभक्तम् divided च yet इव as if स्थितम् existing भूतभर्तृ as sustaining beings च and ग्रसिष्णु devouring प्रभविष्णु as generating च as well तत् It ज्ञेयं is to be known.

16. Impartible, yet It exists as if divided in beings :   It is to be known as sustain-

ing beings ; and devouring, as well as generating (them).

[*Devouring :* at the time of Pralaya.

Generating : at the time of Utpatti or origin of
the universe.]

ज्योतिषामपि तज्ज्योतिस्तमसः परमुच्यते ॥

ज्ञानं ज्ञेयं ज्ञानगम्यं हृदि सर्वस्य धिष्ठितम् ॥१७॥

ज्योतिषां Of lights अपि even ज्योतिः Light तमसः darkness
परं beyond तत् It उच्यते is said (to be) ज्ञानं Knowledge
ज्ञेयं the One Thing to be known ज्ञानगम्यं the Goal of
knowledge सर्वस्य of all हृदि in the heart धिष्ठितं dwelling.

17.   The Light even of lights, It is said
to be beyond darkness ; Knowledge, and the
One Thing to be known, the Goal of knowledge, dwelling in the hearts of all.

[*The Light even of lights :* The illuminator of
all illuminating things, such as the sun, etc., and
Buddhi, etc.   Indeed, these latter shine only when
illuminated by the Light of the consciousness of the
Self.]

इति क्षेत्रं तथा ज्ञानं ज्ञेयं चोक्तं समासतः ॥

मद्भक्त एतद्विज्ञाय मद्भावायोपपद्यते ॥१८॥

इति Thus क्षेत्रं Kshetra तथा and ज्ञानं knowledge ज्ञेयं
that which has to be known च and समासतः briefly उक्तं
have been stated मद्भक्तः My devotee एतत् this विज्ञाय
knowing मद्भावाय for My state उपपद्यते is fitted.

18. Thus Kshetra, knowledge, and that which has to be known, have been briefly stated. Knowing this, My devotee is fitted for My state.

प्रकृतिं पुरुषं चैव विद्ध्यनादी उभावपि ॥

विकारांश्च गुणांश्चैव विद्धि प्रकृतिसम्भवान् ॥१६॥

प्रकृतिं Prakriti पुरुषं Purusha च and एव indeed उभौ both अपि also अनादी beginningless विद्धि know (thou) विकारान् (all) modifications च and गुणान् Gunas च and एव also प्रकृतिसम्भवान् born of Prakriti विद्धि know (thou).

19. Know thou that Prakriti and Purusha are both beginningless ; and know thou also that all modifications and Gunas are born of Prakriti.

[*Modifications*—Vikâras: From Buddhi down to the physical body.]

कार्यकरणकर्तृत्वे हेतुः प्रकृतिरुच्यते ॥

पुरुषः सुखदुःखानां भोक्तृत्वे हेतुरुच्यते ॥२०॥

कार्यकरणकर्तृत्वे In the production of the body and the senses प्रकृतिः Prakriti हेतुः the cause उच्यते is said (to be) पुरुषः Purusha सुखदुःखानां of pleasure and pain भोक्तृत्वे in the experience हेतुः the cause उच्यते is said (to be).

20. In the production of the body and the senses, Prakriti is said to be the cause ; in the experience of pleasure and pain, Purusha is said to be the cause.

[*Senses :* five organs of perception, five of action, mind, intellect, and egoism.

Purusha : the Jiva is meant here.

Kârya : The effect, the physical body. Karana : Senses. Some read Kârana, and explain "Kârya and Kârana" as "effect and cause".]

पुरुषः प्रकृतिस्थो हि भुङ्क्ते प्रकृतिजान्गुणान् ॥

कारणं गुणसङ्गोऽस्य सदसद्योनिजन्मसु ॥२१॥

हि Indeed पुरुषः Purusha प्रकृतिस्थः seated in Prakriti प्रकृतिजान् born of Prakriti गुणान् the Gunas भुङ्क्ते experiences अस्य its सदसद्योनिजन्मसु of birth in good and evil wombs गुणसङ्गः attachment to the Gunas कारणं the reason.

21. Purusha seated in Prakriti, experiences the Gunas born of Prakriti ; the reason of his birth in good and evil wombs is his attachment to the Gunas.

[*Seated in :* identifying himself with.

Gunas : manifesting themselves as pleasure, pain, and delusion.]

उपद्रष्टानुमन्ता च भर्ता भोक्ता महेश्वरः ॥

परमात्मेति चाप्युक्तो देहेऽस्मिन्पुरुषः परः ॥२२॥

अस्मिन् देहे In this body पुरुषः Purusha परः Supreme उपद्रष्टा the Looker-on अनुमन्ता the Permitter च and भर्ता Supporter भोक्ता the Experiencer महेश्वरः the Great Lord परमात्मा the Highest Self च and इति thus अपि also उक्तः is called.

22. And the Supreme Purusha in this body is also called the Looker-on, the Permitter, the Supporter, the Experiencer, the Great Lord, and the Highest Self.

[*Looker-on, the Permitter :* He himself does not participate in the activities of the bodily organs, the mind and the Buddhi, being quite apart from them, yet appears to be so engaged. And being a looker-on, He never stands in the way of the activities of Prakriti as manifested in the body. Indeed, all the consciousness or intelligence that manifests itself in the activities of life is but the reflection of the All-pervading, Absolute, and Perfect Intelligence—the Supreme Spirit.]

य एवं वेत्ति पुरुषं प्रकृतिं च गुणैः सह ॥

सर्वथा वर्तमानोऽपि न स भूयोऽभिजायते ॥२३॥

य: Who एवं thus पुरुषं the Purusha गुणैः सह with Gunas प्रकृतिं Prakriti च and वेत्ति knows सः he सर्वथा in whatever way वर्तमानः living अपि even भूयः again न not अभिजायते is born.

23. He who thus knows the Purusha and Prakriti together with the Gunas, whatever his life, is not born again.

[*Whatever his life, etc.*: Whether he be engaged in prescribed or forbidden acts, he is not born again. For, the acts, the seeds of rebirth, of a knower of

Truth are burnt by the fire of knowledge, and thus
cannot be effective causes to bring about births. In
his case they are mere semblances of Karma ; a burnt
cloth, for instance, cannot serve the purposes of a
cloth.]

ध्यानेनात्मनि पश्यन्ति केचिदात्मानमात्मना ॥
अन्ये सांख्येन योगेन कर्मयोगेन चापरे ॥२४॥

केचित् Some ध्यानेन by meditation आत्मनि in their own
intelligence आत्मना by the purified heart आत्मानं the
Self पश्यन्ति behold अन्ये others सांख्येन योगेन by the path of
knowledge अपरे others च again कर्मयोगेन by Karma-
Yoga.

24. Some by meditation behold the Self
in their own intelligence by the purified heart,
others by the path of knowledge, others again by
Karma-Yoga.

अन्ये त्वेवमजानन्तः श्रुत्वान्येभ्य उपासते ॥
तेऽपि चातितरन्त्येव मृत्युं श्रुतिपरायणाः ॥२५॥

अन्ये Others तु again एवम् thus अजानन्तः not knowing
अन्येभ्यः from others श्रुत्वा as (they have) heard उपासते
worship ते these अपि च and also श्रुतिपरायणाः regarding
what they have heard as the Supreme Refuge मृत्युं
death अतितरन्ति go beyond एव even.

25. Others again not knowing thus,
worship as they have heard from others.

Even these go beyond death, regarding what
they have heard as the Supreme Refuge.

[*Not knowing thus* : not able to know the Self
described above, by one of the several methods as
pointed out.

From others : Âchâryas or spiritual teachers.

Regarding : following with Shraddhâ.

What they have heard : i.e., they solely depend
upon the authority of others' instructions.]

यावत्सञ्जायते किञ्चित्सत्त्वं स्थावरजङ्गमम् ।।
क्षेत्रक्षेत्रज्ञसंयोगात्तद्विद्धि भरतर्षभ ।।२६।।

भरतर्षभ O bull of the Bhâratas यावत् किञ्चित् whatever
स्थावरजङ्गमम् the moving and the unmoving सत्त्वं being
सञ्जायते is born तत् it क्षेत्रक्षेत्रज्ञसंयोगात् from the union of
Kshetra and Kshetrajna विद्धि know (to be).

26. Whatever being is born, the
moving or the unmoving, O bull of the Bhâratas, know it to be from the union of Kshetra
and Kshetrajna.

[*Union . . . Kshetrajna* : The union of Kshetra
and Kshetrajna, of the object and the subject,
is of the nature of mutual Adhyâsa which consists
in confounding them as well as their attributes with
each other, owing to the absence of discrimination
of their real nature. This false knowledge vanishes
when one is able to separate Kshetra from
Kshetrajna.]

समं सर्वेषु भूतेषु तिष्ठन्तं परमेश्वरम् ॥

विनश्यत्स्वविनश्यन्तं यः पश्यति स पश्यति ॥२७॥

सर्वेषु All भूतेषु in beings समं equally तिष्ठन्तं existing विनश्यत्सु in the dying अविनश्यन्तं deathless परमेश्वरं the Lord Supreme यः who पश्यति sees सः he पश्यति sees.

27.   He sees, who sees the Lord Supreme, existing equally in all beings, deathless in the dying.

समं पश्यन् हि सर्वत्र समवस्थितमीश्वरम् ॥

न हिनस्त्यात्मनात्मानं ततो याति परां गतिम् ॥२८॥

हि Since सर्वत्र everywhere समं equally समवस्थितम् existent ईश्वरम् the Lord पश्यन् seeing आत्मना by self आत्मानं Self न not हिनस्ति injures ततः so परां highest गतिं the Goal याति (he) goes to.

28.   Since seeing the Lord equally existent everywhere, he injures not Self by self, and so goes to the highest Goal.

[*He injures...by self :* like the ignorant man either by ignoring the Self in others (Avidyâ or nescience), or regarding the non-Self (physical body, etc.) as the Self (Mithyâ-jnâna or false knowledge)— the two veils that hide the true nature of the Self.]

प्रकृत्यैव च कर्माणि क्रियमाणानि सर्वशः ॥

यः पश्यति तथात्मानमकर्तारं स पश्यति ॥२९॥

यः Who च and कर्माणि actions प्रकृत्या by Prakriti एव alone सर्वशः all क्रियमाणानि being done तथा and आत्मानम् the Self अकर्तारं actionless पश्यति sees सः he पश्यति sees.

29. He sees, who sees that all actions are done by Prakriti alone and that the Self is actionless.

यदा भूतपृथग्भावमेकस्थमनुपश्यति ॥
तत एव च विस्तारं ब्रह्म सम्पद्यते तदा ॥३०॥

यदा When भूतपृथग्भावम् the separate existence of all beings एकस्थम् inherent in the One अनुपश्यति sees ततः from That एव alone विस्तारं (their) expansion च and तदा then ब्रह्म Brahman सम्पद्यते (he) becomes.

30. When he sees the separate existence of all beings inherent in the One, and their expansion from That (One) alone, he then becomes Brahman.

अनादित्वान्निर्गुणत्वात्परमात्मायमव्ययः ॥
शरीरस्थोऽपि कौन्तेय न करोति न लिप्यते ॥३१॥

कौन्तेय O son of Kunti अनादित्वात् being without beginning निर्गुणत्वात् being devoid of Gunas अयम् this अव्ययः immutable परमात्मा Supreme Self शरीरस्थः existing in the body अपि though न neither करोति acts न nor लिप्यते is affected.

21

31.   Being without beginning and devoid of Gunas, this Supreme Self, immutable, O son of Kunti, though existing in the body neither acts nor is affected.

[*Being without beginning:* having no cause.

Neither...affected : Because the Self is not the doer, therefore He is not touched by the fruit of action.]

यथा सर्वगतं सौक्ष्म्यादाकाशं नोपलिप्यते ॥

सर्वत्रावस्थितो देहे तथात्मा नोपलिप्यते ॥३२॥

यथा As सर्वगतं the all-pervading आकाशं Âkâsha सौक्ष्म्यात् because of its subtlety न not उपलिप्यते is tainted तथा so सर्वत्र everywhere देहे in the body अवस्थितः exist- ent आत्मा the Self न not उपलिप्यते is tainted.

32.   As the all-pervading Âkâsha, because of its subtlety, is not tainted, so the Self existent everywhere in the body is not tainted.

यथा प्रकाशयत्येकः कृत्स्नं लोकमिमं रविः ॥

क्षेत्रं क्षेत्री तथा कृत्स्नं प्रकाशयति भारत ॥३३॥

भारत O descendant of Bharata यथा as एकः the one रविः sun इमं this कृत्स्नं all लोकम् world प्रकाशयति illumines तथा so क्षेत्री He who abides in the Kshetra कृत्स्नं the whole क्षेत्रं Kshetra प्रकाशयति illumines.

33. As the one sun illumines all this world, so does He who abides in the Kshetra, O descendant of Bharata, illumine the whole Kshetra.

क्षेत्रक्षेत्रज्ञयोरेवमन्तरं ज्ञानचक्षुषा ॥

भूतप्रकृतिमोक्षं च ये विदुर्यान्ति ते परम् ॥३४॥

एवम् Thus क्षेत्रक्षेत्रज्ञयो: between the Kshetra and the Kshetrajna अन्तरं the distinction भूतप्रकृतिमोक्षं the emancipation from the Prakriti of beings च and (also) ज्ञानचक्षुषा with the eye of knowledge ये who विदु: perceive ते they परम् the Supreme यान्ति go to.

34. They who thus with the eye of knowledge perceive the distinction between the Kshetra and the Kshetrajna, and also the emancipation from the Prakriti of beings, they go to the Supreme.

[*Prakriti of beings:* the material nature or delusion of beings due to Avidyâ.]

इति क्षेत्रक्षेत्रज्ञविभागयोगो नाम त्रयोदशोऽध्याय: ॥

The end of the thirteenth chapter, designated, *The Discrimination of the Kshetra and the Kshetrajna.*

|| चतुर्दशोऽध्यायः ||

FOURTEENTH CHAPTER

श्रीभगवानुवाच ।

परं भूयः प्रवक्ष्यामि ज्ञानानां ज्ञानमुत्तमम् ॥
यज्ज्ञात्वा मुनयः सर्वे परां सिद्धिमितो गताः ॥१॥

श्रीभगवान् The Blessed Lord उवाच said :
ज्ञानानां Of all knowledge उत्तमम् the best परं supreme
ज्ञानम् knowledge भूयः again प्रवक्ष्यामि shall I tell यत् which
ज्ञात्वा having known सर्वं all मुनयः the Munis इतः after
this life परां high सिद्धिं perfection गताः have attained to.

The Blessed Lord said :

1. Again shall I tell thee that supreme
knowledge which is above all knowledge,
having known which all the Munis have
attained to high perfection after this life.

[*After this life*: after being freed from this bondage of the body.]

इदं ज्ञानमुपाश्रित्य मम साधर्म्यमागताः ॥
सर्गेऽपि नोपजायन्ते प्रलये न व्यथन्ति च ॥२॥

इदं This ज्ञानम् knowledge उपाश्रित्य having devoted to मम

साधर्म्यम् My Being आगताः have attained to सर्गे at the time
of creation अपि न neither उपजायन्ते are born प्रलये at the
time of dissolution न च nor व्यथन्ति are (they) troubled.

2. They who, having devoted themselves
to this knowledge, have attained to My
Being, are neither born at the time of
creation, nor are they troubled at the time of
dissolution.

मम योनिर्महद्ब्रह्म तस्मिन् गर्भं दधाम्यहम् ॥
सम्भवः सर्वभूतानां ततो भवति भारत ॥३॥

भारत O descendant of Bharata महत् the great ब्रह्म
Prakriti मम My योनिः womb तस्मिन् in that अहम् I गर्भं the
germ दधामि place ततः thence सर्वभूतानां of all beings
सम्भवः the birth भवति is.

3. My womb is the great Prakriti ;
in that I place the germ ; from thence,
O descendant of Bharata, is the birth of all
beings.

[*Brahma :* This word is derived from Brimh,
"to expand", and means here the vast seed or womb
(the Prakriti) out of which the cosmos is evolved or
expanded.

I place the germ : I infuse the reflection of My
Intelligence, and this act of impregnation is the cause
of the evolution of the cosmos.]

सर्वयोनिषु कौन्तेय मूर्तयः सम्भवन्ति याः ॥
तासां ब्रह्म महद्योनिरहं बीजप्रदः पिता ॥४॥

कौन्तेय O son of Kunti सर्वयोनिषु in all the wombs याः whatever मूर्तयः forms सम्भवन्ति are produced तासां their महत् the great ब्रह्म Prakriti योनिः womb अहं I बीजप्रदः seed-giving पिता Father.

4. Whatever forms are produced, O son of Kunti, in all the wombs, the great Prakriti is their womb, and I the seed-giving Father.

सत्त्वं रजस्तम इति गुणाः प्रकृतिसम्भवाः ॥
निबध्नन्ति महाबाहो देहे देहिनमव्ययम् ॥५॥

महाबाहो O mighty-armed सत्त्वं Sattva रजः Rajas तमः Tamas इति these प्रकृतिसम्भवाः born of Prakriti गुणाः Gunas देहे in the body अव्ययम् the indestructible देहिनम् the embodied one निबध्नन्ति bind fast.

5. Sattva, Rajas, and Tamas—these Gunas, O mighty-armed, born of Prakriti, bind fast in the body the indestructible embodied one.

[*These Gunas:* are the primary constituents of the Prakriti and are the bases of all substances; they cannot therefore be said to be attributes or qualities inhering in the substances as opposed to the substances.

Embodied one : he who abides in the body as if identified therewith.]

तत्र सत्त्वं निर्मलत्वात्प्रकाशकमनामयम् ॥
सुखसङ्गेन बध्नाति ज्ञानसङ्गेन चानघ ॥६॥

अनघ O sinless one तत्र of these निर्मलत्वात् from its stainlessness प्रकाशकम् luminous अनामयम् free from evil सत्त्वं Sattva सुखसङ्गेन by attachment to happiness ज्ञानसङ्गेन by attachment to knowledge च and बध्नाति binds.

6. Of these Sattva, from its stainlessness luminous and free from evil, binds, O sinless one, by attachment to happiness, and by attachment to knowledge.

[*Binds by attachment to happiness, etc.*: Binds the Self by the consciousness of happiness and knowledge in the shape of "I am happy", "I am wise", which belongs properly to the Kshetra, but which is associated with the Self, the Absolute Intelligence and Bliss, through Avidyâ.]

रजो रागात्मकं विद्धि तृष्णासङ्गसमुद्भवम् ॥
तन्निबध्नाति कौन्तेय कर्मसङ्गेन देहिनम् ॥७॥

कौन्तेय O son of Kunti रागात्मकं of the nature of passion रजः Rajas तृष्णासङ्गसमुद्भवम् giving rise to thirst and attachment विद्धि know तत् it कर्मसङ्गेन by attachment to action देहिनम् the embodied one निबध्नाति binds fast.

7. Know Rajas to be of the nature of passion, giving rise to thirst and attachment;

it binds fast, O son of Kunti, the embodied one, by attachment to action.

[*It binds, etc.*: Though the Self is not the agent, Rajas makes him act with the idea, "*I* am the doer."]

तमस्त्वज्ञानजं विद्धि मोहनं सर्वदेहिनाम् ॥
प्रमादालस्यनिद्राभिस्तन्निबध्नाति भारत ॥८॥

भारत O descendant of Bharata तम: Tamas तु and अज्ञानजं born of ignorance सर्वदेहिनाम् all embodied beings मोहनं stupefying विद्धि know तत् it प्रमादालस्यनिद्राभि: by mis-comprehension, indolence, and sleep निबध्नाति binds fast.

8. And know Tamas to be born of ignorance, stupefying all embodied beings ; it binds fast, O descendant of Bharata, by mis-comprehension, indolence, and sleep.

[*Stupefying* : causing delusion or non-discrimination.]

सत्त्वं सुखे सञ्जयति रज: कर्मणि भारत ॥
ज्ञानमावृत्य तु तम: प्रमादे सञ्जयत्युत ॥६॥

भारत O descendant of Bharata सत्त्वं Sattva सुखे to happiness सञ्जयति attaches रज: Rajas कर्मणि to action उत while तम: Tamas तु indeed ज्ञानम् discrimination आवृत्य shrouding प्रमादे to miscomprehension सञ्जयति attaches.

9. Sattva attaches to happiness, and Rajas to action, O descendant of Bharata ; while Tamas, verily, shrouding discrimination, attaches to miscomprehension.

रजस्तमश्चाभिभूय सत्वं भवति भारत ॥

रजः सत्वं तमश्चैव तमः सत्वं रजस्तथा ॥१०॥

भारत O descendant of Bharata सत्त्वं Sattva रजः Rajas तमः Tamas च and अभिभूय predominating over भवति arises रजः Rajas सत्त्वं Sattva तमः Tamas च and तथा so तमः Tamas सत्त्वं Sattva रजः Rajas च and.

10. Sattva arises, O descendant of Bharata, predominating over Rajas and Tamas ; and Rajas over Sattva and Tamas ; so, Tamas over Sattva and Rajas.

[When one or the other of the Gunas asserts itself predominating over the other two, it produces its own effect. Sattva produces knowledge and happiness ; Rajas, action ; Tamas, veiling of discrimination, etc.]

सर्वद्वारेषु देहेऽस्मिन्प्रकाश उपजायते ॥

ज्ञानं यदा तदा विद्याद्विवृद्धं सत्त्वमित्युत ॥११॥

यदा When अस्मिन् this देहे in body सर्वद्वारेषु through every sense ज्ञानं (of) intelligence प्रकाशः light उपजायते shines तदा then उत indeed सत्त्वम् Sattva विवृद्धं (is) predominant इति that विद्यात् (it) should be known.

11. When through every sense in this
body, the light of intelligence shines, then
it should be known that Sattva is predominant.

[*Every sense:* lit., all the gates. All the senses
are for the Self the gateways of perception.]

लोभः प्रवृत्तिरारम्भः कर्मणामशमः स्पृहा ॥

रजस्येतानि जायन्ते विवृद्धे भरतर्षभ ॥१२॥

भरतर्षभ O bull of the Bhâratas लोभः greed प्रवृत्तिः
activity कर्मणाम् of actions आरम्भः the undertaking अशमः
unrest स्पृहा longing एतानि these रजसि Rajas विवृद्धे having
become predominant जायन्ते arise.

12. Greed, activity, the undertaking
of actions, unrest, longing—these arise
when Rajas is predominant, O bull of the
Bhâratas.

[*Unrest:* being agitated with joy, attachment,
etc.]

अप्रकाशोऽप्रवृत्तिश्च प्रमादो मोह एव च ॥

तमस्येतानि जायन्ते विवृद्धे कुरुनन्दन ॥१३॥

कुरुनन्दन O descendant of Kuru अप्रकाशः darkness
अप्रवृत्तिः inertness च and प्रमादः miscomprehension मोहः
delusion एव also च and एतानि these तमसि Tamas विवृद्धे
having become predominant जायन्ते arise.

13. Darkness, inertness, miscomprehension, and delusion—these arise when Tamas is predominant, O descendant of Kuru.

[*Darkness, inertness :* Absence of discrimination and its results, inertness, etc.]

यदा सत्त्वे प्रवृद्धे तु प्रलयं याति देहभृत् ॥
तदोत्तमविदां लोकानमलान्प्रतिपद्यते ॥१४॥

यदा तु When सत्त्वे Sattva प्रवृद्धे having become predominant देहभृत् the embodied one प्रलयं death याति meets तदा then उत्तमविदां of the knowers of the Highest अमलान् the spotless लोकान् worlds प्रतिपद्यते (he) attains.

14. If the embodied one meets death when Sattva is predominant, then he attains to the spotless regions of the worshippers of the Highest.

[*Spotless regions :* The Brahma-loka and the like.

The Highest: Deities such as Hiranyagarbha.]

रजसि प्रलयं गत्वा कर्मसङ्गिषु जायते ॥
तथा प्रलीनस्तमसि मूढयोनिषु जायते ॥१५॥

रजसि In Rajas प्रलयं death गत्वा meeting कर्मसङ्गिषु among those attached to action जायते (he) is born तथा so तमसि in Tamas प्रलीनः dying मूढयोनिषु in the wombs of the irrational जायते (he) is born.

15. Meeting death in Rajas he is born among those attached to action ; so dying in Tamas, he is born in the wombs of the irrational.

[*Meeting...Rajas:* If he dies when Rajas is predominant in him.]

कर्मणः सुकृतस्याहुः सात्त्विकं निर्मलं फलम् ॥
रजसस्तु फलं दुःखमज्ञानं तमसः फलम् ॥१६॥

सुकृतस्य Good कर्मणः of action निर्मलं pure सात्त्विकं Sâttvika फलम् the fruit आहुः they say रजसः of Rajas तु verily दुःखम् pain फलं the fruit तमसः of Tamas अज्ञानं ignorance फलम् the fruit.

16. The fruit of good action, they say, is Sâttvika and pure ; verily, the fruit of Rajas is pain, and ignorance is the fruit of Tamas.

[*Rajas:* means Râjasika action, and Tamas, Tâmasika action, as this section treats of actions.]

सत्त्वात्सञ्जायते ज्ञानं रजसो लोभ एव च ॥
प्रमादमोहौ तमसो भवतोऽज्ञानमेव च ॥१७॥

सत्त्वात् From Sattva ज्ञानं wisdom सञ्जायते arises रजसः from Rajas लोभः greed एव indeed च and तमसः from Tamas अज्ञानम् ignorance प्रमादमोहौ miscomprehension and delusion एव even च and भवतः arise.

17.   From Sattva arises wisdom, and from Rajas greed ; miscomprehension, delusion and ignorance arise from Tamas.

ऊर्ध्वं गच्छन्ति सत्त्वस्था मध्ये तिष्ठन्ति राजसाः ॥

जघन्यगुणवृत्तिस्था अधोगच्छन्ति तामसाः ॥१८॥

सत्त्वस्थाः The Sattva-abiding ऊर्ध्वं upwards गच्छन्ति go राजसाः the Râjasika मध्ये in the middle तिष्ठन्ति dwell जघन्यगुणवृत्तिस्थाः abiding in the function of the lowest Guna तामसाः the Tâmasika अधः downwards गच्छन्ति go.

18.   The Sattva-abiding go upwards ; the Râjasika dwell in the middle ; and the Tâmasika, abiding in the function of the lowest Guna, go downwards.

नान्यं गुणेभ्यः कर्तारं यदा द्रष्टानुपश्यति ॥

गुणेभ्यश्च परं वेत्ति मद्भावं सोऽधिगच्छति ॥१९॥

यदा When द्रष्टा the seer गुणेभ्यः than the Gunas अन्यं other कर्तारं agent न no अनुपश्यति beholds गुणेभ्यः than the Gunas च and परं higher वेत्ति knows तदा then सः he मद्भावं My being अधिगच्छति attains to.

19.   When the seer beholds no agent other than the Gunas and knows That which is higher than the Gunas, he attains to My being.

[*The Gunas*: which transform themselves into the bodies, senses, and sense-objects, and which in all their modifications constitute the agent in all actions.

Knows...the Gunas: Sees Him who is distinct from the Gunas, who is the Witness of the Gunas and of their functions.]

गुणानेतानतीत्य त्रीन्देही देहसमुद्भवान् ॥
जन्ममृत्युजरादुःखैर्विमुक्तोऽमृतमश्नुते ॥२०॥

देहसमुद्भवान् Out of which the body is evolved एतान् these त्रीन् three गुणान् Gunas अतीत्य having gone beyond जन्ममृत्युजरादुःखैः from birth, death, decay, and pain विमुक्तः freed देही the embodied one अमृतम् immortality अश्नुते attains to.

20. The embodied one having gone beyond these three Gunas, out of which the body is evolved, is freed from birth, death, decay, and pain, and attains to immortality.

अर्जुन उवाच ।
कैर्लिंङ्गैस्त्रीन्गुणानेतानतीतो भवति प्रभो ॥
किमाचारः कथं चैतांस्त्रीन्गुणानतिवर्तते ॥२१॥

अर्जुनः Arjuna उवाच said:

प्रभो O Lord कैः by what लिङ्गैः marks एतान् these त्रीन् three गुणान् Gunas अतीतः भवति has gone beyond किमाचारः what (is his) conduct कथं how च and एतान् these त्रीन् three गुणान् Gunas अतिवर्तते does (he) pass beyond.

Arjuna said :

21. By what marks, O Lord, is he (known) who has gone beyond these three Gunas ? What is his conduct, and how does he pass beyond these three Gunas ?

श्रीभगवानुवाच ।

प्रकाशं च प्रवृत्तिं च मोहमेव च पाण्डव ॥
न द्वेष्टि सम्प्रवृत्तानि न निवृत्तानि कांक्षति ॥२२॥

श्रीभगवान् The Blessed Lord उवाच said:

पाण्डव O Pândava प्रकाशं light (the effect of Sattva) प्रवृत्ति activity (the effect of Rajas) मोहम् delusion (the effect of Tamas) एव च and also सम्प्रवृत्तानि (when) come forth न not द्वेष्टि (he) hates निवृत्तानि when absent न nor कांक्षति longs for ;

The Blessed Lord said :

22. He who hates not the appearance of light (the effect of Sattva), activity (the effect of Rajas), and delusion (the effect of Tamas), (in his own mind), O Pândava, nor longs for them when absent ;

[This answers Arjuna's first question. The man of right knowledge does not hate the effects of the three Gunas when they clearly present themselves as objects of consciousness; nor does he long after things which have disappeared.]

उदासीनवदासीनो गुणैर्यो न विचाल्यते ॥

गुणा वर्तन्त इत्येव योऽवतिष्ठति नेङ्गते ॥२३॥

यः Who उदासीनवत् like one unconcerned आसीनः sitting गुणः by the Gunas न not विचाल्यते is moved गुणाः the Gunas वर्तन्ते operate इत्येव (knowing) that अवतिष्ठति is Self-centred न not इङ्गते swerves ;

23. He who, sitting like one unconcerned, is moved not by the Gunas, who knowing that the Gunas operate, is Self-centred and swerves not ;

समदुःखसुखः स्वस्थः समलोष्ट्राश्मकाञ्चनः ॥

तुल्यप्रियाप्रियो धीरस्तुल्यनिन्दात्मसंस्तुतिः ॥२४॥

यः Who समदुःखसुखः alike in pleasure and pain स्वस्थः Self-abiding समलोष्ट्राश्मकाञ्चनः regarding a clod of earth, a stone, and gold alike तुल्यप्रियाप्रियः the same to agreeable and disagreeable धीरः firm तुल्यनिन्दात्मसंस्तुतिः the same in censure and praise ;

24. Alike in pleasure and pain, Self-abiding, regarding a clod of earth, a stone and gold alike ; the same to agreeable and disagreeable, firm, the same in censure and praise ;

[*Self-abiding :* He remains in his own true nature.]

मानापमानयोस्तुल्यस्तुल्यो मित्रारिपक्षयो: ॥

सर्वारम्भपरित्यागी गुणातीत: स उच्यते ॥२५॥

य: Who मानापमानयो: in honour and disgrace तुल्य: the same मित्रारिपक्षयो: to friend and foe तुल्य: the same सर्वारम्भपरित्यागी relinquishing all undertakings स: he गुणातीत: gone beyond the Gunas उच्यते is said.

25. The same in honour and disgrace, the same to friend and foe, relinquishing all undertakings—he is said to have gone beyond the Gunas.

[Inclining to neither of the dual throng, he firmly treads the path of Self-knowledge, and rises above the Gunas.

These three Shlokas are in answer to Arjuna's second question.]

मां च योऽव्यभिचारेण भक्तियोगेन सेवते ॥

स गुणान्समतीत्यैतान् ब्रह्मभूयाय कल्पते ॥२६॥

य: Who च and मां Me अव्यभिचारेण unswerving भक्तियोगेन with devotion सेवते serves स: he एतान् these गुणान् Gunas समतीत्य going beyond ब्रह्मभूयाय for becoming Brahman कल्पते is fitted.

26. And he who serves Me with unswerving devotion, he, going beyond the Gunas, is fitted for becoming Brahman.

[This answers Arjuna's third question.]
22

ब्रह्मणो हि प्रतिष्ठाहममृतस्याव्ययस्य च ॥
शाश्वतस्य च धर्मस्य सुखस्यैकान्तिकस्य च ॥२७॥

हि For अहम् I ब्रह्मणः of Brahman प्रतिष्ठा the abode
अव्ययस्य the Immutable अमृतस्य the Immortal च and शाश्वतस्य
everlasting धर्मस्य of Dharma ऐकान्तिकस्य Absolute सुखस्य
of Bliss च and.

27.   For I am the abode of Brahman, the
Immortal and Immutable, of everlasting
Dharma and of Absolute Bliss.

[*I* : the Pratyagâtman, the true Inner-Self.]

इति गुणत्रयविभागयोगो नाम चतुर्दशोऽध्यायः ॥

The end of the fourteenth chapter, designated, *The Discrimination of the Three
Gunas.*

॥ पञ्चदशोऽध्यायः ॥
FIFTEENTH CHAPTER
श्रीभगवानुवाच ।
ऊर्ध्वमूलमधःशाखमश्वत्थं प्राहुरव्ययम् ॥
छन्दांसि यस्य पर्णानि यस्तं वेद स वेदवित् ॥१॥

श्रीभगवान् The Blessed Lord उवाच said :

ऊर्ध्वमूलम् Rooted above अधःशाखम् branching below अव्ययम् eternal अश्वत्थं Ashvattha प्राहुः they speak of छन्दांसि the Vedas यस्य whose पर्णानि leaves तं it यः who वेद knows सः he वेदवित् (is) Veda-knower.

The Blessed Lord said :

1. They speak of an eternal Ashvattha rooted above and branching below whose leaves are the Vedas ; he who knows it, is a Veda-knower.

[*Ashvattha :* literally, that which does not endure till tomorrow : the Samsâra, the ever-changing, phenomenal world.

Brahman with Its unmanifested energy, Mâyâ, is spoken as the One *"above"*, for It is supreme over all things ; the One above is the root of this Tree of Samsâra, as such it is said to have its root above. Mahat, Ahamkâra, Tanmâtras, etc., are its branches evolving to grosser and grosser states—hence it is said to be branching *"below"*. As leaves protect a tree, so do the Vedas protect the Tree of Samsâra, as treating of Dharma and Adharma, with their causes and fruits.

Eternal : because this Tree of Samsâra rests on a continuous series of births without beginning and end, and it cannot be cut down except by the knowledge, "I am Brahman."]

अधश्चोर्ध्वं प्रसृतास्तस्य शाखाः

गुणप्रवृद्धा विषयप्रवालाः ॥

अधश्च मूलान्यनुसन्ततानि

कर्मानुबन्धीनि मनुष्यलोके ॥२॥

तस्य Its गुणप्रवृद्धाः nourished by the Gunas विषयप्रवालाः sense-objects (are) its buds शाखाः branches अधः below ऊर्ध्वं above च and प्रसृताः spread मनुष्यलोके in the world of man कर्मानुबन्धीनि originating action मूलानि the roots अधः below च and अनुसन्ततानि are stretched forth.

2. Below and above spread its branches, nourished by the Gunas ; sense-objects are its buds ; and below in the world of man stretch forth the roots, originating action.

[*Below :* from man downwards.
Above : up to Brahmâ.
Roots : The tap-root is the Lord "above"; the

secondary roots are the Samskâras, attachment,
aversion, etc. It is these that, being in perpetual
succession the cause and consequence of good and evil
deeds, bind one fast to actions—Dharma and
Adharma.]

न रूपमस्येह तथोपलभ्यते
नान्तो न चादिर्न च सम्प्रतिष्ठा ॥
अश्वत्थमेनं सुविरूढमूल-
मसङ्गशस्त्रेण दृढेन छित्त्वा ॥३॥
ततः पदं तत्परिमार्गितव्यं
यस्मिन्गता न निवर्तन्ति भूयः ॥
तमेव चाद्यं पुरुषं प्रपद्ये
यतः प्रवृत्तिः प्रसृता पुराणी ॥४॥

इह Here अस्य its रूपम् form न not उपलभ्यते is perceived
तथा as such न neither अन्तः (its) end न nor आदिः (its)
origin न च nor सम्प्रतिष्ठा (its) existence एनं this सुविरूढमूलम्
firm-rooted अश्वत्थम् Ashvattha दृढेन strong असङ्गशस्त्रेण with
the axe of non-attachment छित्त्वा having cut asunder
ततः then तत् that पदं goal परिमार्गितव्यं is to be sought for
यस्मिन् whither गताः going भूयः again न not निवर्तन्ति (they)
return यतः whence (एषा the) पुराणी Eternal प्रवृत्तिः Activity
प्रसृता streamed forth तम् in that एव च indeed आद्यं Primeval पुरुषं Purusha प्रपद्ये I seek refuge.

3-4. Its form is not here perceived as
such, neither its end, nor its origin, nor its

existence. Having cut asunder this firm-rooted Ashvattha with the strong axe of non-attachment—then that Goal is to be sought for, going whither they (the wise) do not return again. I seek refuge in that Primeval Purusha whence streamed forth the Eternal Activity.

[*As such :* it cannot be said to exist, because it appears and vanishes every other moment. See commentary on II. 16.

Tat—That : Shankara and Ânandagiri read "Tatah", and explain it as beyond or above the Ashvattha, the Tree of Samsâra.

The Eternal Activity : this ever-passing work of projection, this ever-flowing current of evolution, the world of phenomena.]

निर्मानमोहाजितसङ्गदोषा
अध्यात्मनित्या विनिवृत्तकामाः ॥
द्वन्द्वैर्विमुक्ताः सुखदुःखसंज्ञै-
र्गच्छन्त्यमूढाः पदमव्ययं तत् ॥५॥

निर्मानमोहाः Free from pride and delusion जितसङ्गदोषाः with the evil of attachment conquered अध्यात्मनित्याः ever dwelling in the Self विनिवृत्तकामाः with desires completely receded सुखदुःखसंज्ञैः known as pleasure and pain द्वन्द्वैः from the pairs of opposites विमुक्ताः liberated अमूढाः the undeluded तत् that अव्ययं Eternal पदम् Goal गच्छन्ति reach.

5. Free from pride and delusion, with the evil of attachment conquered, ever dwelling in the Self, with desires completely receded, liberated from the pairs of opposites known as pleasure and pain, the undeluded reach that Goal Eternal.

न तद्भासयते सूर्यो न शशाङ्को न पावकः ॥

यद्गत्वा न निवर्तन्ते तद्धाम परमं मम ॥६॥

यत् Whither गत्वा going न not निवर्तन्ते (they) return तत् that सूर्यः the sun न not भासयते illumines न nor शशाङ्कः the moon न nor पावकः fire तत् that मम My परमं Supreme धाम Abode.

6. That the sun illumines not, nor the moon, nor fire ; that is My Supreme Abode, going whither they return not.

ममैवांशो जीवलोके जीवभूतः सनातनः ॥

मनःषष्ठानीन्द्रियाणि प्रकृतिस्थानि कर्षति ॥७॥

मम एव Of Myself सनातनः eternal अंशः portion जीवभूतः having become a living soul प्रकृतिस्थानि abiding in the Prakriti मनःषष्ठानि with mind as the sixth इन्द्रियाणि the (five) senses जीवलोके in the world of life कर्षति draws (to itself).

7. An eternal portion of Myself having become a living soul in the world of life, draws (to itself) the (five) senses

with mind for the sixth, abiding in
Prakriti.

[The Jiva or the individual soul is that aspect
of the Supreme Self which manifests itself in every
one as the doer and enjoyer, being limited by the
Upâdhis set up by Avidyâ; but in reality, both are
the same. It is like the Âkâsha (space) in the jar,
which is a portion of the infinite Âkâsha, and becomes
one with the latter on the destruction of the jar, the
cause of limitation.]

शरीरं यदवाप्रोति यच्चाप्युत्क्रामतीश्वरः ॥
गृहीत्वैतानि संयाति वायुर्गन्धानिवाशयात् ॥८॥

ईश्वरः The Lord यत् when शरीरं a body अवाप्रोति obtains
यत् when च and अपि also उत्क्रामति leaves वायुः the wind
आशयात् from (their) seats गन्धान् the scents इव as एतानि
these गृहीत्वा taking संयाति goes.

8.   When the Lord obtains a body and
when He leaves it, He takes these and goes, as
the wind takes the scents from their seats (the
flowers).

[*Lord :* Jiva spoken of in the preceding Shloka.
When the Jiva leaves the body, then he draws
round himself the senses and the Manas. When he
enters another, he takes these again with him, i.e.,
he is born with these again.]

श्रोत्रं चक्षुः स्पर्शनं च रसनं घ्राणमेव च ॥
अधिष्ठाय मनश्चायं विषयानुपसेवते ॥६॥

अयं He श्रोत्रं the ear चक्षुः the eye स्पर्शनं the (organ of) touch रसनं the (organ of) taste च and घ्राणं the (organ of) smell एव च as also मनः the mind अधिष्ठाय presiding over विषयान् objects उपसेवते experiences.

9. Presiding over the ear, the eye, the touch, the taste, and the smell, as also the mind, He experiences objects.

उत्क्रामन्तं स्थितं वापि भुञ्जानं वा गुणान्वितम् ॥

विमूढा नानुपश्यन्ति पश्यन्ति ज्ञानचक्षुषः ॥१०॥

उत्क्रामन्तं Transmigrating (from one body to another) स्थितं residing (in the same) वापि or भुञ्जानं experiencing गुणान्वितम् united with the Gunas विमूढाः the deluded न not अनुपश्यन्ति do see (Him) ज्ञानचक्षुषः those who have the eye of wisdom पश्यन्ति do see (Him)

10. Him while transmigrating (from one body to another), or residing (in the same) or experiencing, or when united with the Gunas—the deluded do not see; but those who have the eye of wisdom behold Him.

[Though Âtman is nearest and comes most easily within the range of their consciousness in a variety of functions, still all do not see Him, because of their complete subservience to sense-objects.]

यतन्तो योगिनश्चैनं पश्यन्त्यात्मन्यवस्थितम् ॥

यतन्तोऽप्यकृतात्मानो नैनं पश्यन्त्यचेतसः ॥११॥

यतन्तः Striving (for perfection) योगिनः the Yogis एनं
Him आत्मनि in themselves अवस्थितम् dwelling पश्यन्ति behold
यतन्तः striving अपि even though अकृतात्मानः the men of
unrefined self अचेतसः unintelligent एनं Him न not
पश्यन्ति see.

11. The Yogis striving (for perfection)
behold Him dwelling in themselves ; but the
unrefined and unintelligent, even though striving, see Him not.

[*The unrefined :* Whose mind has not been re-
generated by Tapas and subjugation of the senses,
whose mind is not purified.]

यदादित्यगतं तेजो जगद्भासयतेऽखिलम् ॥

यच्चन्द्रमसि यच्चाग्नौ तत्तेजो विद्धि मामकम् ॥१२॥

आदित्यगतं Residing in the sun यत् which तेजः light
अखिलम् the whole जगत् world भासयते illumines चन्द्रमसि in
the moon च and यत् which अग्नौ in the fire च and यत्
which तत् that तेजः light मामकम् Mine विद्धि know.

12. The light which residing in the sun
illumines the whole world, that which is in the
moon and in the fire—know that light to be
Mine.

[*Light :* may also be understood to mean the
light of consciousness.]

गामाविश्य च भूतानि धारयाम्यहमोजसा ॥

पुष्णामि चौषधीः सर्वाः सोमो भूत्वा रसात्मकः ॥१३॥

अहम् I ओजसा with my energy गाम् the earth आविश्य
entering भूतानि all beings धारयामि (I) support रसात्मकः
watery सोमः moon च and भूत्वा becoming सर्वाः all औषधीः
the herbs पुष्णामि I nourish.

13. Entering the earth with My energy,
I support all beings, and I nourish all the herbs,
becoming the watery moon.

[*Energy*—Ojas : The energy of Ishvara, where-
by the vast heaven and the earth are firmly
held.

Nourish : by infusing sap into them.

The watery moon : The Soma, moon, is considered as the repository or the embodiment of all
fluids (Rasas).]

अहं वैश्वानरो भूत्वा प्राणिनां देहमाश्रितः ॥

प्राणापानसमायुक्तः पचाम्यन्नं चतुर्विधम् ॥१४॥

अहं I वैश्वानरः (the fire) Vaishvânara भूत्वा becoming
प्राणिनां of living beings देहम् in the body आश्रितः abiding
प्राणापानसमायुक्तः associated with Prâna and Apâna
चतुर्विधम् fourfold अन्नं the food पचामि I digest.

14. Abiding in the body of living
beings as (the fire) Vaishvânara, I, associated
with Prâna and Apâna, digest the fourfold
food.

[See IV. 29.
Vaishvânara : The fire abiding in the stomach.
Fourfold food : Food which has to be eaten by
(1) mastication, (2) sucking, (3) licking, and
(4) swallowing.]

सर्वस्य चाहं हृदि सन्निविष्टो

मत्तः स्मृतिर्ज्ञानमपोहनं च ॥

वेदैश्च सर्वैरहमेव वेद्यो

वेदान्तकृद्वेदविदेव चाहम् ॥१५॥

अहं I सर्वस्य of all हृदि in the heart सन्निविष्टः centred च
and मत्तः from Me स्मृतिः memory ज्ञानम् perception अपोहनं
(their) loss च as well as सर्वैः all वेद: by the Vedas च and
अहम I एव verily वेद्यः that which has to be known वेदान्तकृत्
the Author of the Vedânta वेदवित् the Knower of the
Veda च and अहम् I एव indeed.

15. I am centred in the hearts of all ;
memory and perception as well as their loss
come from Me. I am verily that which has
to be known by all the Vedas, I indeed am the
Author of the Vedânta, and the Knower of the
Veda am I.

[*Memory :* of what is experienced in the past
births; and *knowledge*—of things transcending the
ordinary limits of space, time, and visible nature.—
Ânandagiri.

Come from Me: as the result of their good or
evil deeds.

I indeed...Vedânta: It is I who am the
Teacher of the wisdom of the Vedânta, and cause it
to be handed down in regular succession.]

द्राविमौ पुरुषौ लोके क्षरश्चाक्षर एव च ॥

क्षरः सर्वाणि भूतानि कूटस्थोऽक्षर उच्यते ॥१६॥

क्षरः The Perishable अक्षरः the Imperishable च and
द्वौ two एव indeed इमौ these पुरुषौ (two) Purushas (beings) लोके in the world सर्वाणि all भूतानि beings क्षरः (are)
the Perishable कूटस्थः the Kutastha अक्षरः the Imperishable उच्यते is called.

16.   There are two Purushas in the world
—the Perishable and the Imperishable. All
beings are the Perishable, and the Kutastha is
called Imperishable.

[*Two Purushas:* Two categories—arranged in
two separate groups of beings—spoken of as "Purushas", as they are the Upâdhis of the Purusha.

Imperishable : Mâyâ-Shakti of the Lord, the
germ from which the perishable being takes its birth.

Kutastha : That which manifests Itself in various
forms of illusion and deception. It is said to be imperishable, as the seed of Samsâra is endless—in the
sense that it does not perish in the absence of
Brahma-Jnâna.]

उत्तमः पुरुषस्त्वन्यः परमात्मेत्युदाहृतः ॥
यो लोकत्रयमाविश्य बिभर्त्यव्यय ईश्वरः ॥१७॥

अन्यः Another तु but उत्तमः the Supreme पुरुषः Purusha
परमात्मा the Highest Self इति thus उदाहृतः called यः who
ईश्वरः Lord अव्ययः the immutable लोकत्रयम् the three
worlds आविश्य pervading बिभर्ति sustains (them).

17. But (there is) another, the Supreme
Purusha, called the Highest Self, the immutable
Lord, who pervading the three worlds, sustains
them.

[*Another :* quite distinct from the two.

The three worlds : Bhuh (the Earth), Bhuvah
(the Mid-Region), and Svah (the Heaven).]

यस्मात्क्षरमतीतोऽहमक्षरादपि चोत्तमः ॥
अतोऽस्मि लोके वेदे च प्रथितः पुरुषोत्तमः ॥१८॥

यस्मात् As अहम् I क्षरं the Perishable अतीतः transcend
अक्षरात् than (to) the Imperishable अपि even उत्तमः
superior च and अतः therefore लोके in the world वेदे in
the Veda च and पुरुषोत्तमः Purushottama (the
Highest Purusha) इति as प्रथितः celebrated अस्मि am I.

18. As I transcend the Perishable and
am above even the Imperishable, therefore
am I in the world and in the Veda celebrated
as Purushottama, (the Highest Purusha).

[*The Perishable :* The Tree of Samsâra called Ashvattha.

The Imperishable : Which constitutes the seed of the Tree of Samsâra.]

यो मामेवमसम्मूढो जानाति पुरुषोत्तमम् ॥
स सर्वविद्भजति मां सर्वभावेन भारत ॥१९॥

भारत O descendant of Bharata यः who एवम् thus असम्मूढः free from delusion पुरुषोत्तमम् the Supreme Purusha माम् Me जानाति knows सः he सर्ववित् knowing all सर्वभावेन with all his heart मां Me भजति worships.

19. He who, free from delusion, thus knows Me, the Highest Spirit, he knowing all, worships Me with all his heart, O descendant of Bharata.

इति गुह्यतमं शास्त्रमिदमुक्तं मयाऽनघ ॥
एतद्बुद्ध्वा बुद्धिमान्स्यात्कृतकृत्यश्च भारत ॥२०॥

अनघ O sinless one भारत O descendant of Bharata इति thus गुह्यतमं most profound इदम् this शास्त्रम् teaching मया by Me उक्तं has been imparted एतत् this बुद्ध्वा knowing बुद्धिमान् possessed of (the highest) intelligence कृतकृत्यः (who has) accomplished all the duties च and स्यात् becomes.

20. Thus, O sinless one, has this most profound teaching been imparted by Me. Knowing this one attains the highest intelli-

gence and will have accomplished all one's
duties, O descendant of Bharata.

[*Highest intelligence:* which realises the Brahman.

Will have accomplished...duties: Whatever
duty one has to do in life, all that duty has been done,
when the Brahman is realised.]

इति पुरुषोत्तमयोगो नाम पञ्चदशोऽध्यायः ॥

The end of the fifteenth chapter, designated, *The Way to the Supreme Spirit.*

॥ षोडशोऽध्यायः ॥

SIXTEENTH CHAPTER

श्रीभगवानुवाच ।

अभयं सत्त्वसंशुद्धिर्ज्ञानयोगव्यवस्थितिः ॥
दानं दमश्च यज्ञश्च स्वाध्यायस्तप आर्जवम् ॥१॥

श्रीभगवान् The Blessed Lord उवाच said:

अभयं Fearlessness सत्त्वसंशुद्धिः purity of heart ज्ञानयोग-
व्यवस्थितिः steadfastness in knowledge and Yoga दानं
almsgiving दमः control of the senses यज्ञः Yajna
स्वाध्यायः reading of the Shâstras तपः austerity आर्जवम्
uprightness:

The Blessed Lord said :
1. Fearlessness, purity of heart, steadfastness in knowledge and Yoga ; almsgiving,
control of the senses, Yajna, reading of the
Shâstras, austerity, uprightness ;

[*Yoga:* consists in making what has been learnt
from the Shâstras and the Âchârya an object of one's
own direct perception, by concentration and self-
control.]

23

अहिंसा सत्यमक्रोधस्त्यागः शान्तिरपैशुनम् ॥
दया भूतेष्वलोलुप्त्वं मार्दवं ह्रीरचापलम् ॥२॥

अहिंसा Non-injury सत्यम् truth अक्रोधः absence of anger
त्यागः renunciation शान्तिः tranquillity अपैशुनम् absence of
calumny भूतेषु to beings दया compassion अलोलुप्त्वं uncovetousness मार्दवं gentleness ह्रीः modesty अचापलम् absence
of fickleness;

2. Non-injury, truth, absence of anger,
renunciation, tranquillity, absence of calumny,
compassion to beings, uncovetousness, gentleness, modesty, absence of fickleness ;

[*Uncovetousness :* Unaffectedness of the senses
when in contact with their objects.

Absence of fickleness : Avoidance of useless actions.—*Shridhara.*]

तेजः क्षमा धृतिः शौचमद्रोहो नातिमानिता ॥
भवन्ति सम्पदं दैवीमभिजातस्य भारत ॥३॥

तेजः Boldness क्षमा forgiveness धृतिः fortitude शौचम्
purity अद्रोहः absence of hatred नातिमानिता absence of
pride दैवीम् divine सम्पदं state अभिजातस्य to one born for
भवन्ति (these) belong भारत O descendant of Bharata.

3. Boldness, forgiveness, fortitude, purity,
absence of hatred, absence of pride ; these

belong to one born for a divine state, O descendant of Bharata.

दम्भो दर्पोऽभिमानश्च क्रोध: पारुष्यमेव च ॥
अज्ञानं चाभिजातस्य पार्थ सम्पदमासुरीम् ॥४॥

पार्थ O Pârtha दम्भः ostentation दर्पः arrogance च and अभिमानः self-conceit क्रोधः anger पारुष्यं harshness च and अज्ञानं ignorance च एव as well as आसुरीम् an Âsurika सम्पदं state अभिजातस्य to one who is born for.

4. Ostentation, arrogance, and self-conceit, anger as also harshness and ignorance, belong to one who is born, O Pârtha, for an Âsurika state.

[*Âsurika* : demoniac.]

देवी सम्पद्विमोक्षाय निबन्धायासुरी मता ॥
मा शुच: सम्पदं दैवीमभिजातोऽसि पाण्डव ॥६॥

देवी The divine सम्पत् state विमोक्षाय for liberation आसुरी the Âsurika निबन्धाय for bondage मता is deemed (as mature) पाण्डव O Pândava मा not शुचः grieve देवीम् the divine सम्पदं state अभिजातः born for असि (thou) art.

5. The divine state is deemed to make for liberation, the Âsurika for bondage; grieve not, O Pândava, thou art born for a divine state.

द्वौ भूतसर्गौ लोकेऽस्मिन् दैव आसुर एव च ॥

दैवो विस्तरशः प्रोक्त आसुरं पार्थ मे शृणु ॥६॥

पार्थ O Pârtha अस्मिन् लोके in this world दैव: the divine आसुर: the Âsurika च and द्वौ two भूतसर्गौ types of beings दैव: the divine विस्तरशः at length प्रोक्त:has been described आसुरं of the Âsurika मे from Me शृणु hear.

6. There are two types of beings in this world, the divine and the Âsurika. The divine have been described at length ; hear from Me, O Pârtha, of the Âsurika.

प्रवृत्तिं च निवृत्तिं च जना न विदुरासुराः ॥

न शौचं नापि चाचारो न सत्यं तेषु विद्यते ॥७॥

आसुरा: The Âsurika जनाः persons प्रवृत्तिं what to do च and निवृत्तिं what to refrain from न not विदुः know तेषु in them न neither शौचं purity न nor आचार: good conduct न च nor सत्यं truth विद्यते is.

7. The persons of Âsurika nature know not what to do and what to refrain from ; neither is purity found in them nor good conduct, nor truth.

[*What to do...from :* What acts they should perform to achieve the end of man, nor what acts they should abstain from to avert evil.]

असत्यमप्रतिष्ठं ते जगदाहुरनीश्वरम् ॥

अपरस्परसम्भूतं किमन्यत्कामहैतुकम् ॥८॥

जगत् The universe असत्यम् (is) without truth अप्रतिष्ठं without (moral) basis अनीश्वरम् without a God अपरस्परसम्भूतं brought about by mutual union किमन्यत् what else कामहैतुकं with lust for its cause ते आहुः they say.

8.   They say, "The universe is without truth, without a (moral) basis, without a God, brought about by mutual union, with lust for its cause ; what else ?"

[*Without truth* : As we are unreal so this universe is unreal, and the sacred scriptures that declare the truth are unreal.

What else: but lust can be the cause of the universe ?—This is the view of the Lokâyatikas, the materialists.]

एतां दृष्टिमवष्टभ्य नष्टात्मानोऽल्पबुद्धयः ॥
प्रभवन्त्युग्रकर्माणः क्षयाय जगतोऽहिताः ॥९॥

अल्पबुद्धयः Of small intellect एतां this दृष्टिम् view अवष्टभ्य holding नष्टात्मानः ruined souls उग्रकर्माणः of fierce deeds अहिताः the enemies जगतः of the world क्षयाय for (its) destruction प्रभवन्ति rise.

9.   Holding this view, these ruined souls of small intellect and fierce deeds, rise as the enemies of the world for its destruction.

[*Small intellect:* as it concerns itself only with sense-objects and cannot soar higher.]

काममाश्रित्य दुष्पूरं दम्भमानमदान्विता: ॥

मोहाद्गृहीत्वाऽसद्ग्राहान्प्रवर्तन्तेऽशुचिव्रता:॥१०॥

दुष्पूरं Insatiable कामं desire आश्रित्य abiding in दम्भमान-
मदान्विता: full of hypocrisy, pride, and arrogance
मोहात् through delusion असद्ग्राहान् evil ideas गृहीत्वा holding अशुचिव्रता: with impure resolve प्रवर्तन्ते they work.

10. Filled with insatiable desires, full of
hypocrisy, pride, and arrogance, holding evil
ideas through delusion, they work with impure
resolve.

चिन्तामपरिमेयां च प्रलयान्तामुपाश्रिता: ॥

कामोपभोगपरमा एतावदिति निश्चिता: ॥११॥

प्रलयान्तां Ending only with death अपरिमेयां immense
चिन्ताम् cares उपाश्रिता: beset with कामोपभोगपरमा: regarding
gratification of lust as the highest एतावत् that is all
इति that निश्चिता: feeling sure;

11. Beset with immense cares ending
only with death, regarding gratification of
lust as the highest, and feeling sure that that is
all ;

[*Cares:* as to the means of acquiring and pre-
serving the innumerable objects of desire.]

आशापाशशतैर्बद्धा: कामक्रोधपरायणा: ॥

ईहन्ते कामभोगार्थमन्यायेनार्थसञ्चयान् ॥१२॥

आशापाशशतै: By a hundred ties of hope बद्धा: bound कामक्रोधपरायणा: given over to lust and wrath कामभोगार्थम् for sensual enjoyment अन्यायेन by unjust means अर्थ-सञ्चयान् hoards of wealth ईहन्ते (they) strive (to secure).

12. Bound by a hundred ties of hope, given over to lust and wrath, they strive to secure by unjust means hoards of wealth for sensual enjoyment.

इदमद्य मया लब्धमिदं प्राप्स्ये मनोरथम् ॥
इदमस्तीदमपि मे भविष्यति पुनर्धनम् ॥१३॥

अद्य Today मया by me इदं this लब्धम् has been gained इदं this मनोरथम् desire प्राप्स्ये I shall obtain इदं this अस्ति is पुन: again (in future) मे mine इदम् this अपि also धनम् wealth भविष्यति shall be.

13. "This today has been gained by me; this desire I shall obtain; this is mine, and this wealth also shall be mine in future.

असौ मया हत: शत्रुर्हनिष्ये चापरानपि ॥
ईश्वरोऽहमहं भोगी सिद्धोऽहं बलवान्सुखी ॥१४॥

असौ That शत्रु: enemy मया by me हत: has been slain अपरान् others च and अपि also हनिष्ये shall I slay अहम् I ईश्वर: Lord अहं I भोगी enjoyer अहं I सिद्ध: (am) successful बलवान् powerful सुखी happy.

14. "That enemy has been slain by

me, and others also shall I slay. I am the
Lord, I enjoy, I am successful, powerful, and
happy.

आढ्योऽभिजनवानस्मि कोऽन्योऽस्ति सदृशो मया ॥

यक्ष्ये दास्यामि मोदिष्य इत्यज्ञानविमोहिताः ॥१५॥

आढ्यः Rich अभिजनवान् well-born अस्मि I am मया to
me सदृशः equal अन्यः else कः who अस्ति is यक्ष्ये I will
sacrifice दास्यामि I will give मोदिष्ये I will rejoice इति
thus अज्ञानविमोहिताः deluded by ignorance,

15. "I am rich and well-born. Who
else is equal to me ? I will sacrifice, I will
give, I will rejoice." Thus deluded by
ignorance,

अनेकचित्तविभ्रान्ता मोहजालसमावृताः ॥

प्रसक्ताः कामभोगेषु पतन्ति नरकेऽशुचौ ॥१६॥

अनेकचित्तविभ्रान्ताः Bewildered by many a fancy मोह-
जालसमावृताः covered by the meshes of delusion कामभोगेषु
to the gratification of lust प्रसक्ताः addicted अशुचौ foul
नरके into a hell पतन्ति they fall.

16. Bewildered by many a fancy, covered by the meshes of delusion, addicted to the
gratification of lust, they fall down into a foul
hell.

आत्मसम्भाविताः स्तब्धा धनमानमदान्विताः ॥

यजन्ते नामयज्ञैस्ते दम्भेनाविधिपूर्वकम् ॥१७॥

आत्मसम्भाविताः Self-conceited स्तब्धाः haughty धनमान
मदान्विताः filled with the pride and intoxication of
wealth ते they दम्भेन out of ostentation नामयज्ञैः sacrifices in name अविधिपूर्वकम् disregarding ordinance यजन्ते
they perform ;

17. Self-conceited, haughty, filled with
the pride and intoxication of wealth, they perform sacrifices in name, out of ostentation, disregarding ordinance ;

अहङ्कारं बलं दर्पं कामं क्रोधं च संश्रिताः ॥
मामात्मपरदेहेषु प्रद्विषन्तोऽभ्यसूयकाः ॥१८॥

अहङ्कारं Egoism बलं power दर्पं insolence कामं lust क्रोधं
wrath च and संश्रिताः possessed of आत्मपरदेहेषु in their own
bodies and in those of others माम् Me (the Self within)
प्रद्विषन्तः hating अभ्यसूयकाः (these) malignant people.

18. Possessed of egoism, power, insolence,
lust, and wrath, these malignant people hate
Me (the Self within) in their own bodies and
those of others.

तानहं द्विषतः क्रूरान्संसारेषु नराधमान् ॥
क्षिपाम्यजस्रमशुभानासुरीष्वेव योनिषु ॥१९॥

अहं I द्विषतः malicious क्रूरान् cruel नराधमान् most
degraded of men अशुभान् evil-doers संसारेषु in these

worlds आसुरीषु of Asuras योनिषु into the wombs एव only
अजस्रम् perpetually क्षिपामि (I) hurl.

19. These malicious and cruel evil-
doers, most degraded of men, I hurl perpetually into the wombs of Asuras only, in these
worlds.

[*Wombs of Asuras* : Wombs of the most cruel
beings, as tigers, snakes, etc.

Worlds : Paths of Samsâra passing through
many a hell.]

आसुरीं योनिमापन्ना मूढा जन्मनि जन्मनि ॥
मामप्राप्यैव कौन्तेय ततो यान्त्यधमां गतिम् ॥२०॥

कौन्तेय O son of Kunti मूढाः deluded जन्मनि जन्मनि
birth after birth आसुरीं Âsurika योनिम् wombs आपन्नाः
obtaining माम् Me अप्राप्य not attaining एव still ततः than
that अधमां lower गतिम् condition यान्ति (they) fall into.

20. Obtaining the Âsurika wombs, and
deluded birth after birth, not attaining to Me,
they thus fall, O son of Kunti, into a still lower
condition.

त्रिविधं नरकस्येदं द्वारं नाशनमात्मनः ॥
कामः क्रोधस्तथा लोभस्तस्मादेतत्त्रयं त्यजेत् ॥२१॥

कामः Lust क्रोधः anger तथा and लोभः greed इदं this
त्रिविधं triple नरकस्य of hell द्वारं the gate आत्मनः of the
self नाशनम् destructive एतत् these त्रयं three त्यजेत् (one)
should forsake.

21.   Triple is this gate of hell, destructive
of the self—lust, anger and greed ; therefore
one should forsake these three.

[*Destructive of the self :* making the self fit for
no human end whatever.]

एतैर्विमुक्तः कौन्तेय तमोद्वारैस्त्रिभिर्नरः ॥
आचरत्यात्मनः श्रेयस्ततो याति परां गतिम् ॥२२॥

कौन्तेय O son of Kunti एतैः from these त्रिभिः three
तमोद्वारैः gates of darkness (hell) विमुक्तः free नरः the man
आत्मनः for himself श्रेयः what is good आचरति practises
ततः and then परां Supreme गतिम् Goal याति goes to.

22.   The man who has got beyond these
three gates of darkness, O son of Kunti, practises what is good for himself, and thus goes to
the Goal Supreme.

[*Gates of darkness :* leading to hell (Naraka)
which is full of pain and delusion.]

यः शास्त्रविधिमुत्सृज्य वर्तते कामकारतः ॥
न स सिद्धिमवाप्नोति न सुखं न परां गतिम् ॥२३॥

यः Who शास्त्रविधिम् the ordinance of the Shâstra उत्सृज्य
setting aside कामकारतः under the impulse of desire वर्तते
acts सः he सिद्धिम् perfection न not अवाप्नोति attains to न
nor सुखं happiness न nor परां Supreme गतिम् Goal.

23. He who, setting aside the ordinance of the Shâstra, acts under the impulse of desire, attains not to perfection, nor happiness, nor the Goal Supreme.

[*Perfection :* fitness for attaining the end of man.]

तस्माच्छास्त्रं प्रमाणं ते कार्याकार्यव्यवस्थितौ ॥
ज्ञात्वा शास्त्रविधानोक्तं कर्म कर्तुमिहार्हसि ॥२४॥

तस्मात् So कार्याकार्यव्यवस्थितौ in ascertaining what ought to be done and what ought not to be done शास्त्रं the Shâstra ते thy प्रमाणं (be) authority इह here शास्त्रविधानोक्तं what is said in the ordinance of the Shâstra ज्ञात्वा having known कर्म action कर्तुम् to do अर्हसि thou shouldst.

24. So let the Shâstra be thy authority in ascertaining what ought to be done and what ought not to be done. Having known what is said in the ordinance of the Shâstra, thou shouldst act here.

[*Here :* in this world.]

इति देवासुरसम्पद्विभागयोगो नाम षोडशोऽध्यायः ॥

The end of the sixteenth chapter, designated, *The Classification of the Divine and the Non-divine Attributes.*

|| सप्तदशोऽध्यायः ||

SEVENTEENTH CHAPTER

अर्जुन उवाच ।

ये शास्त्रविधिमुत्सृज्य यजन्ते श्रद्धयान्विताः ॥
तेषां निष्ठा तु का कृष्ण सत्त्वमाहो रजस्तमः ॥१॥

अर्जुनः Arjuna उवाच said :

कृष्ण O Krishna ये who शास्त्रविधिम् the ordinance of the Shâstra उत्सृज्य setting aside श्रद्धया with Shraddhâ तु but अन्विताः endued यजन्ते perform sacrifice तेषां their निष्ठा condition का what सत्त्वम् Sattva रजः Rajas आहो or तमः Tamas.

Arjuna said :

1. Those who setting aside the ordinance of the Shâstra, perform sacrifice with Shraddhâ, what is their condition, O Krishna ? (Is it) Sattva, Rajas, or Tamas ?

[Setting...Shraddhâ : not that they believe the ordinance of the Shâstra to be false, but out of laziness or because of the difficulty in adhering to them

strictly, they let them alone and worship the gods, endued with Shraddhâ.]

श्रीभगवानुवाच ।

त्रिविधा भवति श्रद्धा देहिनां सा स्वभावजा ॥

सात्त्विकी राजसी चैव तामसी चेति तां शृणु ॥२॥

श्रीभगवान् The Blessed Lord उवाच said :

देहिनां Of the embodied सात्त्विकी the Sâttvika राजसी
the Râjasika तामसी Tâmasika च and इति thus त्रिविधा
threefold एव indeed श्रद्धा the Shraddhâ भवति is सा which
स्वभावजा (is) inherent in (their) nature तां of it शृणु hear
(thou).

The Blessed Lord said :

2.   Threefold is the Shraddhâ of the embodied, which is inherent in their nature—the
Sâttvika, the Râjasika and the Tâmasika.   Do
thou hear of it.

[*Inherent...nature :* born of their past Samskâras.   *It :* the threefold Shraddhâ.]

सत्त्वानुरूपा सर्वस्य श्रद्धा भवति भारत ॥

श्रद्धामयोऽयं पुरुषो यो यच्छ्रद्धः स एव सः ॥३॥

भारत O descendant of Bharata सर्वस्य of each श्रद्धा
Shraddhâ सत्त्वानुरूपा according to his natural disposition भवति is अयं the पुरुषः man श्रद्धामयः consists of

(his) Shraddhâ यः he यच्छ्रद्धः what (his) Shraddhâ is सः
he एव verily सः that (is).

3. The Shraddhâ of each is according to his natural disposition, O descendant
of Bharata. The man consists of his
Shraddhâ ; he verily is what his Shraddhâ
is.

[*Natural disposition:* the specific tendencies or
Samskâras.]

यजन्ते सात्त्विका देवान्यक्षरक्षांसि राजसाः ॥

प्रेतान्भूतगणांश्चान्ये यजन्ते तामसा जनाः ॥४॥

सात्त्विकाः Sâttvika men देवान् the Devas यजन्ते worship
राजसाः the Râjasika यक्षरक्षांसि the Yakshas and the
Râkshasas अन्ये the others तामसाः the Tâmasika जनाः
men प्रेतान् the Pretas भूतगणान् the hosts of Bhutas च
and यजन्ते worship.

4. Sâttvika men worship the Devas ;
Râjasika, the Yakshas and the Râkshasas ; the
others—the Tâmasika men—the Pretas and the
hosts of Bhutas.

अशास्त्रविहितं घोरं तप्यन्ते ये तपो जनाः ॥

दम्भाहङ्कारसंयुक्ताः कामरागबलान्विताः ॥५॥

कर्शयन्तः शरीरस्थं भूतग्राममचेतसः ॥

मां चैवान्तःशरीरस्थं तान्विद्ध्यासुरनिश्चयान् ॥६॥

दम्भाहङ्कारसंयुक्ताः Given to ostentation and egoism
कामरागबलान्विताः possessed with the power of lust and
attachment ये who अचेतसः senseless जनाः men शरीरस्थं
in the body भूतग्राममम् all the organs अन्तःशरीरस्थं that
dwell in the body within मां Me च and कर्शयन्तःtorturing
अशास्त्रविहितं not enjoined by the Shâstras घोरं severe तपः
austerity तप्यन्ते practise तान् them आसुरनिश्चयान् to be of
Âsurika resolve विद्धि know.

5-6. Those men who practise severe
austerities not enjoined by the Shâstras,
given to ostentation and egoism, possessed
with the power of lust and attachment,
torture, senseless as they are, all the
organs in the body, and Me dwelling in the
body within ; know them to be of Âsurika
resolve.

[*Austerities:* which cause pain to himself and to
other living beings.

Possessed...attachment: may also be interpreted as, "possessed of lust, attachment and power".

All the organs of the body : the aggregate of all
the elements composing the body.]

आहारस्त्वपि सर्वस्य त्रिविधो भवति प्रियः ॥
यज्ञस्तपस्तथा दानं तेषां भेदमिमं श्रृणु ॥७॥

सर्वस्य By each of them अपि also आहारः food तु indeed
त्रिविधः threefold प्रियः liked भवति is तथा as also यज्ञः Yajna

तप: austerity दानं almsgiving च and तेषां their इमं this
भेदम् distinction श्रृणु do thou hear.

7. The food also which is liked by each
of them is threefold, as also Yajna, austerity,
and almsgiving. Do thou hear this, their
distinction.

आयुःसत्त्वबलारोग्यसुखप्रीतिविवर्धना: ॥
रस्या: स्निग्धा: स्थिरा हृद्या आहारा: सात्त्विकप्रिया: ॥८॥

आयुःसत्त्वबलारोग्यसुखप्रीतिविवर्धना: Those which augment
आयु: vitality सत्त्वम् energy बलम् strength आरोग्यम् health सुखम्
cheerfulness and प्रीति: appetite रस्या: which are savoury
स्निग्धा: oleaginous स्थिरा: substantial हृद्या: agreeable आहारा:
the foods सात्त्विकप्रिया: (are) liked by the Sâttvika.

8. The foods which augment vitality,
energy, strength, health, cheerfulness, and
appetite, which are savoury and oleaginous,
substantial and agreeable, are liked by the
Sâttvika.

कट्वम्ललवणात्युष्णतीक्ष्णरूक्षविदाहिन: ॥
आहारा राजसस्येष्टा दु:खशोकामयप्रदा: ॥९॥

कट्वम्ललवणात्युष्णतीक्ष्णरूक्षविदाहिन: Those that are कटु: bitter
अम्ल: sour लवण: saline अत्युष्ण: excessively hot तीक्ष्ण: pungent
रूक्ष: dry and विदाहिन: burning दु:खशोकामयप्रदा: are productive
of pain, grief, and disease आहारा: the foods राजसस्य by
the Râjasika इष्टा: are liked.

24

9. The foods that are bitter, sour, saline, excessively hot, pungent, dry, and burning, are liked by the Râjasika, and are productive of pain, grief, and disease.

[*Excessively:* this word should be construed with each of the seven; thus, excessively bitter, excessively sour, and so on.]

यातयामं गतरसं पूति पर्युषितं च यत् ॥
उच्छिष्टमपि चामेध्यं भोजनं तामसप्रियम् ॥१०॥

यत् Which यातयामं (is) stale गतरसं is tasteless पूति stinking पर्युषितं cooked overnight उच्छिष्टम् refuse अमेध्यं impure च and भोजनं the food तामसप्रियम् liked by the Tâmasika.

10. That which is stale, tasteless, stinking, cooked overnight, refuse, and impure, is the food liked by the Tâmasika.

[*Stale—Yâtayâmam* : lit., cooked three hours ago.

Refuse: left on the plate after a meal.]

अफलाकांक्षिभिर्यज्ञो विधिदृष्टो य इज्यते ॥
यष्टव्यमेवेति मनः समाधाय स सात्त्विकः ॥११॥

अफलाकांक्षिभिः By men desiring no fruit यष्टव्यम् to be performed for its own sake एव only इति as मनः (their)

mind समाधाय fixing विधिदृष्टः as enjoined by ordinance यः
which यज्ञः Yajna इज्यते is performed सः that सात्त्विकः is
Sâttvika.

11. That Yajna is Sâttvika which is
performed by men desiring no fruit, as
enjoined by ordinance, with their mind fixed
on the Yajna only, for its own sake.

अभिसन्धाय तु फलं दम्भार्थमपि चैव यत् ॥
इज्यते भरतश्रेष्ठ तं यज्ञं विद्धि राजसम् ॥१२॥

फलं Fruit अभिसन्धाय seeking for तु but दम्भार्थम् for
ostentation अपि also एव indeed च and यत् which इज्यते is
performed भरतश्रेष्ठ O best of the Bhâratas तं that यज्ञं
Yajna राजसं Râjasika विद्धि know (it to be).

12. That which is performed, O best
of the Bhâratas, seeking for fruit and for
ostentation, know it to be a Râjasika
Yajna.

विधिहीनमसृष्टान्नं मन्त्रहीनमदक्षिणम् ॥
श्रद्धाविरहितं यज्ञं तामसं परिचक्षते ॥१३॥

विधिहीनम् Without keeping to ordinance असृष्टान्नं in
which no food is distributed मन्त्रहीनम् which is devoid of
Mantras अदक्षिणम् which is devoid of gifts श्रद्धाविरहितं
devoid of Shraddhâ यज्ञं Yajna तामसं Tâmasika परिचक्षते
is said to be.

13. The Yajna performed without heed to ordinance, in which no food is distributed, which is devoid of Mantras, gifts, and Shraddhâ, is said to be Tâmasika.

देवद्विजगुरुप्राज्ञपूजनं शौचमार्जवम् ॥
ब्रह्मचर्यमहिंसा च शारीरं तप उच्यते ॥१४॥

देवद्विजगुरुप्राज्ञपूजनं Worship of the Devas, the twice-born, the Gurus, and the wise शौचम् purity आर्जवम् straight-forwardness ब्रह्मचर्यम् continence अहिंसा non-injury च and शारीरं of the body तप: the austerity उच्यते is called.

14. Worship of the Devas, the twice-born, the Gurus, and the wise ; purity, straightfor-wardness, continence, and non-injury are called the austerity of the body.

अनुद्वेगकरं वाक्यं सत्यं प्रियहितं च यत् ॥
स्वाध्यायाभ्यसनं चैव वाङ्मयं तप उच्यते ॥१५॥

अनुद्वेगकरं Causing no vexation सत्यं true प्रियहितं agreeable and beneficial च as also यत् which वाक्यं speech स्वाध्यायाभ्यसनं regular study of the Vedas च एव and also वाङ्मयं of speech तप: the austerity उच्यते is said (to form).

15. Speech which causes no vexation, and is true, as also agreeable and beneficial and regular study of the Vedas—these are said to form the austerity of speech.

[Speech, to be an austerity, must form an in-
variable combination of all the four attributes mentioned in the Shloka ; if it lacks in one or other of
them, it will no longer be an austerity of speech.]

मनःप्रसादः सौम्यत्वं मौनमात्मविनिग्रहः ॥
भावसंशुद्धिरित्येतत्तपो मानसमुच्यते ॥१६॥

मनःप्रसादः Serenity of mind सौम्यत्वं kindliness मौनम्
silence आत्मविनिग्रहः self-control भावसंशुद्धिः honesty of
motive इति एतत् this मानसम् mental तपः the austerity उच्यते
is called.

16. Serenity of mind, kindliness,
silence, self-control, honesty of motive—this
is called the mental austerity.

[*Silence*—Maunam : is the result of the control
of thought so far as it concerns speech. Or it may
mean, the condition of the Muni, i.e., practice of
meditation.]

श्रद्धया परया तप्तं तपस्तत्त्रिविधं नरैः ॥
अफलाकांक्षिभिर्युक्तैः सात्त्विकं परिचक्षते ॥१७॥

अफलाकांक्षिभिः Desiring no fruit युक्तैः steadfast नरैः by
men परया great श्रद्धया with Shraddhâ तप्तं practised तत्
that त्रिविधं threefold तपः austerity सात्त्विकं Sâttvika
परिचक्षते (sages) call.

17.   This threefold austerity practised by steadfast men, with great Shraddhâ, desiring no fruit, is said to be Sâttvika.

[*Steadfast:* unaffected in success and failure.]

सत्कारमानपूजार्थं तपो दम्भेन चैव यत् ॥

क्रियते तदिह प्रोक्तं राजसं चलमध्रुवम् ॥१८॥

सत्कारमानपूजार्थं With the object of gaining welcome, honour, and worship दम्भेन with ostentation च एव and यत् which तप: austerity क्रियते is practised इह here चलम् unstable अध्रुवम् transitory तत् that राजसं Râjasika प्रोक्तं is said (to be).

18.   That austerity which is practised with the object of gaining welcome, honour, and worship, and with ostentation, is here said to be Râjasika, unstable, and transitory.

[*With ostentation :* for mere show, hypocritically, with no sincere belief.

Here: is explained also in the sense of "of this world", i.e., yielding fruit only in this world.]

मूढग्राहेणात्मनो यत्पीडया क्रियते तप: ॥

परस्योत्सादनार्थं वा तत्तामसमुदाहृतम् ॥१९॥

मूढग्राहेण Out of a foolish notion आत्मन: of self पीडया with torture परस्य of another उत्सादनार्थं for the purpose

of ruining वा or यत् which तप: austerity क्रियते is practised तत् that तामसम् Tâmasika उदाहृतम् is declared (to be).

19.   That austerity which is practised out
of a foolish notion, with self-torture or for the
purpose of ruining another, is declared to be
Tâmasika.

दातव्यमिति यद्दानं दीयतेऽनुपकारिणे ॥

देशे काले च पात्रे च तद्दानं सात्त्विकं स्मृतम् ॥२०॥

देशे In a fit place काले in a fit time च and पात्रे to a
worthy person च and दातव्यम् to give is right इति with
this idea अनुपकारिणे to one who does no service (in
return) यत् which दानं gift दीयते is given तत् that दानं
gift सात्त्विकं Sâttvika स्मृतम् is held to be.

20.   "To give is right"—gift given with
this idea, to one who does no service in return,
in a fit place and to a worthy person, that gift
is held to be Sâttvika.

[*Who...return:* one who cannot, or who
though able is not expected to return the good.]

यत्तु प्रत्युपकारार्थं फलमुद्दिश्य वा पुनः ॥

दीयते च परिक्लिष्टं तद्दानं राजसं स्मृतम् ॥२१॥

यत् What तु and प्रत्युपकारार्थं with a view to receiving
in return फलम् च and the fruit उद्दिश्य looking for वा or पुनः
again परिक्लिष्टं reluctantly दीयते is given तत् that दानं
gift राजसं Râjasika स्मृतं is held to be.

21. And what is given with a view to receiving in return, or looking for the fruit, or again reluctantly, that gift is held to be Râjasika.

अदेशकाले यद्दानमपात्रेभ्यश्च दीयते ॥

असत्कृतमवज्ञातं तत्तामसमुदाहृतम् ॥२२॥

अदेशकाले At the wrong place or time अपात्रेभ्यः च and to unworthy persons असत्कृतम् without regard अवज्ञातं with disdain यत् that दानं gift दीयते is given तत् that तामसम् Tâmasika उदाहृतं is declared to be.

22. The gift that is given at the wrong place or time, to unworthy persons, without regard or with disdain, that is declared to be Tâmasika.

ॐ तत्सदिति निर्देशो ब्रह्मणस्त्रिविधः स्मृतः ॥

ब्राह्मणास्तेन वेदाश्च यज्ञाश्च विहिताः पुरा ॥२३॥

ॐ Om तत् Tat सत् Sat इति this ब्रह्मणः of Brahman त्रिविधः triple निर्देशः designation स्मृतः has been declared तेन by that ब्राह्मणाः the Brâhmanas च and वेदाः the Vedas च and यज्ञाः the Yajnas पुरा of old विहिताः were made.

23. "Om, Tat, Sat": this has been declared to be the triple designation of Brahman. By that were made of old the Brâhmanas, the Vedas, and the Yajnas.

[*Om, Tat, Sat :* Om is the principal name of

the Lord, because it means all that is manifest and the beyond. It also means "Yes". Tat means "That"; the Indefinable, that which can only be described indirectly as "That which". Sat means Reality; which is ever permanent in one mode of being.]

तस्मादोमित्युदाहृत्य यज्ञदानतपःक्रियाः ॥
प्रवर्तन्ते विधानोक्ताः सततं ब्रह्मवादिनाम् ॥२४॥

तस्मात् Therefore ओम् Om इति उदाहृत्य uttering ब्रह्मवादि-नाम् of the followers of the Vedas विधानोक्ताः as enjoined in the ordinances यज्ञदानतपःक्रियाः the acts of sacrifice, gift, and austerity सततं always प्रवर्तन्ते begun.

24. Therefore, uttering "Om", are the acts of sacrifice, gift, and austerity as enjoined in the ordinances, always begun by the followers of the Vedas.

तदित्यनभिसन्धाय फलं यज्ञतपःक्रियाः ॥
दानक्रियाश्च विविधाः क्रियन्ते मोक्षकांक्षिभिः ॥२५॥

तत् Tat इति thus (uttering) फलं the fruit अनभिसन्धाय without aiming at मोक्षकांक्षिभिः by the seekers of Moksha विविधाः various यज्ञतपः क्रियाः acts of Yajna and austerity दानक्रियाः acts of gift च and क्रियन्ते are performed.

25. Uttering "Tat", without aiming at fruits, are the various acts of Yajna, austerity, and gift performed by the seekers of Moksha.

सद्भावे साधुभावे च सदित्येतत्प्रयुज्यते ॥

प्रशस्ते कर्मणि तथा सच्छब्द: पार्थ युज्यते ॥२६॥

पार्थं O Pârtha सद्भावे in the sense of reality साधुभावे in the sense of goodness च and सत् Sat इति as एतत् this प्रयुज्यते is used तथा so long प्रशस्ते auspicious कर्मणि in (the sense of) an act च and सत् Sat शब्द: the word युज्यते is used.

26.   The word "Sat" is used in the sense of reality and of goodness ; and so also, O Pârtha, the word "Sat" is used in the sense of an auspicious act.

यज्ञे तपसि दाने च स्थिति: सदिति चोच्यते ॥

कर्म चैव तदर्थीयं सदित्येवाभिधीयते ॥२७॥

यज्ञे In Yajna तपसि in austerity दाने in gift च and स्थिति: steadiness सत् Sat इति so उच्यते is called च also तदर्थीयं in connection with these, or, for the sake of the Lord कर्म action च एव as also सत् Sat इति एव so अभिधीयते is called.

27.   Steadiness   in   Yajna,   austerity, and gift is also called "Sat": as also action in connection with these (or, action for the sake of the Lord) is called "Sat".

अश्रद्धया हुतं दत्तं तपस्तप्तं कृतं च यत् ॥

असदित्युच्यते पार्थ न च तत्प्रेत्य नो इह ॥२८॥

अश्रद्धया Without Shraddhâ हुतं is sacrificed दत्तं given तपं is practised तपः austerity च and यत् whatever कृतं performed असत् Asat इति so उच्यते is called पार्थ O Pârtha तत् it न च neither प्रेत्य hereafter (after death) नो nor इह here.

28. Whatever is sacrificed, given, or performed and whatever austerity is practised without Shraddhâ, it is called Asat, O Pârtha ; it is naught here or hereafter.

[*It is naught here or hereafter :* Though costing much trouble it is of no use here as it is not acceptable to the wise ones, nor can it produce any effect conducive to good hereafter.]

इति श्रद्धात्रयविभागयोगो नाम सप्तदशोऽध्यायः ॥

The end of the seventeenth chapter, designated, *The Enquiry into the Threefold Shraddha.*

EIGHTEENTH CHAPTER

अर्जुन उवाच ।

संन्यासस्य महाबाहो तत्त्वमिच्छामि वेदितुम् ॥
त्यागस्य च हृषीकेश पृथक्केशिनिषूदन ॥१॥

अर्जुनः Arjuna उवाच said :

हृषीकेश O Hrishikesha महाबाहो O mighty-armed केशिनिषूदन O Slayer of Keshi संन्यासस्य of Sannyâsa त्यागस्य of Tyâga च as also पृथक् severally तत्त्वं truth वेदितुं to know इच्छामि I desire.

Arjuna said :

1. I desire to know severally, O mighty-armed, the truth of Sannyâsa, O Hrishikesha, as also of Tyâga, O slayer of Keshi.

[*Sannyâsa* and *Tyâga* both mean renunciation. *Keshi:* was an Asura.]

श्रीभगवानुवाच ।

काम्यानां कर्मणां न्यासं संन्यासं कवयो विदुः ॥
सर्वकर्मफलत्यागं प्राहुस्त्यागं विचक्षणाः ॥२॥

श्रीभगवान् The Blessed Lord उवाच said :

कवयः The sages काम्यानां Kâmya कर्मणां of actions न्यास the renunciation संन्यासं (as) Sannyâsa विदुः understand विचक्षणाः the wise सर्वकर्मफलत्यागं the abandonment of the fruit of all works त्यागं (as) Tyâga प्राहुः declare.

The Blessed Lord said:

2. The renunciation of Kâmya actions, the sages understand as Sannyâsa : the wise declare the abandonment of the fruit of all works as Tyâga.

[*Kâmya :* which are accompanied with a desire for fruits.]

त्याज्यं दोषवदित्यके कर्म प्राहुर्मनीषिणः ॥

यज्ञदानतपःकर्म न त्याज्यमिति चापरे ॥३॥

एके Some मनीषिणः philosophers कर्म (all) actions दोषवत् as an evil इति that त्याज्यं should be relinquished प्राहुः declare अपरे others च whilst यज्ञदानतपःकर्म the work of Yajna, gift, and austerity न not त्याज्यं should be relinquished इति that.

3. Some philosophers declare that all actions should be relinquished as an evil, whilst others (say) that the work of Yajna, gift, and austerity should not be relinquished.

निश्चयं शृणु मे तत्र त्यागे भरतसत्तम ॥
त्यागो हि पुरुषव्याघ्र त्रिविधः सम्प्रकीर्तितः ॥४॥

भरतसत्तम O best of the Bhâratas पुरुषव्याघ्र O tiger among men तत्र about that त्यागे in relinquishment मे from Me निश्चयं the final truth शृणु hear त्यागः relinquishment हि for त्रिविधः of three kinds सम्प्रकीर्तितः has been declared (to be).

4. Hear from Me the final truth about relinquishment, O best of the Bhâratas. For relinquishment has been declared to be of three kinds, O tiger among men.

यज्ञदानतपःकर्म न त्याज्यं कार्यमेव तत् ॥
यज्ञो दानं तपश्चैव पावनानि मनीषिणाम् ॥५॥

यज्ञदानतपःकर्म The work of Yajna, gift, and austerity न not त्याज्यं should be relinquished तत् it कार्यम् should be performed एव indeed यज्ञः Yajna दानं gift तप: austerity च and एव indeed मनीषिणां to the wise पावनानि are purifying.

5. The work of Yajna, gift, and austerity should not be relinquished, but it should indeed be performed ; (for) Yajna, gift, and austerity are purifying to the wise.

एतान्यपि तु कर्माणि सङ्गं त्यक्त्वा फलानि च ॥
कर्तव्यानीति मे पार्थ निश्चितं मतमुत्तमम् ॥६॥

पार्थ O Pârtha एतानि these कर्माणि works अपि even तु but सङ्गं attachment फलानि the fruits च and त्यक्त्वा leaving कर्तव्यानि should be performed इति such मे my निश्चितं certain उत्तमम् best मतम् conviction.

6. But even these works, O Pârtha, should be performed, leaving attachment and the fruits ; such is My best and certain conviction.

नियतस्य तु संन्यासः कर्मणो नोपपद्यते ॥
मोहात्तस्य परित्यागस्तामसः परिकीर्तितः ॥७॥

नियतस्य Obligatory कर्मणः of action तु but संन्यासः the renunciation न not उपपद्यते is proper मोहात् from delusion तस्य of the same परित्यागः abandonment तामसः Tâmasika परिकीर्तितः is declared.

7. But the renunciation of obligatory action is not proper. Abandonment of the same from delusion is declared to be Tâmasika.

[Since it is purifying in the case of the ignorant.]

दुःखमित्येव यत्कर्म कायक्लेशभयात्त्यजेत् ॥
स कृत्वा राजसं त्यागं नैव त्यागफलं लभेत् ॥८॥

दुःखम् (It is) painful इति because एव only कायक्लेशभयात् from fear of bodily trouble यत् which कर्म action त्यजेत् relinquishes सः he राजसं Râjasika त्यागं relinquishment कृत्वा performing त्यागफलं the fruit of relinquishment न not एव लभेत् obtains.

8. He who from fear of bodily trouble relinquishes action, because it is painful, thus performing a Râjasika relinquishment, he obtains not the fruit thereof.

[*Fruit:* i.e., Moksha, which comes out of the renunciation of all actions accompanied with wisdom.]

कार्यमित्येव यत्कर्म नियतं क्रियतेऽर्जुन ॥
सङ्गं त्यक्त्वा फलं चैव स त्यागः सात्त्विको मतः ॥६॥

अर्जुन O Arjuna सङ्गं attachment फलं fruit च एव and त्यक्त्वा leaving कार्यं it ought to be done इति because एव only यत् which नियतं obligatory कर्म action क्रियते is performed सः such त्यागः relinquishment सात्त्विकः Sâttvika मतः is regarded.

9. When obligatory work is performed, O Arjuna, only because it ought to be done, leaving attachment and fruit, such relinquishment is regarded as Sâttvika.

न द्वेष्ट्यकुशलं कर्म कुशले नानुषज्जते ॥

त्यागी सत्त्वसमाविष्टो मेधावी छिन्नसंशयः ॥१०॥

सत्त्वसमाविष्टः Endued with Sattva मेधावी with a steady understanding छिन्नसंशयः with his doubts dispelled त्यागी the relinquisher अकुशलं disagreeable कर्म action न not द्वेष्टि hates कुशले to an agreeable one न nor अनुषज्जते is attached.

10. The relinquisher endued with Sattva and a steady understanding and with his doubts dispelled, hates not a disagreeable work nor is attached to an agreeable one.

न हि देहभृता शक्यं त्यक्तुं कर्माण्यशेषतः ॥

यस्तु कर्मफलत्यागी स त्यागीत्यभिधीयते ॥११॥

देहभृता by an embodied being अशेषतः entirely कर्माणि actions त्यक्तुं to relinquish न not हि indeed शक्यं can be यः who तु but कर्मफलत्यागी relinquisher of the fruits of action सः he त्यागी relinquisher इति thus अभिधीयते is called.

11. Actions cannot be entirely relinquished by an embodied being, but he who relinquishes the fruits of action is called a relinquisher.

अनिष्टमिष्टं मिश्रं च त्रिविधं कर्मणः फलम् ॥

भवत्यत्यागिनां प्रेत्य न तु संन्यासिनां कचित् ॥१२॥

25

अत्यागिनां To non-relinquishers प्रेत्य after death अनिष्टम् disagreeable इष्टं agreeable मिश्रं mixed च and त्रिविधं threefold कर्मणः of action फलम् fruit भवति accrues तु but संन्यासिनां to relinquishers क्वचित् ever न not.

12. The threefold fruit of action— disagreeable, agreeable, and mixed—accrues to non-relinquishers after death, but never to relinquishers.

पञ्चैतानि महाबाहो कारणानि निबोध मे ॥
साङ्ख्ये कृतान्ते प्रोक्तानि सिद्धये सर्वकर्मणाम् ॥१३॥

महाबाहो O mighty-armed साङ्ख्ये in the wisdom कृतान्ते which is the end of all action सर्वकर्मणाम् of all works सिद्धये for the accomplishment प्रोक्तानि as declared एतानि these पञ्च five कारणानि causes मे from Me निबोध learn.

13. Learn from Me, O mighty-armed, these five causes for the accomplishment of all works as declared in the wisdom which is the end of all action :

[*Wisdom* : Sânkhya—literally, in which all the things that are to be known are expounded, therefore, the highest wisdom.]

अधिष्ठानं तथा कर्ता करणं च पृथग्विधम् ॥
विविधाश्च पृथक् चेष्टा दैवं चैवात्र पञ्चमम् ॥१४॥

अधिष्ठानं The body तथा also कर्ता the agent पृथग्विधम्
various करणं the senses विविधाः of a manifold kind पृथक्
different चेष्टाः functions अत्र of these पञ्चमम् the fifth दैवं
the presiding divinity च एव and also.

14. The body, the agent, the various
senses, the different functions of a manifold
kind, and the presiding divinity, the fifth of
these ;

[*Presiding divinity* : Each of the senses has its
god who presides over it, and by whose aid it dis-
charges its own functions; e.g., Āditya (the Sun) is
the presiding divinity of the eye, by whose aid it sees
and acts; and so on with the other senses.]

शरीरवाङ्मनोभिर्यत्कर्म प्रारभते नरः ॥

न्याय्यं वा विपरीतं वा पञ्चैते तस्य हेतवः ॥१५॥

नरः A man शरीरवाङ्मनोभिः by (his) body, speech, and
mind यत् whatever न्याय्यं right वा or विपरीतं the reverse
कर्म action प्रारभते performs एते these पञ्च five तस्य its हेतवः
causes.

15. Whatever action a man performs
by his body, speech, and mind—whether
right or the reverse—these five are its
causes.

तत्रैवं सति कर्तारमात्मानं केवलं तु यः ॥

पश्यत्यकृतबुद्धित्वान्न स पश्यति दुर्मतिः ॥१६॥

एवं Thus सति being तत्र there (the case) केवलं the Absolute आत्मानं the Self तु verily अकृतबुद्धित्वात् through a non-purified understanding यः who कर्तारम् as the agent पश्यति looks upon सः he दुर्मतिः of perverted mind न not पश्यति sees.

16. Such being the case, he who through a non-purified understanding looks upon his Self, the Absolute, as the agent—he of perverted mind sees not.

यस्य नाहंकृतो भावो बुद्धिर्यस्य न लिप्यते ॥
हत्वापि स इमाँल्लोकान्न हन्ति न निबध्यते ॥१७॥

यस्य Whose अहंकृतः of egoism भावः the notion न not यस्य whose बुद्धिः intelligence न not लिप्यते is affected सः he इमान् these लोकान् people हत्वा killing अपि though न not हन्ति kills न nor निबध्यते is bound ;

17. He who is free from the notion of egoism, whose intelligence is not affected (by good or evil), though he kills these people, he kills not, nor is bound (by the action);

[He whose self-consciousness, by the force of long, strenuous, and properly-trained self-concentration, is ever identified with Brahman, and not with the five causes of action as mentioned in Shloka 14— he whose self-consciousness never mistakes itself for the body, mind, and the like, even when performing

physical acts—he is ever free from the taint of
action.]

ज्ञानं ज्ञेयं परिज्ञाता त्रिविधा कर्मचोदना ॥
करणं कर्म कर्तेति त्रिविधः कर्मसंग्रहः ॥१८॥

ज्ञानं Knowledge ज्ञेयं the known परिज्ञाता the knower
त्रिविधा threefold कर्मचोदना the cause of action करणं the
instrument कर्म the object कर्ता the agent इति the त्रिविधः
threefold कर्मसंग्रहः the basis of action.

18. Knowledge, the known, and the
knower form the threefold cause of action.
The instrument, the object, and the agent are
the threefold basis of action.

[*Basis :* because the threefold action inheres in
these three.]

ज्ञानं कर्म च कर्ता च त्रिधैव गुणभेदतः ॥
प्रोच्यते गुणसंख्याने यथावच्छृणु तान्यपि ॥१६॥

गुणसंख्याने In the (science of) enumeration of the
Gunas (Sânkhya philosophy) ज्ञानं knowledge कर्म action
च and कर्ता agent च and गुणभेदतः from the distinction of
Gunas त्रिधा of three kinds एव only प्रोच्यते are declared
(to be) तानि them अपि also यथावत् duly शृणु hear.

19. Knowledge, action, and agent are
declared in the Sânkhya philosophy to be

of three kinds only, from the distinction of Gunas : hear them also duly.

[*Sânkhya* :   the Science of the Gunas by Kapila. Though the Sânkhya view is in conflict with the supreme Truth of Vedânta—the oneness or non-duality of Brahman—yet the former view is given here, because it is an authority on the science of Gunas.

Duly : described according to the science, according to reason.]

सर्वभूतेषु येनैकं भावमव्ययमीक्षते ॥

अविभक्तं विभक्तेषु तज्ज्ञानं विद्धि सात्त्विकम् ॥२०॥

येन By which विभक्तेषु in the separate सर्वभूतेषु (in) all beings अविभक्तं inseparate एकं the one अव्ययम् indestructible भावम् Substance ईक्षते (one) sees तत् that ज्ञानं knowledge सात्त्विकम् to be Sâttvika विद्धि know (thou).

20. That by which the one indes-tructible Substance is seen in all beings, inseparate in the separated, know that knowledge to be Sâttvika.

[*Inseparate* :   undifferentiated ; permeating all.]

पृथक्त्वेन तु यज्ज्ञानं नानाभावान्पृथग्विधान् ॥

वेत्ति सर्वेषु भूतेषु तज्ज्ञानं विद्धि राजसम् ॥२१॥

पृथक्त्वेन As different from one another तु but यत् which ज्ञानं knowledge सर्वेषु all भूतेषु in beings पृथग्विधान् of

distinct kinds नानाभावान् various entities वेत्ति knows तत्
that ज्ञानं knowledge राजसम् as Râjasika विद्धि know (thou).

21. But that knowledge which sees in
all beings various entities of distinct kinds as
different from one another, know thou that
knowledge as Râjasika.

[*Entities* : Souls.
Different from one another : Different in different bodies.]

यत्तु कृत्स्नवदेकस्मिन् कार्ये सक्तमहैतुकम् ॥

अतत्त्वार्थवदल्पं च तत्तामसमुदाहृतम् ॥२२॥

यत् which तु but एकस्मिन् one single कार्ये to effect
कृत्स्नवत् as if it were the whole सक्तम् confined अहैतुकम्
without reason अतत्त्वार्थवत् without foundation in truth
अल्पं trivial च and तत् that तामसम् Tâmasika उदाहृतम् is
declared.

22. Whilst that which is confined to
one single effect as if it were the whole,
without reason, without foundation in
truth, and trivial—that is declared to be
Tâmasika.

[*One single effect* : such as the body—thinking
it to be the Self.]

नियतं सङ्गरहितमरागद्वेषतः कृतम् ॥

अफलप्रेप्सुना कर्म यत्तत्सात्त्विकमुच्यते ॥२३॥

अफलप्रेप्सुना By one not desirous of the fruit नियत

ordained संङ्गरहितम् free from attachment अरागद्वेषतः without love or hatred कृतम् done यत् which कर्म action तत् that सात्त्विकम् Sâttvika उच्यते is declared.

23. An ordained action done without love or hatred by one not desirous of the fruit and free from attachment, is declared to be Sâttvika.

यत्तु कामेप्सुना कर्म साहंकारेण वा पुनः ॥
क्रियते बहुलायासं तद्राजसमुदाहृतम् ॥२४॥

कामेप्सुना By one desiring desires साहंकारेण with self-conceit वा or बहुलायासं with much effort यत् which तु but पुनः again कर्म the action क्रियते is performed तत् that राजसम् Râjasika उदाहृतम् is declared.

24. But the action which is performed desiring desires, or with self-conceit and with much effort, is declared to be Râjasika.

अनुबन्धं क्षयं हिंसामनपेक्ष्य च पौरुषम् ॥
मोहादारभ्यते कर्म यत्तत्तामसमुच्यते ॥२५॥

अनुबन्धं The consequence क्षयं loss (of power and wealth) हिंसाम् injury (to others) पौरुषम् (one's own) ability च and अनपेक्ष्य without heeding मोहात् through delusion यत् which कर्म action आरभ्यते is undertaken तत् that तामसम् Tâmasika उच्यते is declared.

25. That action is declared to be Tâmasika which is undertaken through delusion, without heed to the consequence, loss (of power and wealth), injury (to others), and (one's own) ability.

मुक्तसङ्गोऽनहंवादी धृत्युत्साहसमन्वितः ॥
सिद्ध्यसिद्ध्योर्निर्विकारः कर्ता सात्त्विक उच्यते ॥२६॥

मुक्तसङ्गः Who is free from attachment अनहंवादी non-egotistic धृत्युत्साहसमन्वितः endued with fortitude and enthusiasm सिद्ध्यसिद्ध्योः in success or failure निर्विकारः un-affected कर्ता an agent सात्त्विकः Sâttvika उच्यते is called.

26. An agent who is free from attachment, non-egotistic, endued with fortitude and enthusiasm, and unaffected in success or failure, is called Sâttvika.

रागी कर्मफलप्रेप्सुर्लुब्धो हिंसात्मकोऽशुचिः ॥
हर्षशोकान्वितः कर्ता राजसः परिकीर्तितः ॥२७॥

रागी Passionate कर्मफलप्रेप्सुः desirous of the fruits of action लुब्धः greedy हिंसात्मकः malignant अशुचिः impure हर्षशोकान्वितः (easily) affected by elation or dejection कर्ता (such) an agent राजसः Râjasika परिकीर्तितः is called.

27. He who is passionate, desirous of the fruits of action, greedy, malignant, impure, easily elated or dejected, such an agent is called Râjasika.

[*Elated or dejected* : at the success or failure of the action in which he is engaged.]

अयुक्तः प्राकृतः स्तब्धः शठो नैष्कृतिकोऽलसः ॥

विषादी दीर्घसूत्री च कर्ता तामस उच्यते ॥२८॥

अयुक्तः Unsteady प्राकृतः vulgar स्तब्धः arrogant शठः dishonest नैष्कृतिकः malicious अलसः indolent विषादी desponding दीर्घसूत्री procrastinating च and कर्ता (such) an agent तामसः Tâmasika उच्यते is called.

28.   Unsteady,   vulgar,   arrogant,   dis-honest,   malicious,   indolent,   desponding,   and   procrastinating,   such   an   agent   is   called Tâmasika.

बुद्धेर्भेदं धृतेश्चैव गुणतस्त्रिविधं श्रृणु ॥

प्रोच्यमानमशेषेण पृथक्त्वेन धनञ्जय ॥२९॥

धनञ्जय O Dhananjaya बुद्धेः of intellect धृतेः of for-titude च एव and also गुणतः according to the Gunas त्रिविधं triple पृथक्त्वेन severally अशेषेण exhaustively प्रोच्यमानम् as I declare भेद the distinction श्रृणु hear (thou).

29.   Hear thou the triple distinction of intellect and fortitude, according to the Gunas, as I declare them exhaustively and severally, O Dhananjaya.

[*Dhananjaya* :   the conqueror of wealth—human and divine, earthly and celestial ; an epithet of Arjuna.]

प्रवृत्तिं च निवृत्तिं च कार्याकार्ये भयाभये ॥

बन्धं मोक्षं च या वेत्ति बुद्धिः सा पार्थ सात्त्विकी ॥३०॥

पार्थ O Pârtha या which प्रवृत्ति the path of work निवृत्ति the path of renunciation च and कार्याकार्ये right and wrong action भयाभये fear and fearlessness बन्धं bondage मोक्षं liberation च and वेत्ति knows सा that सात्त्विकी Sâttvika बुद्धिः intellect.

30 That which knows the paths of work and renunciation, right and wrong action, fear and fearlessness, bondage and liberation, that intellect, O Pârtha, is Sâttvika.

[*Fear...liberation :* the cause of fear and the cause of fearlessness ; similarly, the cause of bondage and the cause of liberation.]

यया धर्ममधर्मं च कार्यं चाकार्यमेव च ॥

अयथावत्प्रजानाति बुद्धिः सा पार्थ राजसी ॥३१॥

पार्थ O Pârtha यया by which धर्मम् Dharma अधर्मम् Adharma कार्यम् right action अकार्यम् wrong action च and अयथावत् in a distorted way प्रजानाति apprehends सा that राजसी Râjasika बुद्धिः intellect.

31. That which has a distorted apprehension of Dharma and its opposite and also of right action and its opposite, that intellect, O Pârtha, is Râjasika.

अधर्मं धर्ममिति या मन्यते तमसावृता ॥
सर्वार्थान्विपरीतांश्च बुद्धिः सा पार्थ तामसी ॥३२॥

पार्थ O Pârtha या which अधर्मम् Adharma धर्मं Dharma
इति as मन्यते regards सर्वार्थान् all things विपरीतान् perverted
च and तमसा in darkness आवृता enveloped सा that बुद्धिः
intellect तामसी Tâmasika.

32. That which, enveloped in darkness,
regards Adharma as Dharma and views all
things in a perverted light, that intellect, O
Pârtha, is Tâmasika.

धृत्या यया धारयते मनःप्राणेन्द्रियक्रियाः ॥
योगेनाव्यभिचारिण्या धृतिः सा पार्थ सात्त्विकी ॥३३॥

पार्थ O Pârtha अव्यभिचारिण्या unswerving यया which
धृत्या by fortitude मनःप्राणेन्द्रियक्रियाः the functions of the
mind, the Prâna, and the senses योगेन through Yoga
धारयते (one) regulates सा that धृतिः fortitude सात्त्विकी
Sâttvika.

33. The fortitude by which the functions of the mind, the Prâna, and the
senses, O Pârtha, are regulated, that fortitude, unswerving through Yoga, is
Sâttvika.

यया तु धर्मकामार्थान् धृत्या धारयतेऽर्जुन ॥
प्रसङ्गेन फलाकांक्षी धृतिः सा पार्थ राजसी ॥३४॥

पार्थ O Pârtha अर्जन O Arjuna यया which धृत्या by fortitude तु but धर्मकामार्थान् Dharma, desire, and wealth धारयते (one) regulates प्रसङ्गेन from attachment फलाकांक्षी desirous of the fruit of action सा that धृति: fortitude राजसी Râjasika.

34. But the fortitude by which one regulates (one's mind) to Dharma, desire, and wealth, desirous of the fruit of each from attachment, that fortitude, O Pârtha, is Râjasika.

यया स्वप्नं भयं शोकं विषादं मदमेव च ॥
न विमुञ्चति दुर्मेधा धृति: सा पार्थ तामसी ॥३५॥

पार्थ O Pârtha दुर्मेधा a stupid man यया by which स्वप्नं sleep भयं fear शोकं grief विषादं despondency मदम् overweening conceit एव च and also न not विमुञ्चति gives up सा that धृति: fortitude तामसी Tâmasika.

35. That by which a stupid man does not give up sleep, fear, grief, despondency, and also overweening conceit, that fortitude, O Pârtha, is Tâmasika.

[*Does not give up sleep, etc.:* is inordinately addicted to sleep, etc., regarding these to be only proper.]

सुखं त्विदानीं त्रिविधं शृणु मे भरतर्षभ ॥
अभ्यासाद्रमते यत्र दुःखान्तं च निगच्छति ॥३६॥

भरतर्षभ O bull of the Bhâratas इदानीं now त्रिविधं threefold सुखं happiness तु and मे from Me श्रृणु hear यत्र in which अभ्यासात् by habit रमते learns to enjoy दुःखान्तं the end of pain च and निगच्छति (he) attains to ;

36. And now hear from Me, O bull of the Bhâratas, of the threefold happiness that one learns to enjoy by habit, and by which one comes to the end of pain.

यत्तदग्रे विषमिव परिणामेऽमृतोपमम् ॥
तत्सुखं सात्त्विकं प्रोक्तमात्मबुद्धिप्रसादजम् ॥३७॥

यत् which तत् that अग्रे at first विषम् poison इव like परिणामे at the end अमृतोपमं like nectar आत्मबुद्धिप्रसादजं born of the translucence of intellect due to Self-realisation तत् that सुखं happiness सात्त्विकं Sâttvika प्रोक्तम् is declared (to be).

37. That which is like poison at first, but like nectar at the end ; that happiness is declared to be Sâttvika, born of the translucence of intellect due to Self-realisation.

विषयेन्द्रियसंयोगाद्यत्तदग्रेऽमृतोपमम् ॥
परिणामे विषमिव तत्सुखं राजसं स्मृतम् ॥३८॥

विषयेन्द्रियसंयोगात् from the contact of object with sense यत् which तत् that अग्रे at first अमृतोपमम् like nectar

परिणामे at the end विषम् poison इव like तत् that सुखं happiness राजसं Râjasika स्मृतम् is declared.

38. That which arises from the contact of object with sense, at first like nectar, but at the end like poison, that happiness is declared to be Râjasika.

[*At the end like poison:* because it leads to deterioration in strength, vigour, complexion, wisdom, intellect, wealth, and energy.]

यदग्रे चानुबन्धे च सुखं मोहनमात्मनः ॥
निद्रालस्यप्रमादोत्थं तत्तामसमुदाहृतम् ॥३६॥

निद्रालस्यप्रमादोत्थं Arising from निद्रा sleep आलस्यं indolence and प्रमादः miscomprehension यत् what सुखं happiness अग्रे in the beginning अनुबन्धे in the sequel च and आत्मनः to the self मोहनं causing delusion तत् that तामसम् Tâmasika उदाहृतम् is declared.

39. That happiness which begins and results in self-delusion arising from sleep, indolence, and miscomprehension, that is declared to be Tâmasika.

न तदस्ति पृथिव्यां वा दिवि देवेषु वा पुनः ॥
सत्त्वं प्रकृतिजैर्मुक्तं यदेभिः स्यात्त्रिभिर्गुणैः ॥४०॥

पृथिव्यां On earth दिवि in heaven वा or देवेषु among the Devas तु again तत् that सत्त्वं entity न no अस्ति there is

यत् which एभिः these प्रकृतिजैः born of Prakriti त्रिभिः three गुणैः (by) Gunas मुक्तं devoid of स्यात् is.

40. There is no entity on earth, or again in heaven among the Devas, that is devoid of these three Gunas, born of Prakriti.

ब्राह्मणक्षत्रियविशां शूद्राणां च परन्तप ॥
कर्माणि प्रविभक्तानि स्वभावप्रभवैर्गुणैः ॥४१॥

परन्तप O scorcher of foes ब्राह्मणक्षत्रियविशां of Brâhmanas, Kshatriyas, and Vaishyas शूद्राणां of Shudras च as also कर्माणि duties स्वभावप्रभवैः born of (their) own nature गुणैः according to the Gunas प्रविभक्तानि are distributed.

41. Of Brâhmanas and Kshatriyas and Vaishyas, as also of Shudras, O scorcher of foes, the duties are distributed according to the Gunas born of their own nature.

[According to the Karma or habits and tendencies formed by desire, action, and association in the past life manifesting themselves in the present as effects. Or, nature (Svabhâva) may here mean the Mâyâ made up of the three Gunas, the Prakriti of the Lord.]

शमो दमस्तपः शौचं क्षान्तिरार्जवमेव च ॥
ज्ञानं विज्ञानमास्तिक्यं ब्रह्मकर्म स्वभावजम् ॥४२॥

शमः Control of mind दमः control of these senses तपः austerity शौचं purity क्षान्तिः forbearance आर्जवम् upright-

ness ज्ञानं knowledge विज्ञानम् realisation आस्तिक्यं belief
in a hereafter एव also च and स्वभावजम् born of the nature
ब्रह्मकर्म (are) the duties of Brâhmanas.

42. The control of the mind and the
senses, austerity, purity, forbearance, and
also uprightness, knowledge, realisation,
belief in a hereafter—these are the duties
of the Brâhmanas, born of (their own)
nature.

शौर्यं तेजो धृतिर्दाक्ष्यं युद्धे चाप्यपलायनम् ॥

दानमीश्वरभावश्च क्षात्रं कर्म स्वभावजम् ॥४३॥

शौर्यं Prowess तेज: boldness धृति: fortitude दाक्ष्यं dexterity युद्धे in the battle च and अपि also अपलायनम् not flying
दानम् generosity ईश्वरभाव: sovereignty च and स्वभावजम् born
of the nature क्षात्रं of Kshatriyas कर्म the duties.

43. Prowess, boldness, fortitude, dexterity, and also not flying from battle,
generosity and sovereignty are the duties
of the Kshatriyas, born of (their own)
nature.

कृषिगौरक्ष्यवाणिज्यं वैश्यकर्म स्वभावजम् ॥

परिचर्यात्मकं कर्म शूद्रस्यापि स्वभावजम् ॥४४॥

कृषिगौरक्ष्यवाणिज्यं agriculture, cattle-rearing, and trade
स्वभावजम् born of the nature वैश्यकर्म the duties of Vaishya
शूद्रस्य of a Shudra अपि also परिचर्यात्मकं consisting of
service कर्म action स्वभावजम् born of the nature.

26

44.   Agriculture, cattle-rearing, and trade are the duties of the Vaishyas, born of (their own) nature ; and action consisting of service is the duty of the Shudras, born of (their own) nature.

स्वे स्वे कर्मण्यभिरतः संसिद्धिं लभते नरः ॥

स्वकर्मनिरतः सिद्धिं यथा विन्दति तच्छृणु ॥४५॥

स्वे स्वे Each his own कर्मणि to duty अभिरतः devoted नरः man संसिद्धिं the highest perfection लभते attains स्वकर्म-निरतः engaged in his own duty यथा how सिद्धि perfection विन्दति attains तत् that शृणु hear.

45.   Devoted each to his own duty, man attains the highest perfection. How engaged in his own duty, he attains perfection, that hear.

[Own : according to his nature.

The Âpastamba Dharma-Shâstra says : "Men of several castes and orders, each devoted to his respective duties, reap the fruits of their actions after death, and then by the residual Karma attain to births in superior countries, castes, and families, possessed of comparatively superior Dharma, span of life, learning, conduct, wealth, happiness, and intelligence."]

यतः प्रवृत्तिर्भूतानां येन सर्वमिदं ततम् ॥

स्वकर्मणा तमभ्यर्च्य सिद्धिं विन्दति मानवः ॥४६॥

यतः From whom भूतानां of all beings प्रवृत्तिः (is) the
evolution येन by whom इदं this सर्वम् all ततम् is pervaded
मानवः man स्वकर्मणा with his own duty तम् him अभ्यर्च्य worshipping सिद्धिं perfection विन्दति attains.

46.　From whom is the evolution of all
beings, by whom all this is pervaded, worshipping Him with his own duty, a man attains
perfection.

[The highest worship to the Lord consists in the
closest approach to Him. The veil of Mâyâ comprising Karma or habits, tendencies and actions
prevents a man from nearing the Lord, i.e., realising
his own Self. By working out one's Karma alone,
according to the law of one's being, can this veil
be rent and the end accomplished.]

श्रेयान् स्वधर्मो विगुणः परधर्मात्स्वनुष्ठितात् ।।
स्वभावनियतं कर्म कुर्वन्नाप्नोति किल्बिषम् ।।४७।।

विगुणः (Though) imperfect स्वधर्मः one's own Dharma
स्वनुष्ठितात् well-performed परधर्मात् than the Dharma of
another श्रेयान् better　(is) स्वभावनियतं ordained by his own
nature कर्म the duty कुर्वन् doing किल्बिषम् evil न no आप्नोति
(he) incurs.

47.　Better　is　one's　own　Dharma,
(though)　imperfect　than　the　Dharma　of
another well-performed.　He who does the
duty ordained by his own nature incurs
no evil.

[As a poisonous substance does not injure the
worm born in that substance, so he who does his
Svadharma incurs no evil.]

सहजं कर्म कौन्तेय सदोषमपि न त्यजेत् ।।
सर्वारम्भा हि दोषेण धूमेनाग्निरिवावृताः ।।४८।।

कौन्तेय O son of Kunti सदोषम् attended with evil अपि
though सहजं which is born कर्म the duty न not त्यजेत् one
should relinquish हि for सर्वारम्भाः all undertakings धूमेन
by smoke अग्निः fire इव as दोषेण by evil आवृताः are
enveloped.

48.   One should not relinquish, O son
of Kunti, the duty to which one is born,
though it is attended with evil ; for, all
undertakings are enveloped by evil, as fire by
smoke.

[*Duty, etc.*: this need not mean caste duty.

All undertakings : one's own as well as others'
duties.

The greatest evil is bondage, and this endures so
long as one lives in the realm of the Gunas, except
in the case of a freed soul. All action is comprised
in one or the other of the Gunas. All action therefore involves the evil of bondage.]

असक्तबुद्धिः सर्वत्र जितात्मा विगतस्पृहः ।।
नैष्कर्म्यसिद्धिं परमां संन्यासेनाधिगच्छति ।।४९।।

सर्वत्र Everywhere असक्तबुद्धि: whose intellect is unattached जितात्मा who has subdued his heart विगतस्पृह:
whose desires have fled संन्यासेन by renunciation परमां
the supreme नैष्कर्म्यसिद्धिं the perfection consisting in
freedom from action अधिगच्छति (he) attains to.

49. He whose intellect is unattached
everywhere, who has subdued his heart,
whose desires have fled, he attains by
renunciation to the supreme perfection,
consisting of freedom from action.

[He attains...renunciation : This may also be
interpreted to mean: he attains the supreme state
in which he remains as the actionless Self, by his
renunciation of all actions, for which he is prepared
by his right knowledge.]

सिद्धिं प्राप्तो यथा ब्रह्म तथाप्नोति निबोध मे ॥
समासेनैव कौन्तेय निष्ठा ज्ञानस्य या परा ॥५०॥

कौन्तेय O son of Kunti सिद्धिं perfection प्राप्त: reaching
यथा how ब्रह्म Brahman आप्नोति he attains to तथा that
समासेन in brief मे from Me निबोध learn ज्ञानस्य of knowledge या which परा supreme निष्ठा consummation.

50. Learn from Me in brief, O son of
Kunti, how reaching such perfection, he
attains to Brahman, that supreme consummation of knowledge.

बुद्ध्या विशुद्धया युक्तो धृत्यात्मानं नियम्य च ॥
शब्दादीन्विषयांस्त्यक्त्वा रागद्वेषौ व्युदस्य च ॥५१॥

विशुद्धया Pure बुद्ध्या with an intellect युक्तः endued धृत्या
with fortitude आत्मानं the body and the senses नियम्य
subduing च and शब्दादीन् sound and such other विषयान्
sense-objects त्यक्ता relinquishing रागद्वेषौ attraction and
hatred च and व्युदस्य abandoning;

51. Endued with a pure intellect;
subduing the body and the senses with
fortitude; relinquishing sound and such
other sense-objects; abandoning attraction and
hatred;

[*Pure*: free from doubt and misconception,
being merged in Brahman through the elimination
of all alien attributes ascribed to It.

Relinquishing sound, etc.: abandoning all super-
fluous luxuries, all objects, except those only which
are necessary for the bare maintenance of the body,
and laying aside attraction and hatred even for those
objects.]

विविक्तसेवी लघ्वाशी यतवाक्कायमानसः ॥
ध्यानयोगपरो नित्यं वैराग्यं समुपाश्रितः ॥५२॥

विविक्तसेवी Resorting to a sequestered spot लघ्वाशी eating but little यतवाक्कायमानसः body, speech, and mind controlled नित्यं ever ध्यानयोगपरःengaged in meditation and
concentration वैराग्यं dispassion समुपाश्रितः possessed of;

52. Resorting to a sequestered spot;
eating but little; body, speech, and mind

controlled; ever engaged in meditation and concentration; possessed of dispassion ;

[*Eating but little :* as conducive to the serenity of thought by keeping off languor, sleepiness, and the like.

Meditation : upon the nature of the Self.

Concentration : one-pointedness of thought, on one feature of the Self.

Dispassion : for the seen and the unseen.]

अहंकारं बलं दर्पं कामं क्रोधं परिग्रहम् ॥

विमुच्य निर्ममः शान्तो ब्रह्मभूयाय कल्पते ॥५३॥

अहंकारं Egoism बलं power दर्पं pride कामं lust क्रोधं wrath परिग्रहम् property विमुच्य forsaking निर्ममः freed from the notion of "mine" शान्तः tranquil ब्रह्मभूयाय for becoming Brahman कल्पते (he) is fit.

53. Forsaking egoism, power, pride, lust, wrath, and property; freed from the notion of "mine"; and tranquil;—he is fit for becoming Brahman.

[*Power :* that power which is combined with passion and desire.

Property : Though a man who is free from all passions of the mind and the senses, may own so much of external belongings as is necessary for bodily sustenance and for the observance of his religious duties (Dharma), yet this the aspirant abandons, even if this comes of itself, because he does not regard

the bodily life as his; thus he becomes a Parama-
hamsa Parivrâjaka, a Sannyâsin of the highest
order.]

ब्रह्मभूतः प्रसन्नात्मा न शोचति न कांक्षति ॥

समः सर्वेषु भूतेषु मद्भक्तिं लभते पराम् ॥५४॥

ब्रह्मभूतः Brahman-become प्रसन्नात्मा tranquil-minded
न neither शोचति (he) grieves न nor कांक्षति desires सर्वेषु
all भूतेषु to beings समः the same पराम् supreme मद्भक्तिं
devotion unto Me लभते attains to.

54. Brahman-become, tranquil-minded,
he neither grieves nor desires ; the same to
all beings, he attains to supreme devotion
unto Me.

[*Brahman-become :* not that he is yet freed and
become the Absolute, but is firmly grounded in the
knowledge that he is Brahman. His attainment of
freedom is described in the next verse.

Supreme devotion : the devotion stated in
VII. 17.]

भक्त्या मामभिजानाति यावान्यश्चास्मि तत्त्वतः ॥

ततो मां तत्त्वतो ज्ञात्वा विशते तदनन्तरम् ॥५५॥

यावान् What यः who च and अस्मि I am माम् Me भक्त्या
by devotion तत्त्वतः in reality अभिजानाति (he) knows ततः
then मां Me तत्त्वतः in reality ज्ञात्वा having known तदनन्तरम्
forthwith मां into Me विशते enters.

55. By devotion he knows Me in

reality, what and who I am; then having
known Me in reality, he forthwith enters into
Me.

सर्वकर्माण्यपि सदा कुर्वाणो मद्व्यपाश्रयः ॥
मत्प्रसादादवाप्नोति शाश्वतं पदमव्ययम् ॥५६॥

सदा Always सर्वकर्माणि all actions कुर्वाणः doing अपि
even मद्व्यपाश्रयः taking refuge in Me मत्प्रसादात् by My
grace शाश्वतं the eternal अव्ययम् immutable पदम् State
अवाप्नोति (he) attains to.

56.   Even doing all actions always, taking
refuge in Me—by My grace he attains to the
eternal, immutable State.

चेतसा सर्वकर्माणि मयि संन्यस्य मत्परः ॥
बुद्धियोगमुपाश्रित्य मच्चित्तः सततं भव ॥ ५७ ॥

चेतसा Mentally सर्वकर्माणि all deeds मयि in Me संन्यस्य
resigning मत्परः having Me as the highest goal बुद्धियोगम्
Buddhi-Yoga उपाश्रित्य resorting to सततं ever मच्चित्तः with
the mind fixed on Me भव be.

57.   Resigning mentally all deeds to
Me, having Me as the highest goal, resorting
to Buddhi-Yoga do thou ever fix thy mind on
Me.

मच्चित्तः सर्वदुर्गाणि मत्प्रसादात्तरिष्यसि ॥
अथ चेत्त्वमहंकारान्न श्रोष्यसि विनंक्ष्यसि ॥५८॥

त्वम् Thou मच्चित्तः fixing the mind on Me मत्प्रसादात्
by My grace सर्वदुर्गाणि all obstacles तरिष्यसि (thou) shalt
overcome अथ but चेत् if अहंकारात् from self-conceit न not
श्रोष्यसि (thou) wilt hear विनंक्ष्यसि (thou) shalt perish.

58.   Fixing thy mind on Me, thou shalt, by
My grace, overcome all obstacles; but if from
self-conceit thou wilt not hear Me, thou shalt
perish.

यदहंकारमाश्रित्य न योत्स्य इति मन्यसे ॥
मिथ्यैष व्यवसायस्ते प्रकृतिस्त्वां नियोक्ष्यति ॥ ५६ ॥

अहंकार Self-conceit आश्रित्य abiding in न not योत्स्ये (I)
will fight यत् if इति thus मन्यसे (thou) thinkest ते thy एषः
this व्यवसायः resolve मिथ्या (is) vain प्रकृतिः (thy) Prakriti
त्वां thee नियोक्ष्यति will constrain.

59.   If, filled with self-conceit, thou thinkest, "I will not fight", vain is this thy resolve;
thy Prakriti will constrain thee.

[*Thy Prakriti :* Thy nature as a Kshatriya.]

स्वभावजेन कौन्तेय निबद्धः स्वेन कर्मणा ॥
कर्तुं नेच्छसि यन्मोहात्करिष्यस्यवशोऽपि तत् ॥ ६० ॥

कौन्तेय O son of Kunti मोहात् from delusion यत् what
कर्तुं to do न not इच्छसि thou desirest स्वभावजेन born of
(thy) own nature स्वेन (thy) own कर्मणा by Karma निबद्धः
fettered अवशः helpless, in spite of thyself तत् that अपि
even करिष्यसि (thou) shalt (have to) do.

60.   Fettered, O son of Kunti, by thy own Karma, born of thy own nature, what thou, from delusion, desirest not to do, thou shalt have to do in spite of thyself.

ईश्वरः सर्वभूतानां हृद्देशेऽर्जुन तिष्ठति ॥

भ्रामयन्सर्वभूतानि यन्त्रारूढानि मायया ॥ ६१ ॥

अर्जुन O Arjuna ईश्वरः the Lord मायया by Mâyâ यन्त्रारूढानि mounted on a machine सर्वभूतानि all beings भ्रामयन् causing to revolve सर्वभूतानां of all beings हृद्देशे in the hearts तिष्ठति dwells.

61.   The Lord, O Arjuna, dwells in the hearts of all beings, causing all beings, by His Mâyâ, to revolve, (as if) mounted on a machine.

[See commentary to IX. 10.

Arjuna means "white", and here it signifies— "O pure-hearted one".]

तमेव शरणं गच्छ सर्वभावेन भारत ॥

तत्प्रसादात्परां शान्तिं स्थानं प्राप्स्यसि शाश्वतम् ॥६२॥

भारत O Bhârata सर्वभावेन with all thy heart तम् in Him एव even शरणं गच्छ take refuge तत्प्रसादात् by His grace परां supreme शान्तिं peace शाश्वतम् eternal स्थानं the abode प्राप्स्यसि shalt (thou) attain.

62.   Take refuge in Him with all thy heart, O Bhârata ; by His grace shalt thou

attain supreme peace (and) the eternal
abode.

इति ते ज्ञानमाख्यातं गुह्याद्गुह्यतरं मया ॥

विमृश्यैतदशेषेण यथेच्छसि तथा कुरु ॥६३॥

इति Thus गुह्यात् than all profundities गुह्यतरं more
profound ज्ञानम् wisdom ते to thee मया by Me आख्यातं has
been declared अशेषेण fully एतत् it विमृश्य reflecting over
यथा as इच्छसि thou likest तथा so कुरु act.

63. Thus has wisdom, more profound
than all profundities, been declared to
thee by Me ; reflecting over it fully, act as
thou likest.

[*It* : the Shâstra, the teaching as declared
above.]

सर्वगुह्यतमं भूयः श्रृणु मे परमं वचः ॥

इष्टोऽसि मे दृढमिति ततो वक्ष्यामि ते हितम् ॥६४॥

मे My सर्वगुह्यतमं the profoundest of all परमं supreme
वचः word भूयः again श्रृणु hear thou मे of Me दृढम् dearly
इष्टः beloved असि thou art ततः therefore ते to thee हितं
what is good वक्ष्यामि will I speak.

64. Hear thou again My supreme
word, the profoundest of all ; because thou
art dearly beloved of Me, therefore will I
speak what is good to thee.

[*Again* : though more than once declared.]

मन्मना भव मद्भक्तो मद्याजी मां नमस्कुरु ॥

मामेवैष्यसि सत्यं ते प्रतिजाने प्रियोऽसि मे ॥६६॥

मन्मनाः With mind occupied with Me मद्भक्तःdevoted
to Me मद्याजी sacrificing to Me भव be thou मां to Me
नमस्कुरु bow down मामेव Myself एष्यसि thou shalt reach
अहं I ते unto thee सत्यं truly प्रतिजाने promise मे to Me
प्रियः dear असि thou art.

65.   Occupy thy mind with Me, be
devoted to Me, sacrifice to Me, bow down
to Me.   Thou shalt reach Myself ; truly do
I promise unto thee, (for) thou art dear
to Me.

[*Thou shalt reach Myself :* Thus acting, i.e.,
looking upon the Lord alone as thy aim, means and
end—thou shalt attain the Highest.

Truly do I promise unto thee : Have implicit
faith in the declarations of Me, the Lord, as I pledge
thee My troth.]

सर्वधर्मान्परित्यज्य मामेकं शरणं व्रज ॥

अहं त्वा सर्वपापेभ्यो मोक्षयिष्यामि मा शुचः ॥६६॥

सर्वधर्मान् All Dharmas परित्यज्य relinquishing एकं alone
माम् in Me शरणं refuge व्रज take अहं I त्वा thee सर्वपापेभ्यः
from all sins मोक्षयिष्यामि will liberate मा (do) not शुचः
grieve.

66.   Relinquishing all Dharmas   take

refuge in Me alone ; I will liberate thee
from all sins ; grieve not.

[*All Dharmas :* including Adharma also : all
actions, righteous or unrighteous, since absolute
freedom from the bondage of all action is intended
to be taught here.

Take refuge in Me alone : knowing that there
is naught else except Me, the Self of all, dwelling
the same in all.

Liberate thee : by manifesting Myself as thy own
Self.

All sins : all bonds of Dharma and Adharma.

Shankara in his commentary here very strongly
combats the opinion of those who hold that highest
spiritual realisation (Jnâna) and ritualistic work
(Karma) may go together in the same person. For
Karma is possible only in the relative world
(Samsâra), which is the outcome of ignorance; and
knowledge dispels this ignorance. So neither the
conjunction of Jnâna with Karma, nor Karma alone
conduces to the absolute cessation of Samsâra,
but it is only the Right Knowledge of the Self which
does so.]

इदं ते नातपस्काय नाभक्ताय कदाचन ॥
न चाशुश्रूषवे वाच्यं न च मां योऽभ्यसूयति ॥ ६७॥

अतपस्काय To one who is devoid of austerities ते by
thee इदं this न कदाचन never वाच्यं to be spoken न nor

अभक्ताय to one without devotion न च nor अशुश्रूषवे to one who does not render service य: who मां at Me अभ्यसूयति cavils न च nor.

67. This is never to be spoken by thee to one who is devoid of austerities or devotion, nor to one who does not render service, nor to one who cavils at Me.

[*This :* Shâstra which has been taught to you. *Service :* to the Guru; अशुश्रूषवे also means—to one who does not wish to hear.]

य इदं परमं गुह्यं मद्भक्तेष्वभिधास्यति ॥
भक्तिं मयि परां कृत्वा मामेवैष्यत्यसंशयः ॥६८॥

य: Who परमं deeply गुह्यं profound philosophy इदं this मद्भक्तेषु to My devotees अभिधास्यति will teach मयि to Me परां supreme भक्तिं devotion कृत्वा doing असंशयः (being) doubtless माम् एव Me alone एष्यति shall come to.

68. He who with supreme devotion to Me will teach this deeply profound philosophy to My devotees, shall doubt-less come to Me alone.

[*Teach :* in the faith that he is thus doing service to the Lord, the Supreme Teacher.
Doubtless : or, freed from doubts.]

न च तस्मान्मनुष्येषु कश्चिन्मे प्रियकृत्तमः ॥
भविता न च मे तस्मादन्यः प्रियतरो भुवि ॥ ६९ ॥

मनुष्येषु Among men तस्मात् than he कश्चित् any मे to Me प्रियकृत्तमः one who does dearer service च and न not तस्मात् than he अन्यः another मे to Me प्रियतरः dearer च and भुवि on earth न not भविता shall be.

69. Nor among men is there any who does dearer service to Me, nor shall there be another on earth dearer to Me, than he.

[*He :* who hands down the Shâstra to a fit person.]

अध्येष्यते च य इमं धर्म्यं संवादमावयोः ॥
ज्ञानयज्ञेन तेनाहमिष्टः स्यामिति मे मतिः ॥७०॥

यः Who च and आवयोः of ours इमं this धर्म्यं sacred संवादम् dialogue अध्येष्यते will study तेन by him अहम् I ज्ञान-यज्ञेन by the Yajna of knowledge इष्टः worshipped स्याम् (I) shall have been इति such मे My मतिः conviction.

70. And he who will study this sacred dialogue of ours, by him shall I have been worshipped by the Yajna of knowledge ; such is My conviction.

[*Yajna of knowledge :* A Yajna can be performed in four ways, such as (1) Vidhi or ritual, (2) Japa, (3) Upâmshu, or a prayer uttered in a low voice, or (4) Mânasa or prayer offered with the mind. Jnâna-yajna or the Yajna of knowledge comes under the head of Mânasa, and is therefore the highest.

The study of the Gitâ will produce an effect equal to that of the Yajna of knowledge.]

श्रद्धावाननसूयश्च शृणुयादपि यो नरः ॥
सोऽपि मुक्तः शुभाँल्लोकान्प्राप्नुयात्पुण्यकर्मणाम् ॥७१॥

श्रद्धावान् Full of Shraddhâ अनसूय: free from malice च
and य: who नर: man शृणुयात् will hear अपि even स: he
अपि too मुक्त: liberated पुण्यकर्मणाम् of those of righteous
deeds शुभान् happy लोकान् the worlds प्राप्नुयात् shall
attain to.

71. And even that man who hears
this, full of Shraddhâ and free from malice,
he too, liberated, shall attain to the happy
worlds of those of righteous deeds.

[*Even that man :* much more so he who under-
stands the doctrine.]

कच्चिदेतच्छ्रुतं पार्थ त्वयैकाग्रेण चेतसा ॥
कच्चिदज्ञानसंमोहः प्रनष्टस्ते धनञ्जय ॥७२॥

पार्थ O Pârtha त्वया by thee एकाग्रेण attentive चेतसा
with mind एतत् this कच्चित् whether श्रुतं has been heard
धनञ्जय O Dhananjaya ते thy अज्ञानसंमोह: the delusion of
ignorance कच्चित् whether प्रनष्ट: has been destroyed ?

72. Has this been heard by thee, O
Pârtha, with an attentive mind ? Has the
delusion of thy ignorance been destroyed,
O Dhananjaya ?

27

अर्जुन उवाच ।

नष्टो मोह: स्मृतिर्लब्धा त्वत्प्रसादान्मयाच्युत ॥

स्थितोऽस्मि गतसन्देह: करिष्ये वचनं तव ॥७३॥

अर्जुन: Arjuna उवाच said :

अच्युत O Achyuta मोह: the delusion नष्ट: is destroyed मया by me त्वत्प्रसादात् through Thy grace स्मृति: memory लब्धा has been gained स्थित: firm अस्मि I am गतसन्देह: freed from doubts तव Thy वचनं word करिष्ये I will do.

Arjuna said :

73. Destroyed is my delusion, and I have gained my memory through Thy grace, O Achyuta. I am firm ; my doubts are gone. I will do Thy word.

[*Memory :* of the true nature of the Self.
Firm : in Thy command.

The purpose of the knowledge of the Shâstras is the destruction of doubts and delusions, and the recognition of the true nature of the Self. Here, the answer of Arjuna conclusively shows that that purpose has been fulfilled in him.

The teaching of the Shâstra is over here. The rest is only to connect it with the main narrative.]

सञ्जय उवाच ।

इत्यहं वासुदेवस्य पार्थस्य च महात्मन: ॥

संवादमिममश्रौषमद्भुतं रोमहर्षणम् ॥७४॥

सञ्जय: Sanjaya उवाच said :

अहं I इति thus वासुदेवस्य of Vâsudeva महात्मन: high-souled पार्थस्य of Pârtha च and इमम् this रोमहर्षणम् which causes the hair to stand on end अद्भुतं wonderful संवादम् dialogue अश्रौषम् (I) have heard.

Sanjaya said :

74. Thus have I heard this wonder-ful dialogue between Vâsudeva and the high-souled Pârtha, causing my hair to stand on end.

व्यासप्रसादाच्छ्रुतवानिमं गुह्यमहं परम् ॥
योगं योगेश्वरात्कृष्णात्साक्षात्कथयत: स्वयम् ॥७५॥

अहं I व्यासप्रसादात् through the grace of Vyâsa इमं this परम् supreme गुह्यम् most profound योगं Yoga कथयत: speaking स्वयम् Himself साक्षात् direct योगेश्वरात् from the Lord of Yoga कृष्णात् from Krishna श्रुतवान् I have heard.

75. Through the grace of Vyâsa have I heard this supreme and most profound Yoga, direct from Krishna, the Lord of Yoga. Himself declaring it.

[Through...Vyâsa : by obtaining from him the Divya-chakshu or divine vision.]

राजन्संस्मृत्य संस्मृत्य संवादमिममद्भुतम् ॥
केशवार्जुनयो: पुण्यं हृष्यामि च मुहुर्मुहु: ॥७६॥

राजन् O King केशवार्जुनयो: between Keshava and Arjuna इमम् this पुण्यं holy अद्भुतम् wonderful संवादं dialogue संस्मृत्य संस्मृत्य as I remember and remember मुहु: मुहु: again and again हृष्यामि I rejoice.

76. O King, as I remember and remember this wonderful and holy dialogue between Keshava and Arjuna, I rejoice again and again.

[*King :* Dhritarâshtra.]

तच्च संस्मृत्य संस्मृत्य रूपमत्यद्भुतं हरे: ॥

विस्मयो मे महान् राजन् हृष्यामि च पुन: पुन: ॥७७॥

राजन् O King हरे: of Hari तत् that अद्भुतं wonderful रूपम् Form संस्मृत्य संस्मृत्य as I remember and remember च and मे my महान् great विस्मय: wonder च and अहं I पुन: पुन: again and again हृष्यामि rejoice.

77. And as I remember and remember that most wonderful Form of Hari, great is my wonder, O King ; and I rejoice again and again.

[*Form :* Vishvarupa, the Universal Form.]

यत्र योगेश्वर: कृष्णो यत्र पार्थो धनुर्धर: ॥

तत्र श्रीर्विजयो भूतिर्ध्रुवा नीतिर्मतिर्मम ॥७८॥

यत्र Wherever योगेश्वर: the Lord of Yoga कृष्ण: Krishna यत्र wherever धनुर्धर: the wielder of the bow पार्थ: Pârtha

तत्र there श्री: prosperity विजय: victory भूति: expansion ध्रुवा
sound नीति: policy इति such मे my मति: conviction.

78. Wherever is Krishna, the Lord of
Yoga, wherever is Pârtha, the wielder of
the bow, there are prosperity, victory, expansion, and sound policy : such is my
conviction.

[*The bow :* called the Gândiva.]

इति श्रीमद्भगवद्गीतासूपनिषत्सु ब्रह्मविद्यायां योग-
शास्त्रे श्रीकृष्णार्जुनसंवादे मोक्षसंन्यासयोगो
नामाष्टादशोऽध्याय: ॥

Thus in the Shrimad-Bhagavad-Gitâ, the
Essence of the Upanishads, the Science
of the Brahman, the Scripture of
Yoga, the Dialogue between Shri
Krishna and Arjuna, ends the
eighteenth chapter, designated,

The Way of Liberation in Renunciation.
Here the Bhagavad-Gitâ ends.

ओं शान्ति: शान्ति: शान्ति: ॥

Om ! Peace ! Peace ! Peace be to all !

|| अथ श्रीगीतामाहात्म्यम् ||

THE GREATNESS OF THE GITA

श्रीगणेशाय नमः || श्रीराधारमणाय नमः ||

Salutation to Shri Ganesha !
Salutation to Shri Râdhâramana !

[Ganesha is the god of wisdom and remover of obstacles; hence he is invoked and worshipped at the commencement of every important undertaking. Râdhâramana, the Lover of Râdhâ, Shri Krishna.]

धरोवाच ।

भगवन्परमेशान भक्तिरव्यभिचारिणी ||

प्रारब्धं भुज्यमानस्य कथं भवति हे प्रभो || १ ||

Dharâ (the Earth) said :

1. O Blessed Lord, O Supreme Ruler, how may one, who is held back by his Prârabdha Karma, obtain unswerving devotion ?

[*Prârabdha Karma :* There are three kinds of Karma: (1) Sanchita or accumulated and stored up in past lives ; (2) Âgâmi or that which is yet to be done; (3) Prârabdha or that which is already bearing fruit. This last is that part of the accumulated actions (Sanchita) which has brought about the

present life and will influence it until its close. The
knowledge of Brahman destroys all accumulated
Karma and makes the current work abortive. But
the Prârabdha Karma must run out its course,
though the balanced mind of a liberated man is not
affected by it.]

विष्णुरुवाच ।

प्रारब्धं भुज्यमानो हि गीताभ्यासरतः सदा ॥

स मुक्तः स सुखी लोके कर्मणा नोपलिप्यते ॥ २ ॥

The Lord Vishnu said :

2. If one be devoted to the constant
practice of the Gitâ, even though he be
restrained by Prârabdha Karma, yet is
he Mukta, happy, in this very world. He
is not tainted by (new) Karma.

महापापातिपापानि गीताध्यानं करोति चेत् ॥

क्वचित्स्पर्शं न कुर्वन्ति नलिनीदलमम्बुवत् ॥ ३ ॥

3. No evil, however great, can affect
him who meditates on the Gitâ. He is like
the lotus leaf untouched by the water.

गीतायाः पुस्तकं यत्र यत्र पाठः प्रवर्तते ॥

तत्र सर्वाणि तीर्थानि प्रयागादीनि तत्र वै ॥ ४ ॥

सर्वे देवाश्च ऋषयो योगिनः पन्नगाश्च ये ॥

गोपाला गोपिका वापि नारदोद्धवपार्षदैः ॥ ५ ॥

4-5. Where there is the book of the Gîtâ, where its study is proceeded with, there are present all the holy places, there verily, are Prayâga and the rest. There also are all the Devas, Rishis, Yogis, and Pannagas, so also the Gopâlas and Gopi-kâs, with Nârada, Uddhava, and their whole train of comrades.

सहायो जायते शीघ्रं यत्र गीता प्रवर्तते ॥

यत्र गीताविचारश्च पठनं पाठनं श्रुतम् ॥

तत्राहं निश्चितं पृथ्वि निवसामि सदैव हि ॥६॥

6. Where the Gîtâ is read, forthwith comes help. Where the Gîtâ is discussed, recited, taught, or heard, there, O Earth, beyond a doubt, do I Myself unfailingly reside.

गीताश्रयेऽहं तिष्ठामि गीता मे चोत्तमं गृहम् ॥

गीताज्ञानमुपाश्रित्य त्रील्लोकान्पालयाम्यहम् ॥ ७ ॥

7. In the refuge of the Gîtâ I abide ; the Gîtâ is My chief abode. Standing on the wisdom of the Gîtâ, I maintain the three worlds.

गीता मे परमा विद्या ब्रह्मरूपा न संशयः ॥

अर्धमात्राक्षरा नित्या स्वानिर्वाच्यपदात्मिका ॥८॥

चिदानन्देन कृष्णेन प्रोक्ता स्वमुखतोऽर्जुनम् ॥

वेदत्रयी परानन्दा तत्त्वार्थज्ञानसंयुता ॥ ८ ॥

8-9. The Gitâ is My Supreme Knowledge ; it is undoubtedly inseparable from
Brahman—this Knowledge is absolute,
Imperishable, eternal, of the essence of
My inexpressible State—the Knowledge
comprising the whole of the three Vedas,
supremely blissful, and consisting of the
realisation of the true nature of the Self—
declared by the All-knowing and Blessed
Krishna, through his own lips, to Arjuna.

[*Ardhamâtrâ* : lit., the half-syllable, and refers
to the dot on the ओं ; symbolically, it stands for the
Turiya state, hence the Absolute.]

योऽष्टादशजपो नित्यं नरो निश्चलमानसः ॥

ज्ञानसिद्धिं स लभते ततो याति परं पदम् ॥ १० ॥

10. That man who with steady mind
recites the eighteen chapters daily, attains
the perfection of knowledge and thus reaches
the highest plane.

पाठे समग्रेऽसम्पूर्णे ततोऽर्धं पाठमाचरेत् ॥

तदा गोदानजं पुण्यं लभते नात्र संशयः ॥ ११ ॥

11. If the whole cannot be recited,
then half of it may be read ; and he who

does this acquires merit, equal to that of
the gift of a cow. There is no doubt about
this.

त्रिभागं पठमानस्तु गङ्गास्नानफलं लभेत् ॥

षडंशं जपमानस्तु सोमयागफलं लभेत् ॥ १२ ॥

12. By the recitation of a third part,
he gains the same merit as by bathing
in the Ganges. By the repetition of a
sixth part, he obtains the fruit of the
Soma-sacrifice.

एकाध्यायं तु यो नित्यं पठते भक्तिसंयुतः ॥

रुद्रलोकमवाप्नोति गणो भूत्वा वसेच्चिरम् ॥ १३ ॥

13. He who reads, full of devotion,
even one chapter daily, attains to the
Rudraloka, and lives there for a long time,
having become one of those who wait on
Shiva.

[*Become, etc.*: lit., attained to Ganahood.]

अध्यायं श्लोकपादं वा नित्यं यः पठते नरः ॥

स याति नरतां यावन्मन्वन्तरं वसुन्धरे ॥ १४ ॥

14. The man who daily reads a quarter of a chapter, or of a Shloka, O Earth,
attains to human birth throughout the duration
of a Manu.

[*Attains to human birth :* is born every time in a man-body.]

गीतायाः श्लोकदशकं सप्त पञ्च चतुष्टयम् ॥

द्वौ त्रीनेकं तदर्धं वा श्लोकानां यः पठेन्नरः ॥ १५ ॥

चन्द्रलोकमवाप्नोति वर्षाणामयुतं ध्रुवम् ॥

गीतापाठसमायुक्तो मृतो मानुषतां व्रजेत् ॥ १६ ॥

15-16.   The man who recites ten, seven, five, four, three, or two Shlokas, or even one or half a Shloka of the Gitâ, certainly lives in Chandraloka for ten thousand years. He who leaves the body while reading the Gitâ, obtains the world of Man.

गीताभ्यासं पुनः कृत्वा लभते मुक्तिमुत्तमाम् ॥

गीतेत्युच्चारसंयुक्तो म्रियमाणो गतिं लभेत् ॥ १७ ॥

17.   Again, practising the Gitâ, he attains Supreme Mukti. The dying man uttering the word "Gitâ" will attain the goal.

गीतार्थश्रवणासक्तो महापापयुतोऽपि वा ॥

वैकुण्ठं समवाप्नोति विष्णुना सह मोदते ॥ १८ ॥

18.   One who loves to hear the meaning of the Gitâ, even though he has committed heinous sins, attains to heaven, and lives in beatitude with Vishnu.

गीतार्थं ध्यायते नित्यं कृत्वा कर्माणि भूरिशः ॥

जीवन्मुक्तः स विज्ञेयो देहान्ते परमं पदम् ॥ १६ ॥

19. He who constantly meditates on the meaning of the Gitâ, even though he performs Karma incessantly, he is to be regarded as a Jivanmukta; and after the destruction of his body he attains to the highest plane of knowledge.

गीतामाश्रित्य बहवो भूभुजो जनकादयः ॥

निर्धूतकल्मषा लोके गीता याताः परं पदम् ॥२०॥

20. By the help of this Gitâ, many kings like Janaka became free from their impurities and attained to the highest goal. It is so sung.

गीतायाः पठनं कृत्वा माहात्म्यं नैव यः पठेत् ॥

वृथा पाठो भवेत्तस्य श्रम एव ह्युदाहृतः ॥ २१ ॥

21. He, who having finished the reading of the Gitâ, does not read its Mâhâtmya as declared here, his reading is in vain; it is all labour wasted.

एतन्माहात्म्यसंयुक्तं गीताभ्यासं करोति यः ॥

स तत्फलमवाप्नोति दुर्लभां गतिमाप्नुयात् ॥ २२ ॥

22. He who studies the Gitâ, accompanied with this discourse on its Mâhâ-

tmya, obtains the fruit stated herein, and reaches that goal which is difficult to attain.

सूत उवाच ।

माहात्म्यमेतद्गीताया मया प्रोक्तं सनातनम् ॥

गीतान्ते च पठेद्यस्तु यदुक्तं तत्फलं लभेत ॥ २३ ॥

Suta said :

23. He who will read this eternal Greatness of the Gitâ, declared by me, after having finished the reading of the Gitâ itself, will obtain the fruit described herein.

[These declarations will, no doubt, seem to be mere flights of extravagant fancy, if they are taken in their literal sense. They may be explained either (1) as mere Arthavâda or a statement of glorification meant to stimulate a strong desire for the study of the Gitâ, which being performed from day to day, may, by the force of the truth and grandeur of one or other of its teachings, strike an inner chord of the heart some time, so much so as to change the whole nature of the man for good; (2) or, the "reading" and "reciting" and so forth, of the whole or a part, may not perhaps be taken in their ordinary sense, as meaning lip-utterance and the like; but in view of the great results indicated, they may be reasonably construed to mean the assimilation of the essence of the Gitâ teaching into the practical daily life of the individual. What wonder, then, that such a one who is the embodiment of the Gitâ would be a true Jnâni, or a Jivanmukta, or that he would, in proportion to his success of being so, attain the intermediate spheres of evolution and finally obtain Mukti ?]

इति श्रीवाराहपुराणे श्रीगीतामाहात्म्यं संपूर्णम् ॥

Thus ends in the Vârâha Purâna the discourse designated, *The Greatness of the Gita*.

INDEX TO FIRST LINES

28

INDEX TO TOPICS